# DEMOCRACY
## AND **PUNISHMENT**

# DEMOCRACY

# AND **PUNISHMENT**

Disciplinary Origins of the United States

## THOMAS L. DUMM

The University of Wisconsin Press

Published 1987

The University of Wisconsin Press
114 North Murray Street
Madison, Wisconsin 53715

The University of Wisconsin Press, Ltd.
1 Gower Street
London WC1E 6HA, England

First printing

Printed in the United States of America

For LC CIP information see the colophon

ISBN 0-299-11400-7 cloth;  0-299-11404-X paper

# Contents

# Preface

Of what use is the prison? Since it has never been of value for constraining or rehabilitating those who are found guilty of breaking laws, is it better understood as a sign for certain experiences? Perhaps it is coldhearted to think this way. The men and women who inhabit the interiors of penitentiaries suffer much, and it seems a cruel and even callous gesture to reduce their pain—what in some contexts can be called their infinite pain—to the category of metaphor. Yet this is what I have tried to do in this book. I hope readers understand that I did not write this book without an appreciation of the pain suffered by prisoners.

The passion of reformers seems to me to be rooted in a sentimental view of the world, one which reflects a horrifying banality. If one thinks of what the world would be like should reformers succeed in liberating all prisoners, one would, I think, need to fear not a catharsis of violence so much as an agony of boredom. Perhaps to think this thought is to be on the way to subverting the notion of reform. Yet this is what I have tried to do in this book. I hope readers understand that I did not do so without an appreciation of the emotions that sometimes underlie the sentimentality of reformers.

One might describe this book by saying that it is an exploration into certain customs of American citizens. In it, I develop some technical terms—fear, danger, desolation, to name a few—in order to shed a peculiar light on how the Europeans who invaded and later named the United States sought to order themselves as they ordered others. To summarize what I have concluded would be to participate in the most transparent lie of the prefatory text. I do not wish to be so unsubtle. But I do feel compelled to issue certain cautions. First I must caution the historian: should you argue that I have horribly distorted the history of the era I describe here, I will respond by asking you, what is history? Next, I must caution the moralist: should you argue that I have irreverently attempted to undermine the grounds of moral valuation, I will ask you, what are morals? And to those who call themselves political scientists: should you argue that my work is useless for understanding policy, I will ask you, what is policy if not the ordering of others so as to keep things clean for yourself?

At the same time, I do not claim as my privilege the neutrality of the "happy positivist," an artful term that has been used to discuss (and dismiss) certain poststructuralist thinkers, among them one whose work is crucial to this book's genesis and completion, Michel Foucault. Were this a post-face, rather than preface, I might engage in a discussion of the consequences, beyond incoherence, of the position I have taken in this work. A colleague of mine once explained to another colleague my reluctance to issue pre-scriptive statements concerning moral action as the result of my deep moral sensitivity. That explanation sounded good to me at the time, so I let the observation pass as a kind interpretation of my hostility to the project of seeking certainty. I understand the search for certainty to have its origins in a mistaken, if understandable, fear. I have shared that fear. I am perhaps too attracted to fear, for it represents to me the shape my own *amor mundi* has taken. For that reason I subject the search for certainty to as ruthless a critique as I can muster.

So, should a preface, as a posterior statement of intent, be an expression of warning, this is mine to the reader: I wish to implicate you in fear so as to contribute to dispersing and diffusing some prominent dangers present in the late modern era. Only by writing this book was I able to realize this purpose.

# Acknowledgments

In an earlier incarnation, this book was a dissertation. Fortunately, or disastrously, depending on one's perspective, this book only vaguely resembles, in style and in substance, that first text. I thank the following citizens from Cornell University, who helped me along the way of making this book: Theodore Lowi, who continues to try to make me comprehensible, if not coherent, Susan Buck-Morss, Eldon Eisenach, Isaac Kramnick, John Forester, and Benjamin Ginsberg. Ben especially inspired my work as my dissertation adviser at Cornell by emphasizing that it is much more important to be interesting than it is to be correct.

Friends and colleagues who helped me formulate the ideas in this book include James Curtis, Greg Delaurier, Mark Silverstein, Nancy Love, Michael Busch, Aline Kuntz, Alphonso Lingis, Kathy Ferguson, Alex Hooke, Jean Bethke-Elshtain, Michael Ryan, Gary Aller, Peter Kardas, Lin Nelson, Elizabeth Long, Dani Thomas, Bob Fisher, Michael Dressman, Austin Sarat, Diane Rubenstein, George Lipsitz, Nat Herold, George Kateb, Jane Bennett, Alan Stone, Anthony Barnett, and especially William Connolly. My gratitude to Larry Weil, who encouraged/criticized this work at every point in its development, and also saw me through difficult times during the course of its writing. Extra thanks as well go to Brenda Bright, for her love, friendship, and presence, as well as for her insights as an artist, architect, and anthropologist.

Lurline Dowell word processed the whole of the final draft of the manuscript. She has my heartfelt thanks. Susan Tarcov aided immeasurably by copyediting a manuscript in bad need of pruning.

This book was written during the years that I underwent a now common academic ritual—seeking a tenure-track position. Two schools were generous in their support of me knowing I was only a visitor, Wartburg College in Waverly, Iowa, and the University of Houston, Downtown, in Houston, Texas. I completed this book at Amherst College, a place I have found conducive to writing because of the generous time made available to the faculty to pursue research. I learn from my colleagues in the Political Science Department at Amherst every day.

Thanks for support received to attend a seminar directed by William Connolly on interpretation and genealogy at the University of Massachusetts, Amherst, in the summer of 1984, go to the National Endowment for the Humanities. Parts of Chapters 3 and 4 of this book appeared in a different form in *Political Theory* 13 (August 1985), © Sage Publications, Inc. A draft of the conclusion was presented to the Honors Seminar on Political Theory and Public Policy at Pennsylvania State University in February of 1986. I thank Larry Spence, Nancy Love, and James Curtis for their hospitality.

This book is dedicated to John Wikse. He taught me what it means to be in the estate of a desperate debtor. He also taught me how one might escape that plight, thus giving me permission to be his friend. In that special sense, he is my first teacher.

# DEMOCRACY

# AND **PUNISHMENT**

# Introduction:
# On the Genealogy of Danger

The American prison presents itself as Hobbes's state of nature reproduced in miniature. It is a place where life is nasty, brutish, and short, where human beings abandon themselves to ferocious and insatiable lusts. It is a seething cauldron of evil, a distillation of the worst characteristics of all people into a few, a resting place for the misfit, malformed, despised, and violent men and women who have proved unwilling or unable to obey the laws of the land. Only prison walls separate these unfortunate and unhappy creatures from the citizenry. Only prison walls can constrain those who have lost, or have never had, the capacity to be human.

Prison protects with its walls. But prison punishes, too, not through its more spectacular cruelties, not by its allowance of rape, murder, humiliation, and boredom, but instead by depriving those who enter it of their most cherished possession, their freedom. In America, everyone is free; prison is the negation of that freedom. Hence the prison experience is a negation of the conditions which allow one to define oneself as a person, for when the ability to choose is taken away, one ceases to be a willing entity. Put succinctly, prison punishes by eliminating the conditions which allow one to behave oneself.

Thus, prison is in a dialectical relationship with freedom, as its necessary negation. It constitutes a realm of unfreedom in an otherwise free world. In establishing such a realm, the founders of American society may be said to have completed a circle, to have drawn the connecting lines between an individual whose freedom is a possession and an individual who has lost the right to possess and hence is not free. Adorno and Horkheimer put this matter in stark yet now familiar terms:

3

> Absolute solitude, the violent turning inward on the self, whose whole being consists in the mastery of material and in the monotonous rhythm of work, is the specter which outlines the existence of man in the modern world. Radical isolation and radical reduction to the same hopeless nothingness are identical. Man in prison is the virtual image of the bourgeois type which he still has to become in reality.[1]

On the margin of social existence, the prison outlines, provides the sharp relief which illuminates the meaning of freedom in a world where existence is commodified, where being is defined under the sign of capital.

Such a compelling and exhaustive statement of the meaning of the prison leaves little left to say on the subject. It blasts asunder the arguments of apologists of the prison, those who have so profoundly misread the prison as a humanitarian reform. For these apologists, the punishment that literally tore bodies to pieces, concentrating pain on purpose, operating with such a surplus of horror as to become obscene once men and women shook off the sleep of unreason which marked the Dark Ages, is always the worst horror. They fear pain of the body, and perhaps think that souls float free. But for those who have grasped the insidiousness of the operations of capitalist domination, the reason of imprisonment is revealed as the belly of the beast of modernity, the deception of Enlightenment, the price of an exacting rule, in short, the internal violence of capitalistic order. The prison is more, not less, horrible for having been constituted as a humanitarian reform.

Yet such a presentation of the nature of the modern prison paradoxically trivializes it. The prison becomes a mere mirror of capitalism's subject, the bourgeoisie. For radical critics of capitalism, the prison at most plays an ancillary role in the development and maintenance of the capitalist order. It exists as a mechanism of state authority; the function of the prison is to constrain those who reject the conditions of freedom imposed by the capitalist order. The true conditions of freedom under such circumstances, in this reading, are conditions of alienation. In rejecting the "bargain" offered by the capitalist order—to behave themselves, to submit to the sale of their labor in return for the frugal rewards such a sale brings—criminals find themselves even further in the hole, further in debt, than working proletarians. In capitalist society, where everyone has a role and everybody is absorbed into the logic of capital expansion, their role and their bodies are to demonstrate the consequences of misbehavior. Their disfunctionality is transformed into a function of a stable system. Only when crime becomes politicized, as a consequence of the upheavals that mark the periodic crises afflicting capitalism, can a break with this role occur, and even then the likelihood that the "dangerous classes" will contribute to the overthrow of the system is almost nil. Demoralized, dispossessed of any positive sense of being, they represent the worst wreckage that capitalism leaves in its wake. Their experience in prison is merely one of the dead ends of capitalism, one of the side conflicts distracting from the central conflict between capital and labor, the bourgeoisie and the proletariat. If one should care about the prison, one should care about it only in the terms of the deeper injustice it reflects, or for the sake of the prisoners themselves, but certainly not because it has anything important to offer regarding the central conflicts of the capitalist order.

Such is one view of the prison, perhaps the most persuasive view offered in criminological circles. It represents a neo-Marxian attack upon the concealed assumptions underlying mainstream criminology's explanations of crime, concealed assumptions whose purpose is to enable criminology to assist in the development of state policies for controlling crime. Yet while the attack serves as a valid critique of the pretentions of mainstream policymakers, it fails to appreciate the fuller meaning of prison because of its adherence to its own categorical assumptions. These assumptions have to do with the relative influence of worker and nonworker in the service of revolution. If a connection is drawn too closely between laboring and dangerous classes, responsible radicals fear that ideologues in the interests of continued domination of capital might criminalize the working class. Such criminalization, in fact, has already been accomplished by conservatives such as James Q. Wilson. But that crude connection is hardly the one that illuminates the more essential relationships between criminals and the other subjects of modern, capitalistic societies.

If one assumes rather that the juridical system is crucial to the legitimation of order in the United States, and if one is also critical of the manner in which the prison has shaped legitimate order, then one comes closer to the perspective that informs this book. Rather than understand the prison as a place of enlightened reform, or as a marginal institution, I try to understand it as a place in which new truths are discovered, that is, to understand it as a place where techniques are administered on the bodies of people, and hence as a place where a rehabilitation of being comes about. I focus on the prison's role as the epistemological project of the Enlightenment. Recognizing that the Enlightenment is flawed, I try to remember as well that it is not merely a fraud, however complex a fraud it may be. In short, I start by recognizing the Enlightenment as having constituted a particular regime of truth. By proceeding from these premises, I hope to prepare a way for understanding the regime that liberal democracy has established in the United States, a regime which surely has been fundamentally imprinted by the imperatives of capitalism, but which just as surely has exerted its own influence over the character of American society, and, ironically, over the way in which the capitalistic imperative has been realized.

I argue in this study that the emergence of the penitentiary in the United States was a project *constitutive* of liberal democracy. That is, the penitentiary system formed the epistemological project of liberal democracy, creating conditions of knowledge of self and other that were to shape the political subject required for liberal and democratic values to be realized in practice. The American project, a system of self-rule, involved not only the establishment of representative government with an extensive suffrage, but also the establishment of institutions which would encourage the internalization of liberal democratic values, the creation of individuals who would learn how to rule their selves.

Tensions between liberal and democratic values have diversely been described as contributing to the energy of American politics, as being responsible for the enervating nature of American political discourse, and sometimes as being the source of all crises in its political system. But the most dangerous tensions between liberal and democratic principles, which could not be resolved at the level of public debate and legislative action, could be and were displaced. That is, contradictory demands for individual autonomy and equality were moved, contradictions intact, from the arena of public discourse to the arena of private habit. A primary mechanism for this displacement, and hence the wellspring for the development of the liberal democratic subject, was the penitentiary.

To fully comprehend the implications of this claim, it is necessary to move beyond currently received understandings of the range and limits of liberal and democratic discourse. I argue here that liberal democratic discourse has captured the collective imagination of Americans for so long, and in distorted and stunted forms has persisted as a touchstone for political debate, because it gives modern shape and meaning to an older set of political relationships, relationships threatened by capitalism but rejuvenated and transformed by the "double bind" of liberal democracy. I call these relationships *dangerous* relationships, and it is the purpose of this introduction to delineate briefly a genealogy of danger so as to facilitate a fuller understanding of the complex relationship between liberal democracy and the origins of discipline. Thus I begin a narrative on the modern prison, one appreciative of the irony of narrative, and one which I hope will reach those readers who understand the lucidity (and lack of irony) of Sartre, when he made one of his characters preface a narrative with the qualification, "It's an idiotic story, like all stories."[2]

## Dangerous Relationships

What does it mean to be in danger? The earliest reference to danger in the English language is instructive. *Danger*, derived from the French *dangier*, appeared around A.D. 1100, and was one of the first words to infiltrate from France as a result of the Norman conquest. It is a compound word: *dan-*, an honorific term of address to a lord or master, combined with *-ger*, which means to wage, to bear, and to wear.[3] From its inception, *danger* conveyed multiple meanings designed to express the subtlety and extensiveness of the relationships that exist between rulers and their subjects. To wage, to bear, and to wear a lord, all implied a formal arrangement of domination in which submission to the authority of a lord was closely coupled to the lord's ability to protect subjects. During the feudal era, these relationships of reciprocity were ingrained as *habits;* that is, they expressed moral characteristics of everyday life at a level below the threshold of direct coercion, and while they were forms of exchange that were not of necessity incompatible with the development of the marketplace, they were not directly exploitative.[4] "Being dependent on a dan, being in his power or indebted to him, was expressed as 'being in danger.' "[5]

I do not mean to suggest that the elements of protection and reciprocity conveyed by *danger* were the only ways in which lord and subject related. *Danger*, however, was meant to reflect a mutuality of interest between the two. Although the relationship between lord and peasant was hardly close, in a perilous world there was enough common recognition of the mystery external to the community itself to establish and maintain the bond between them.

This relationship broke down under the pressures that brought an end to the feudal economy. The "great enclosure" is emblematic of this process, with the vision it presents of unattached peasants wandering into towns and cities to fuel the manufactories with their labor. Lords ceased to provide protection to their subjects; subjects no longer bore their lords. The destruction of the feudal economy and the rise of capitalism constitute the frame within which the severing of this relationship has been understood by the most sophisticated chroniclers of this epic.[6]

The argument of this book is premised on the idea that dangerous relationships did not disappear with the breakdown of the feudal order. In fact, they have become more important for making social existence comprehensible, even if they are now less obviously encoded as social conventions. In the modern era, danger has been internalized as a behavioral imperative. The protection once borne as an external social convention is now a structure of personality. Modern subjects might be said to be *gerents*, that is, people who manage, direct, govern, and rule their selves, who *wear* their selfhood, who wage internal battles for the maintenance and control of their selves, who bear their selves, learning to live as their selves.[7] A logic of self-possession informs these people's lives. This logic is acted out largely through the processes by which subjects identify themselves with commodities. The motto of the modern gerent is "You are what you own," and they cling to it ever more desperately as ownership becomes more ambiguous in late capitalist society. They seek a safety zone within which they might construct stable and continuous self-identities. But they are finding out in increasing numbers that the chief strategy for finding safety, disappearing into one's collection, is available only so long as the collection is *worth* something, and in an age of inflation the market for things cheapens even as it exaggerates value.[8]

Few modern subjects possess the kind of resources necessary to be successful gerents. They would need to live more marginalized lives than they do, for complementing the devaluation of commodities through inflation has been another logic, not of self-possession but of self-discipline, a logic which is acted out through the processes by which *habits* are inculcated in persons.[9] What might be called the regulatory capacity of modern societies can be depicted as the collective result of these attempts to constitute the modern self as a disciplined body. Coherence and continuity of self depend upon the elaboration of controls over the raw and amorphous drives and desires of bodies so as to transform them into self-ruled subjects.

The modern subject is the product of more than these two complementary processes of reification and disciplinary habit. But other processes, which often do exist as ameliorating practices, and which sometimes actually cultivate alternative notions of selfhood, are overridden by the demands for protection embedded in dominant understandings of the self. Because they represent the contemporary fulfillment of the protective agreement of lord and vassal, the scope of dangerous relationships has expanded in tandem with the expansion of forces which endanger. What is so absurd, however, is that the imperatives of protection as expressed and developed through dangerous relationships not only expand the domain of such relationships but also exacerbate the endangerment of the subjects who are to be protected. To "take care of one's self" now has become the most important goal of life for modern subjects, just as it has become the least realizable project of late modernity.

Commodity fetishism, since Marx's analysis, has been relatively well understood in terms of how it impoverishes as it creates a self.[10] Less well known and well documented, however, is the set of processes that contributes to the emergence of discipline and illuminates the full meaning of discipline as it shapes a self-protective subject.

To those readers who are familiar with the various works of Michel Foucault, the general concerns of this study should also seem familiar. The term "Foucauldian" repulses me to the extent that it implies the notion of a school of thought. Such terms generally seem to me to be antithetical to the project of making sense of the world. I learned much from reading Foucault's works, and that learning is reflected in these pages. His study of the emergence of what he called "disciplinary society," *Discipline and Punish,* obviously inspired my study on prisons in the United states. But this study became a long description of certain political developments in the United States, not because of my reading of Foucault, and not because of a serendipitous discovery of the penitentiary's invention in Pennsylvania, but because of my continuing concern to understand how subjects of the United States have sustained such strong dangerous relationships. I have come to recognize an old truth—that a people which breaks with the past also clings even more fearfully to some reassuring vestiges of that past.[11] The sign of progress may also be the sign of recovery, however partial, of relationships that held during an earlier period. Thus, in this "new" land, the inscriptions made by a power that is disciplinary may all the more clearly be traced.

How have I derived such a gloomy vision from the premises and promises of American politics? The United States can claim to be the purest case of liberal democratic society that exists, if for no other reason than that liberal democratic ideas have constituted the ascribed ideology of the United States since its founding, and many have concluded that it has been the continual frustration of the ends of liberal democracy, which in large part might be considered the result of the intimate relationship between liberal democracy and capitalism, that has contributed to the problems the world now is beginning to recognize. Now, faced off against that other great idealistic empire, the Soviet Union, the United States may have become something that it never was intended to be.

Perhaps. But I believe that the current state of affairs represents not a betrayal of liberal democratic values but their strange fruit, the result of an internal dynamic by which freedom and equality have been realized. The evidence I present in the substantive chapters of this work will, I hope encourage a reexamination of that dynamic. While those chapters are devoted to explaining the origins of modern criminal punishment in the United States, and can be read as such, they also present an argument which implies that the problem of criminal punishment in the United States is closely tied to questions concerning the legitimacy of authority more generally. In fact, these case studies, from the era when the United States was forming itself as a liberal democracy, can be read as an alternative, or at least supplemental, history of the constitution of the United States.[12]

To suggest that the United States is a disciplinary society is to make a claim about the ontological status of those who inhabit it, as will become more apparent as this argument unfolds. Perhaps I also need to state, especially given the emphasis I have placed on danger, that regardless of the dark hues of this study, I do not intend it to be a pessimistic work. Ultimately I wish to show that disciplinary societies develop only to the extent that the people who live within them fail to face the strategies of power that constitute them as subjects, and who thus continue to resist mistaken things. In order to resist properly, subjects must constantly disillusion themselves, so as to know better which dangers they must face, which ones they might welcome, and which ones they should probably run from.

All authors attempt to impose order over texts. By beginning this book with a discussion of the genealogy of danger I have offered readers a way of ordering; the subsequent divisions of this study represent my attempt to persuade, to seduce the reader with my argument, and to enlist support for the project of understanding the consequences for politics when dangerous relationships have reached certain terminal points.

I offer a continuation of the argument for understanding dangerous relationships as a form of power in the first two chapters of this book. I ground the argument in the various critical perspectives from which the trajectory of liberal democratic discourse might be traced. My object is to clarify the specific project of this study, initiate an argument regarding the uses of genealogy, and, finally, provide a context within which the second half of the book may be understood.

The second half traces the birth of the prison in the United States, and there I attempt to sustain the initial argument regarding the development of liberal democratic theory and practice. I have resisted an urge to present this section of the book first and thus to allow the readers the luxury of applying their own arguments to a collection of jumbled documents. I believe however that, given such an invitation, those who inevitably respect the authority of authors would follow the tyranny of consecutive pages as though the text were a narrative. Such readers do that violence every time they read, just as other readers do their violence by skipping from introduction to conclusion. As they do what they will, I hope the text accommodates them, for it is my intention to do no more here than to problematize a series of what have too often seemed to me to be (either because of their acceptance or dismissal) unproblematic assumptions concerning the nature of politics under the domination of liberal democratic discourse. That, of course, is my own way of trying to seduce the reader. Hence I say:

Read this book as you will. *Nolo contendere.*

# PART

# I

# 1

## Liberal Democratic Discourse

How might one date the origin of liberal democratic discourse? This question is not as useless as one might guess. Answering it entails illuminating the power of that discourse, seeing through the cracks and fissures that surround, penetrate, and ultimately pattern the discourse itself. It is a question designed as a dodge; it avoids the one-dimensionality of a more direct interrogatory, that which asks, what is liberal democratic discourse? That latter question guides one to a well-worn path, shuttling between the equally specious claims of two fictive entities—autonomous individuals and integrative communities.

The question about origins, though, allows one to dig into those fictions, to see the machinery in motion. The artificiality of a discourse can be revealed in the investigation of the conditions of its emergence. Here is such an explanation: Liberal democratic discourse began at the moment when the principle of sovereignty escaped from the prison of the king's body and began to invest itself in the procedures and techniques which would allow it to be reproduced in "the least body of the condemned man."[1] Such a moment is recurrent, so that the discourse itself in time takes on the qualities of a refined truth; a continually reinstituted and always profoundly moving discovery, through research, of the truth of the discourse will satisfy the demands of the critical questioner of sovereignty. For what mesmerizes those enraptured by truth is precisely that it shows itself as a beginning.[2] But in order to fulfill this project of seeking an origin, one must overcome a certain fear—the fear of discourse. For to chase down the radically contingent systematicities which shape discourse, to sort through the piles of shifting, uncertifiable debris at the foundations of that

15

discourse, is no less frightening that the experience of practices crumbling and settling that constitutes the discursive moment itself.[3] This project, if it may be labeled a genealogical one, consistently turns discourse in against itself so as to bring its machinery to a stop, makes it crack open so as to reveal what it cannot, by itself, show: its own moment of practice, the shift from the idea to its realization, from the alea to the event.

If, after all that effort, one wished to claim that this task had explained liberal democratic discourse, could one do so without provoking too much laughter? The first temptation is to say yes, to assert that liberal democratic discourse is a practice that untangles the confused lines of power that had been knotted together in the two bodies of the king. It clarifies the principle of sovereignty as it secularizes it, and shows the face of power to be the rule of law. Sovereignty becomes the power-that-matters in a liberal democratic regime. Sovereignty makes a clean order in political affairs, it separates public from private, it synthesizes separate spheres of being for both, and gives directions to all who seek political solutions to problems of life. Answer yes, and understand the rule of law that governs modern subjects as a sovereign being outside of self.

Answer no, and risk being cast out of the society of ordered subjects. Understand the "no" to be a refusal of the terms of discourse, a resistance to an easy forgetfulness that will allow one to reconstruct comfortably the order of discourse along new lines, lines amenable to the expression of yet another power. Understand a description of this type to be the expression of a rupture, a discontinuity, a root shift which informs the tracings of power itself. When sovereignty migrated from the king's body to that of the modern subject, perhaps *then* that modern subject was born. But against intention, that birth remains a problem, because it falls into place as the product of a series of events, the aleatoric patterning which has been forced into order, in order for modern subjects to understand the "history of the present."[4]

In seeking the places where tensions within the discourse of liberal democracy play themselves out and become the sources of powerful habits, I seek to describe the discursive practices in operation, but not yet to make judgments about the legitimacy or illegitimacy of the order of discourse. It is meaningless to question the legitimacy of discourse when that question is posed at the bloodless level of formal theorizing, and liberal democratic discourse as a practice is bloody indeed. Its order, imposed by a seemingly exhaustless inventiveness, can be revealed only when the fear of discourse is itself addressed directly. To address, in fact, to embrace that fear may well be the first step in "cutting off the King's head."[5]

### The Word, the Sword, and the Liberal State

If one wishes to study this modern and bloody power, it is difficult to avoid discussing Thomas Hobbes. Writing in the middle of the seventeenth century, in a sense ushering in the modern age of power, Hobbes might be said to have sunk the cornerstone of modern Western authority. That century was a time of extraordinary upheaval (the parallels between then and now are sometimes astonishing). In fact, Hobbes's political theory sometimes seems to be the direct product of his fear of war, which grew into a conviction that humans, especially men, are naturally creatures of unlimited appetites. But, as familiar as most readers are with Hobbes, his vision is complex enough so that a variety of readings are not only possible, but necessary, if it is to make sense today. The reading of Hobbes that best serves the purpose of this study is that which emphasizes his understanding of the relationship between discourse and power, or as he more eloquently put it, "the word and the sword."[6]

Hobbes sought peace through quiet. In his time, what must have seemed the incessant chatter of thousands of voices constituted a major threat to peace as he understood it. One can read the first two books of the *Leviathan* as Hobbes's vision of the transformation of a noisy society into a quiet one. The key to such a transformation was to be the assertion of a sovereign authority made fully aware of the range and depth of its power. It was to become more powerful by learning that its authority rests upon the word and sword. In fact, if one understands Hobbes to be a strong representative of the origins of modern political theory, then from the very beginning of what might be called the modern era, the relationship between knowledge and power can be characterized as an intimate one. A set of relationships later addressed by almost all modern political theorists is fully elaborated in Hobbes's political epistemology.[7]

The war of every man against every man that Hobbes observed as the English condition was not only a class war, but also a war of and about words. The intensity of sermons, the force with which antinomian doctrines assaulted the very concept of authority, the confusion of meaning that accompanied the ritual observances of Ranters and Seekers and Levelers and Quakers created a general sense of "the world turned upside down."

This war of words was fought as seriously as the war of swords that swelled the ranks of Cromwell's armies and resulted in the beheading of the king.[8] The bonds of guilt that were broken during the Reformation were in dire need of replacement.[9] Otherwise, thought Hobbes, mere anarchy would prevail.

Hobbes advocated the deployment of a form of nominalism in order to separate the demands of temporal authorities from those of God. In some respects, Hobbes's nominalism can be understood as an attempt to protect God from the interrogation of scientific reasoning. Writers as early as William of Ockham had been engaged in such projects. Nominalists asserted that the relationship between words and things is arbitrary, determined in human language by humans. They claimed that while people might understand each other through the use of conventions (words agreed upon), they would never be able to understand God, because God's reason was, is, and always will be God's reason. To challenge the truth value of God's word, as the scientists wished to do, was to revive the assumption, abandoned since the decline of ancient thought, that man is the measure of all things. At the birth of the modern age, such temerity was not very widespread, yet that temerity was recognized by some of the more forward-thinking theologians and philosophers as being the major threat to the medieval order of things. One can interpret the role of nominalism during this period as being an attempt to slow down or halt the advance of such boldness, out of an understanding of the trauma entailed in such a transformation of the human knowledge of self and other.[10] In this context, the nominalism advocated by Hobbes was to serve a double purpose. It was to protect God by showing the incommensurability of human words about God and God's words. Second, and more immediate to the concerns of this work, it was to ensure that the assertions that the sovereign might make concerning the claims of its legitimacy no longer would be closely associated with particular views concerning God's word. While God would be protected from scientific interrogation, the words and actions of humans might be subjected to the interrogation of a ruthless political science that would settle, once and for all, controversies concerning the proper and improper use of power on the part of authorities.[11]

Hobbes's nominalism was thus placed in the service of a constructive enterprise, the conventionalization of authoritative relationships. If, as he claimed, it holds that *"True* and *False* are attributes of Speech, not of Things. And where Speech is not, there is neither *Truth* nor *Falsehood,"* then the legitimacy of authority will be closely bounded by its capacity to determine the meaning of words.[12] In fact, to reiterate one of the central messages of *Leviathan,* the word *authority* means precisely the capacity to own one's words and actions. This definition carries with it an enormous weight of power. Properly speaking, a person is someone who owns his or her own words, who acts upon the basis of his or her own authority. The ownership of words, which resonates so powerfully through Hobbes's text as a metaphor of possession, is synonymous with power.[13] In Hobbesian society, the existence of order depends upon an ontology of behavior in which to be is to have.[14] Ownership becomes one of the most important effects of power in such a society.

This semiotic root of Hobbesian liberalism has not been explored in great detail by students of politics, even by C. B. Macpherson in his justly famous study *The Political Theory of Possessive Individualism.* In Macpherson's reading of Hobbes, the emphasis is on the historical emergence of market society and how it contributed to the creation of a particular type of subject, one who responds more readily to new, acquisitive impulses in himself and others than to a prior set of impulses based upon the epistemological assumptions of feudal economy. Here, my argument parallels Macpherson's, but my emphasis is on the role played by market society in the discourse concerning the state rather than in the discourse concerning the feudal economy. (The classical Marxian connection between these two discourses is compared with the genealogical connection at some length, below.) Hobbesian politics thus can be seen emerging in situations in which, because of the domination of a possessive ontology, people learn that for there to be order, they must give up possessive rights, must come to understand that the retention of life involves a process of bargaining. But the bargaining includes the negotiation of their right to speak for themselves. To give up that right and still retain power is a dubious proposition, which is precisely where Hobbes's great Leviathan runs into a paradox. For the Leviathan to operate, subjects of authority must be willing to give up parts of their behavioral selves, not only as actors in the marketplace but as authors of their own lives. Yet this is also precisely the entity that Hobbes ultimately wished to protect.[15]

The paradox can be illustrated by examining the transactions that result in the establishment of a common authority. The conventional authority that Hobbes envisioned was based on a concept of individual agency, but the individual that Hobbes posited was capable of achieving a high degree of complexity within the terms of the social contract Hobbes subsequently developed. This complexity is hinted at by the careful language that Hobbes used to describe the process.

> The way by which a man either simply Renounceth, or Transferreth his Right, is a Declaration, or Signification, by some voluntary and sufficient signe, or signes, that he doth so Renounce, or Transferre. . . . And these Signes are either Words onely, or Actions onely; or (as it happeneth most often) both Words and Actions.[16]

The sign that is given is ultimately worthless, however, unless backed by the sword. "Covenants, without the Sword, are but Words, and of no strength to secure a man at all," Hobbes argued.[17] While some activities were to be exempt from this ferocious ordering principle, their exemption was problematic, constituting as they did an area that was to generate new words and actions: the realm of commodious living.[18] In the domain of what Hobbes understood to be proper power relationships, the "nominalist moment," so to speak, was to fix all meaning permanently. Just as war is understood by Hobbes to be an inclination to fight, so too must peace be an inclination to rest. But since the Hobbesian political science is also geometric, once peace is established, authority must be univocal; only one set of words and actions can be produced. This absolute authority defines and enforces a single political reality.

Once its word is challenged, sovereign authority must suppress the challenge or disintegrate. Without the sword, a multiplicity of authors/actors might soon emerge. Hobbes feared that emergence, and logically concluded that a univocal authority must be absolute in order to exist at all. The requirement for an absolute authority was not a utopian wish, but instead was an absolute prerequisite for peace. In the absence of the enforcement of the sword, a multiplicity of authors would soon challenge authority. A tower of babble would come into being. This is why crimes of passion are but a secondary concern for Hobbes, being but the setting into motion of the ideas already started by those who cause all threats to civil peace. This primary cause of all crime, "the Presumption of False Principles," leads people to believe that "Justice is but a vain word."[19] When authority is so questioned, civil war follows.

> And that such as have a great, and false opinion of their own Wisedome, take upon them to reprehend the actions, and call in question

the Authority of them that govern, and so to unsettle the Lawes with their publique discourse, as that nothing shall be a Crime, but what their own designes require should be so. It happeneth also to the same men, to be prone to all such Crimes, as consist in Craft, and in deceiving of their Neighbours; because they think their designes are too subtile to be perceived. . . . For of them that are the first movers in the disturbance of Common-wealth, (which can never happen without a Civill Warre), very few are left alive long enough, to see their new Designes established; so that the benefit of their Crimes, redoundeth to Posterity, and such as would least have wished it; which argues that they were not so wise, as they thought they were.[20]

From Hobbes's perspective, then, there is no good reason why anyone should question authority. Thus it is a great irony that his nominalist vision of authority is undermined by one of his most fundamental assertions, that the first natural right is self-preservation.[21] Implicit in that law are two assumptions that serve as the final barriers to the permanent fixing of political authority. First, self-preservation requires that one question authority whenever one's life is placed at risk by that authority.[22] While at first glance, this contingency does not seem to place too great a strain upon the constitution of authority, it becomes obvious, upon reflection, that any determination on the part of authority that life needs to be risked is going to cause legitimation problems (obvious as well is the simple observation that rarely will such demands be couched in straightforward language).

Second, and more directly relevant to understanding danger, preserving oneself demands that one find out who one is in relationship to authority, to the world of power. This search, if limited in the way in which Hobbes wished it to be limited—to an investigation of one's identity vis-à-vis the sovereign authority that he defined—might not by itself have led to the establishment of the modern individual. But Hobbes was unable to limit the inquisitiveness of this new subject to the realm of commodious living. Acting to preserve the king, Hobbes contributed to launching the modern era of politics, not merely by setting selves in search of a new identity in relationship to sovereign authority, but by setting the search for selfhood against a backdrop initially devoid of any but the most starkly defined relationships of power.[23]

Hobbes demonstrated how differentiated authors can be produced from what Foucault later recalled as the "body politic."[24] Hobbes's Leviathan, however, while depicted as a body, is well remembered as a geometric figure held in place by a sword, or, to put it more crudely, as a perpetual-stillness machine. Despite the movements that Hobbes was to allow subjects in other spheres of existence, and despite the limited pattern of change he was to allow in the world of politics, ultimately the only way to constrain the desire of "power after power unto death" was to establish and maintain a regime of silence. It is from this dimension of Hobbes's work that Foucault's understanding of the Leviathan is derived, in terms that complement Hobbes's, even while simultaneously eschewing "the model of the Leviathan," and "grasping subjection in its material instance as a constitution of subjects. This would be the exact opposite of Hobbes's project in *Leviathan.*"[25] The humanitarian project—or, to enter more directly into Foucault's terms, the multiplicity of strategies and tactics that have subjugated bodies over the course of several centuries—is the trajectory that must be traced in tandem with the more explicitly monumental history of the liberal democratic state, if one wishes to understand how the modern self, as an imposed subjectivity, constitutes such a crucial component in the modern exercise of power. But there is no way to pursue the modern imposition of power without following it into the bowels of modern selfhood, without tracing what might be called the deep surfaces, the markings of power as found in the practices that make people as they are. Of course, what happens once these markings are seen will, and probably should, remain a matter of controversy.

To trace the trajectory of these components of liberal democratic discourse, I proceed by asking what may appear to be two equally arbitrary questions. First, what is the *telos* of liberal democracy? Second, how is the frontier of liberal democratic discourse political? The first question is complex enough to require an answer of some length. Even though it has been answered definitively in a variety of ways, ironically it has not ever been answered conclusively, which has been a source of great satisfaction to liberal democrats. The second question has rarely been asked, which is precisely the point of asking it here. Yet the answer to the second question, as well, is by no means simple, even in its most basic formulation.

### The Telos of Liberal Democracy

Martin Heidegger formulated an understanding of *telos* that emphasizes the essentiality of all attempts to completely know and act upon the world:

Circumscribing gives bounds to the thing. With the bounds the thing does not stop; rather, from within them it begins to be what after production it will be. That which gives bounds, that which completes, in this sense is called in Greek *telos*, which is all too often translated as "aim" and "purpose," and so misinterpreted.[26]

Is liberal democracy in this sense teleological? At first glance, it would seem that liberal democracy is boundless. One need only refer to modern defenses of liberal democracy, couched in terms of pluralism, in order to begin a defense of it as being nonteleological. To use an argument of Schumpeter, who provides a benchmark of sorts for this tradition in political theory, representative democracy is a process.[27] Even many of the critics of liberal democracy, most prominently Lowi,[28] share this view, pointing to the incoherence of policymaking in the United States and the listlessness and anomie of its polity as being the results of the absence of clear and comprehensive boundaries endemic to liberal democracy. Such critiques have often united conservatives and radicals in the United States.

But the deep telos of liberal democracy might be said to reside in its dangerous practices. If one shifts the question to "What is the relationship between the theory and practice of liberal democracy?" then its telos becomes clear.

The liberal concept of individuality is acknowledged by most theorists as being in conflict with democratic equality. Indeed, many proponents of liberal democracy point to the tensions between the two as a major source of its strength. Certainly this has been true for those who have celebrated and criticized its American incarnation. Liberalism is rooted in various understandings of the priority of the individual in society.[29] The broad range of liberal views is largely the result of the extent to which different proponents of liberalism have asserted the primacy of the individual over others (others often being equated with their embodiment in sovereign political authority) in the construction of social reality. Liberals usually understand the individual to be a rational actor, or at least a reasonable person. The specific content of individual reason is the basis of various theories of human nature to be found in the liberal tradition. Even Karl Marx can be interpreted as having a place within the liberal tradition, to the extent that one can successfully advance claims that he posited a theory of human nature and had a strong theory of human agency. What separates

Marx from liberals, in this regard, is that he does not give primacy to the individual. He thus provides a bridge to postliberal political theories.

Liberalism is also the first political theory to explore fully the meaning of contract. From its beginning, liberal political theorists have used the contract as what might be called a meta-metaphor, an organizing narrative for the everyday social interactions that are made possible by and enhanced when assumptions about the existence of the reasonable individual are also accepted. Much of the development of liberalism is tied to elaborations of the constraints and freedoms that can be expressed through the delimiting characteristics of the contract metaphor. This is true for Hobbes, and it is also true for John Rawls, who made the most recent systematic attempt to articulate a comprehensive liberal theory of justice. The contract metaphor is also and obviously linked to the theory and practice of market capitalism. The extent to which linkages between the two are made explicit again varies within the liberal tradition of political thought. The contract can be said to provide a means of associating otherwise indifferent and isolated individuals, codifying the reasons and assurances necessary for people to engage in common activity over time. It should also be noted that the contract is also the most explicit link holding individuals to the formal organization of political authority.

Of course, liberalism is more than the interplay of these relatively simple concepts. However, one might argue that liberal theory progressively has grown simpler rather than more complex. If one examines the utilitarian, hedonistic applications of liberal theory to be found in the writings of most contemporary policy analysts, one finds the richness and subtlety of the earlier theory lost, replaced by pseudo-sophisticated mathematical models. Much the same can be said for the pluralist tradition in the United States in general, particularly in regard to the way it has abandoned individuals for abstract "interests" and "interest groups."[30]

This progressive simplification of liberal theory is at first glance puzzling. Some theorists argue that the reasons for it lie in the integration of liberalism with democracy. If liberalism presupposes the primacy of the individual, democracy presupposes the equality of individuals in reference to the sanctions which encourage and discourage the development of individuals and which contribute to the development of institutions that enhance and impede various aspects of individuality. Democracy comes into conflict with liberalism because it gives priority to the equality of all individuals over the full expression of the rights of the specific individual. Of course, there are many ways of imagining the limits and substance of equality so as to make it seem compatible with individualism. In the United States the attempt to integrate the two has most commonly been expressed through the notion of "equal opportunity."[31] Ensuring that all are equally protected in the expression of their individual rights is supposed both to enhance and to preserve individuality.

Nonetheless, the political development of the United States is very often characterized in terms of the conflicts that surround attempts to enhance equality at the price of the preservation of liberal freedom. The two value systems are seen as being intrinsically in opposition, even by those who welcome the tension, who see it as the primary source of the endurance and stability underlying the American political system. George Kateb recently noted this tension in a study of the American transcendentalists, thinkers who made the last systematic and serious attempt to resolve, rather than celebrate, that conflict. Referring specifically to Emerson, Whitman, and Thoreau, he writes,

> They do not, to be sure, expect that all will ever be individuals in the full democratic sense. In any case, democratic individuality is not an ideal that one can ever be certain has been reached. It is not meant to be so unequivocally defined as to be unambiguously reachable. It is not a permanent state of being, but an indefinite project. It allows of degrees, approximations, attenuations. Still, some persons try harder than others; some try *deliberately*.[32]

The ambiguous manner in which these theorists attempt to pull together the opposing tendencies found in liberal and democratic values illuminates one dimension of the sensibility underlying the humanitarian striving of intellectuals and political elites in the era when liberal and democratic values were first explicitly recognized as being in conflict with each other. But one must also ask, what does it reveal about the practice of liberal democracy during this period? How, to use Tocqueville's phrase, does the recognition of the indefinite perfectibility of man inform specific projects? Another question, as well, regarding the role of specific persons in these projects: what *causes* them to try harder, what informs their deliberations?

It is precisely here that Foucault's work critically informs liberal democratic discourse—at the level of its specific projects. His answers to questions concerning practices and motives are rooted in his understanding of the emergence of disciplinary discourse and its implications. What is generally perceived as a dialectic between individuality and equality is, at the level of practice, conflated by Foucault into a unified system of discipline, what might be called organized individuation. Specific disciplinary practices constitute the modern humanitarian project, which is expressed theoretically in the ideal values of liberal individualism and democratic equality. Foucault, coming to an examination of these practices from a perspective that neither assumes nor precludes the possibility of human freedom, pushed aside the claims of liberals that their values can provide insurance against practices oriented toward the totalization of discourses, toward the elimination of free will. In fact, his study of discipline is designed to show how privileging a value like individual freedom results in individual subjugation. These processes of subjugation are necessarily processes of simplification; the imposition of the same model of self upon a variety of peoples results in an equality based upon simple uniformity, a uniformity which shields individuals from differences and supplies them with dangerous protection.

An article by Michael Walzer illustrates the mechanics of this process. Walzer takes to task those left critics who, he says, present the view that liberal freedoms are unreal. Their argument, he claims, "doesn't connect in any plausible way with the actual experience of contemporary politics; it has a quality of abstraction and theoretical willfulness."[33] For him, liberalism, through its art of separation, establishes various spheres of social activity so as to prevent too great a concentration of power in one area. It makes specific freedoms real, and opens their access to many, thus enhancing equality as well.

> Freedom is additive; it consists of rights within settings, and we must understand the settings, one by one, if we are to guarantee the rights. Similarly, each freedom entails a specific form of equality or, better, the absence of a specific inequality—of conquerors and subjects, believers and infidels, trustees and teachers, owners and workers—and the sum of the absences makes an egalitarian society.[34]

While Walzer is convinced that liberalism's art of separation prevents overly great concentrations of power, he also thinks that liberalism has always underestimated the power of the state. Indeed, he argues that it is only when the state is powerful that disciplinary society comes into existence.[35] Only with the breakdown of separation can uniformity be imposed, and for Walzer only the state is powerful enough to destroy the walls between various spheres of social activity. Despite its shortcomings, then, a rigorous liberalism that also imposes its art against the state is the best insurance against the possible establishment of disciplinary society.

From Foucault's perspective, the art of separation celebrated by Walzer constitutes a strategy for the dispersion of disciplinary tactics. Such a strategy can be enhanced by state action. In fact, often a state shows how powerful it is by establishing separation. Regardless of the immediate level of state involvement, however, when human activities are relegated into various spheres dissociated from each other, subjects must fight for rights in each one of these separate spheres, while common linkages, below the level of the state proper, enable those who operate in each sphere to manage and manipulate subjects. Does such a project require the existence of a state to tear down barriers? It would seem that when part of the operating strategy of modern disciplines is itself found in the practices of separation exercised at the local levels of society, then the role of the state is never separate or even separable from that of those localities. Attacks on the state for being the site where this activity occurs are similar to blaming the swallow for bringing the spring. Those agents that Walzer celebrates for acting in different spheres of society—scholars, workers, and parents—all live in institutions not of their own intention, namely schools, factories, and families. The state, in this regard, is always there as the monitor, through law, of the functions of these disciplinary bodies. It either permits incursions or sets up barriers, but it is always involved in decisions allowing or disallowing, or, more accurately, encouraging and discouraging what happens in these institutions.

An example of this impacted state of affairs is the efforts of New Right advocates in the United States to get the national government to pass laws designed, in their words, to protect the family. Arguing as they do for less state intrusion in the realm of individual rights, these people are often viewed as hypocrites by those more comfortable with state intervention. After all, how could they honestly advocate less state intrusion, when they want the state to regulate the sexual habits of teenagers, discourage women's entrance into the job market, and generally enforce a particular religico-ethical standard not shared by all? But if one understands that there is no advocacy position currently available that does not touch upon the use of state power, then their position becomes easier to understand, if not support. However, theorists and policymakers alike continually pretend that there really are separate spheres; the power of the modern state as a coordinator of disciplines thus goes unrecognized, even as its power to influence events generally remains overestimated.

For Walzer, the destruction of barriers by authoritarian states enables power to operate in the manner that Foucault specifies. But the operations of that kind of power are not the result of the systematic destruction of barriers; instead, they are the result of the establishment of localized sites where the disciplines operate. The mistaken association of administration exclusively with a centralized state blinds not only Walzer but most who have written about modern bureaucracy to the fact that bureaucracies are not dependent upon a centralized state in order to act effectively as systems of power. In fact, it is possible that the more localized the actual exercise of power, the more effective the exercise.[36] In the modern era, one may well say that the state, through the administration of power, is itself a conduit through which the transformation of relationships of exploitation and oppression into relationships of danger occurs.

This hardly means that liberal democracy is unimportant. In fact, in the rise of modern power arrangements the strategies adopted by liberal democrats to encourage individual autonomy and to ensure equality contribute directly to this power of the state. Here, I do not wish to imply that there have been no other forces at work; I wish to claim only that the relationships of domination expressed through the Marxian categories of exploitation are insufficient to explain dangerous relationships. Indeed they themselves can be implicated in the exercises of power that contribute to the rise of dangerous relationships. More to the point, the liberal democratic, capitalistic state has served as a matrix through which dangerous relationships have been misunderstood as having to do with the protection of rights (Walzer's walls) rather than as being the instrument of a kind of liberal democratic repression. That repression is instrumental to the establishment of the individual, as any reader of Freud knows, and with apologies to both Freud and C. B. Macpherson, might be called "repressive individualism."[37]

The *telos* of liberal democracy is thus its tendency toward repression. How that came to be is what needs explanation, because the promise was always something else. What, in short, are the connections between liberal democracy and disciplinary society? To answer that, it is necessary to revisit Hobbes, through Foucault.

## Liberal Democracy and Discipline

Foucault took the question of power as seriously as Hobbes did. Yet, unlike Hobbes, he was extremely doubtful that a structure as fragile as the modern state is capable of containing and limiting power's exercise. This is because his understanding of power started at the point where Hobbes left off, in the domain of subjects. Foucault argued,

> Power is everywhere; not because it embraces everything, but because it comes from everywhere. And "Power," insofar as it is permanent, repetitious, inert, and self-reproducing, is simply the over-all effect that emerges from these mobilities, the concatenation that rests on each of them and seeks in turn to arrest their movement. One needs to be a nominalist, no doubt: power is not an institution, and not a structure; neither is it a certain strength we are endowed with; it is the name that one attributes to a complex strategical situation in a particular society.[38]

Foucault's first genealogical analysis of power was his study of the modern prison, *Discipline and Punish*. There he traced authority's word from the point at which Hobbes left off, analyzing its successive transformations, inversions, and multiplications. To describe Foucault's project yet another way, his work can be read as a study of the world of normalization that Hobbes's vision of power made possible.

*Discipline and Punish* is made difficult by the sometimes Aesopian strategies that Foucault employed to enrich the readings of the text. Foucault even outlined the project in an extremely eliptical manner. Following what might be called a rhetorical incision (Foucault's recounting of the drawing and quartering of Damien the regicide, juxtaposed with a description of a prison timetable), the introduction discusses the "king's body" as the departure point for the study of the modern prison. The king's body, Foucault argued, produces its double in "the least body of the condemned man."[39] Foucault continued,

> If the surplus power possessed by the king gives rise to the duplication of his body, has not the power exercised on the subjugated body of the condemned man given rise to another type of duplication? That of a "non-corporal," a "soul" as Mably called it. The history of this "micro-physics" of the punitive power would then be a genealogy of a modern "soul.". . . This real, non-corporal soul is not a substance;

it is the element in which are articulated the effects of a certain type of knowledge, the machinery by which the power relations give rise to a possible corpus of knowledge, and knowledge extends and reinforces the effects of this power.[40]

Foucault subtitled this genealogy *The Birth of the Prison.* Leaving aside Foucault's major debt to Nietzsche (which might lead to considerations of the volume's being a companion to, and modern reflection upon, *The Birth of Tragedy),* it is nonetheless clear that Foucault intended to describe a prison that is far more than a merely physical carceral, the carceral also being a product of the modern era. "The soul," he explained, "is effect and instrument of a political anatomy; the soul is the prison of the body."[41] The soul is the artificial site where the effects of power are manifested; it is, to be brief, where the Leviathan now can be found. Discipline is hidden, is everywhere, if not in the crude instruments of torture, where the least body of the condemned man was ripped apart to release an earlier version of the soul, then in the inscriptions placed upon bodies by petty mechanisms of habituation. This prison is the opposite of the Leviathan as Hobbes imagined it, but is, perhaps, an inevitable product of Hobbesian science. Discipline is headless, multivocal, it turns the chatter of multiplicities of people into the instrumentality that inscribes bodies.

For Foucault, as well as for Hobbes, not only words make up the reality under examination, but actions as well. Foucault considered both as forms of discourse. The multiplicity of discursive formations, and the manner in which seemingly petty mechanisms contribute to the establishment of the modern, subjugated subject, make up the bulk of his genealogical analysis of the modern soul. This was precisely the project that Hobbes undertook, with one crucial exception. For Foucault, a major problem in Hobbes's analysis is that Hobbes misplaced the site of power by concentrating it in one place. The penetration of the body, the elaboration of more complex souls, the rising of new points of resistance, are all possible below the horizon of political authority as conceived by Hobbes. One contemporary alternative to such an analysis, pursued by structuralist theorists such as Althusser and Poulantzas, was to posit the political limits of the state at the point where the state is synonymous with all power relationships.[42] The problem with this formulation is that it renders the specific status of the modern state meaningless, even as it presumes to incorporate into the state all power. The alternative presented by Foucault, on the other hand, leaves room for differentiating various deployments of strategies of power in society. It also presents a specific caution against the focus on sovereignty that any analysis of the exercise of power by the state, qua state, will incorporate.

How does Foucault's analysis proceed? As an example, one might refer to the arrangement of furniture. Foucault presents us with a few pictures of pieces that are almost part of the architecture of the room. The most striking picture is that of a lecture hall.[43] As is not uncommon, all seats are bolted down. The students are looking forward at the lecturer, who is at the podium in the front of the room. In fact, every face is directed toward the front. The most striking feature of these seats is that each is built as an individual room; each has a window out of which its occupant looks, and no one is able to leave his seat, the door to the room being locked from the outside. While everyone has a clear view of the lecturer, no one can communicate with anyone else, or even see them.

This picture is of an auditorium in a French prison. The auditorium is a micromodel of the architectural metaphor that can be found on the frontispiece of Hobbes's *Leviathan*.[44] It is a metaphor made real. It makes up the mechanism, the technology of a particular kind of power that is transferable to other domains of social relationships: factories, schools, and the offices of bureaucrats. It was not so long ago that the desks in American schools were bolted down, that the teacher stood at the front of the room, that all students, under pain of punishment, kept their eyes forward. All communication in such a situation is mediated through the teacher, in a manner similar to that of the sovereign authority that Hobbes established in his writings. While the architectural barriers of the prison are down, they are replaced by more subtle, incorporal fetters. And the students suffer the silence, or resist, fidgeting, passing notes to each other, raising hell occasionally, adjusting to the system. Eventually, they adjust so well that they respond as though physically constrained, even when all such constraints have vanished from sight.

Because the modern age is an age of reform, the unenlightened policies that resulted in this cruel fate for generations of children were eventually rectified. The tyranny of the bolted-down desk came to an end. Furniture was not only rearranged, but made constantly rearrangeable. Some classrooms now even have moving walls. A new device, the learning station, where students consume information in "modules," supplants the lecture and the book. Computers tailor the learning experience to the individual.

Some educators assert that eventually everyone will be "computer literate," and that the classroom and the school will be abolished, replaced by communication links that connect home to information center. The possibilities, as computer company executives are wont to point out, are endless.

But there is a dark side to this process. Under the guise of the liberation of the student, a relatively visible form of power is replaced with a network of finer, less obtrusive techniques of inscription. There is further individualization, a finer tuning of classifications and examinations of subjugated bodies, and a qualitatively higher level of the observatory power of bureaucratic agencies, because the new furniture arrangement and the redeployment of observatory powers allow for a greater access to information about how and what each student learns. Reform results in further penetration of the body, the continual recreation of an increasingly sophisticated soul, and, finally, the creation of more potential points of resistance. If one were to understand Foucault's analysis to be purely critical, one would stop here.

Foucault, however, presents a more specific analysis of the problems of modern power, because he is concerned with what might be termed misplaced resistances to power. The idea that reform is one of the effects of power, is but one more strategy, is an important illustration of how his analysis operates. Later in this work it will become very important to investigate where such an analysis leads, especially because of the often-voiced suspicion that it doesn't lead anywhere. But here the importance of this analysis seems to lie in the way in which it seeks to redirect focus away from traditional concerns of political analysis into areas that are rarely considered to have important, visible political impacts.

Thus Foucault's major objection to Hobbesian analysis was based precisely on the problem of the construction of the sovereign. At the same time, however, Foucault seemed to understand the importance of Hobbes's theory of the state, reading it in a way that no other contemporary theorist has attempted. Modern subjects have allowed the sovereign to remain as the major focus of concern, while the processes by which they are continually renormalized (reformed) proceed apace. For Foucault, if they are to be rid of the afflictions most closely associated with this kind of power, a direct manifestation of the modern will to know, then they must start by realizing that the concern about the powerful role of the modern state is to a large extent misplaced. The "insurrection of subjugated knowledges," as Foucault once called attempts to resist the ongoing processes of normalizing discourses, cannot be advanced by directly attacking the modern state.[45] Such attacks are necessarily subsumed under the same general acceptance of sovereignty that characterizes those who support the state. Those who are directly oppressed by and attack the modern state are acting not out of revolutionary consciousness but out of a desperate identification with the source of their oppression.[46] Regardless of who takes over the apparatus of such a state, the advance of discipline continues, often at a new level of intensity, with the further entrapment of those who resist in the field of power.

There is a monkey trap used in Polynesia that works through a subtle and ingenious mechanism. To catch a monkey, one makes a hole in a coconut large enough to allow its hand to slip inside, but small enough so that when it clenches the food that baited the trap it will be unable to remove its hand. All the monkey has to do to be free is unclench its hand. If it gives up the food, it escapes the trap. But the monkey seems unable to understand.

This simple act is fraught with complexity. In grabbing the food, the monkey simultaneously traps itself and creates the possibilities of its liberation. But there is no going back, and there is no hope of remaining where it is. The monkey is trapped by its desire and its fear. The trapper approaches.

One can apply this metaphor to the experience of rule under the guidance of the sovereign state, that set of institutions which overlies the continued inscriptions of power on bodies, the continued reproductions of the modern selves so necessary for the rule of disciplinary society. Normalization proceeds apace, and in fact is aided by the mistaken belief that in reform lies hope, that the protection of liberal *rights* will impede further subjugation. Like the monkey, modern subjects clamor for privacy acts, sovereign guarantees of the sources and derivations of power, declarations which simply dig them deeper and deeper into the trap, which by virtue of being misplaced resistances to positive exercises of power serve as smoke screens for the further elaboration of dangerous relationships. Modern subjects too are trapped by desire, even though they may not realize it. It is the desire to be both in and out of danger at the same time.

For Foucault, to understand the relationship between words and things was crucial to the development of countermoves on the part of subjugated knowledges. In this sense, his appeal to "nominalism" is the exact opposite of that made by Hobbes. Whereas Hobbes attempted to use the knowledge of the arbitrary connection between words and things to establish a moment in time in which peace can be permanently established, Foucault wished to demonstrate that the Hobbesian project is plausible only as an ongoing ruse, as a *secret*. Foucault once argued that the modern struggle against domination does not involve bringing to consciousness unconscious motives but must be carried out in opposition "to the secretive. It is perhaps more difficult to unearth a secret than it is the unconscious."[47] The purpose of a genealogy of the modern prison, or the modern soul, if one accepts Foucault's understanding, is to make it possible to reveal the secret of the relationship between a particular discourse and the power that it constitutes. Such a project makes one aware of the dangers that are posed by such discourses.

The purpose of studying the genealogy of the prison in the United States is not merely to supplement Foucault's analysis. Paradoxically, a much milder form of liberalism than Hobbes's ferocious brand, coupled with an impulse toward democratic equality, exaggerated rather than ameliorated the effects of disciplinary power during the era of the rise of discipline. The escape from politics supposedly accomplished through the mechanisms of American liberal democratic discourse ultimately played the most important single role in the politicization of all dimensions of life in the United States. That politicization was as thorough, and had the same lingering effects, as that of any "Western societies" Foucault examined. The grounds of legitimate authority in the United States are shaped by the politics of dangerous relationships. While there may be no sovereign, it is important to remember that there are states, and there are multiplicities of factors that hold together these tenuous entities called "nations."[48] In the United States, where most of those interwoven discourses have been frail at best, the strategies of sovereignty have served as a great deception. Underlying that deception, however, is a regime of truth that operates continuously, and that has been met by continuous resistance. Lacking the drama of wars fought through other means, this series of battles has been fought within the bowels of the body politic, which is, by the way, the political frontier of liberal democratic discourse.

# 2

## Genealogy versus History

Genealogy is a way of uncovering the radically contingent systematicities of human being, the habits that give shape to the various orders of political existence—in short, genealogy exposes the regimes of truth under which people live. It is a method of working against the grain of received historical knowledge in order to reveal how history comes to be. Its emphasis on contingency opposes genealogy to the kind of history that incorporates all change within a logic of the progressive realization of reason. Its resistance to fixing a boundary which would delimit (and enable) a primary focus on human agency as the location of power and site of conflict opposes genealogy to the kind of history that identifies necessity as the background and horizon of all historical development. More generally, history, with its "just treatment of the past, its decisive cutting of the roots, its rejection of traditional attitudes of reverence, its liberation of man by presenting him with other origins than those in which he prefers to see himself," fails to diagnose the core nihilisms underlying the development of self-conscious being. Genealogy does so by moving from veneration to parody, from continuity to dissociation, and from truth to a critique of the will to knowledge.[1]

Genealogy counters the deepest intuitions of social scientists, who, in Nietzsche's understanding, confound problems of origin and purpose. As a genealogist Nietzsche protested against such attempts to create an identity between the two, because he thought they concealed the will to power at those points at which it most clearly manifests itself. In fact, the confounding of origin and purpose was for him an ironic sign of the domination of a will to power over the events of humanity.

But purposes and utilities are only *signs* that a will to power has become master of something less powerful and imposed upon it the character of a function; and the entire history of a "thing," an organ, a custom, can in this way be a continuous sign-chain of ever new interpretations and adoptions whose causes do not even have to be related to one another but, on the contrary, in some cases succeed and alternate with one another in a purely chance fashion. The "evolution" of a thing, a custom, an organ is thus by no means its *progressus* toward a goal, even less a logical *progressus* by the shortest route and with the smallest expenditure of force—but a succession of more or less profound, more or less mutually independent processes of subduing, plus the resistances they encounter, the attempts at transformation for the purposes of defense and reaction, and the results of successful counteractions. The form is fluid, but the "meaning" is even more so.[2]

These resistances and counteractions underlie the battles that rage in the name of one or another sign, whether it be in the politics of Plato or Ronald Reagan. Thus genealogy can be a process of exposing signs of power, demystifying the orders of the agents of domination in a given order of being.

It is also a process that is representative of an attempt to assert that power is fundamental to human being. Indeed, Nietzsche is often attacked as a celebrator of domination, owing in part to the nature of his critique of democracy, which he understood to be a simple attack on all forms of domination. His antagonism to democracy is supposedly straightforward. Nietzsche found democracy to be an expression of *ressentiment* on the part of those who are weak. But Nietzsche's view was determined by more than this admittedly aristocratic bias. Democracy, when manifested as an *ordering principle*, acts as a form of endangerment at once insidious and antilife, exists as a form of knowledge *over* life.

The democratic idiosyncrasy which opposes everything that dominates and wants to dominate, the modern *misarchism* (to coin an ugly word for an ugly thing) has permeated the realm of the spirit and disguised itself in the most spiritual forms to such a degree that today it has forced its way, has acquired the *right* to force its way into the strictest, apparently most objective sciences; indeed, it seems to me to have taken charge of all physiology and theory of life—to the detriment of life, as goes without saying, since it has robbed it of a fundamental concept, that of *activity*.[3]

A democracy that pretends to the elimination of power is one that endangers life. The most terrifying expression of this dilemma is the political logic that gambles the lives of *all* subjects of the modern state in hopes of securing their protection. In its most spectacular guise, the democracy of *ressentiment* is the democracy of extinction. Yet such a democracy is specific to a set of practices; no universal rule explains or characterizes all democracy as such.

Moreover, it would be mistaken to conclude that because the greatest peril of extinction is associated in some way with this political logic, a confrontation at the level of life *contra* extinction is necessary if one would oppose contemporary tyrannies. It may be, instead, that Foucault's advice, which emphasizes the particularity of practices, the "micro" exercises of positive power, and hence argues for resistance and insurrections at local levels, is the most helpful way of informing specific counterpractices. That remains open as a question.

Critics of genealogy, paradoxically, argue that ultimately it is a movement that is unambiguously destructive in its supposed celebration of irrationality and its refusal to assert anything positive or affirmative concerning power. Despite such criticisms, genealogists, peculiarly, seem to be consistent in the choices of objects they wish to destroy, seemingly always on the side of problematizing the habits of established power. One commentator has claimed that an implicit Kantianism informs Foucault's work, for instance, and another makes a similar claim in regard to Nietzsche.[4]

But I think it can be claimed, at least, that there is a "counterontology" implicit in genealogical projects, one directed at understanding threats to life, that is, at understanding *danger*.[5] This counterontology, coldly cognizant of the persistence of power in the constitution of truth, holds out the notion that war must be reimagined if humankind is to survive the twentieth century. This task requires also that people realize how universalized war has become, how meaning itself is shot through with conflict. When Nietzsche claimed that the only word possible to define is one with no history, and when Foucault later claimed that "the history that bears and determines us has the form of a war rather than that of language: relations of power, not relations of meaning," they were emphasizing the importance of understanding that no peaceful consensus is possible, and hence that seeking peace is paradoxically dangerous. In fact, by understanding the ways in which power is borne in specific relationships, it may become possible to decode (and defuse) the operation of power and knowledge as a war system.[6] The task is to encourage a new relationship of being to power, or to encourage what Connolly has referred to as "slack in the order."[7] Such is one liberating message of genealogy.

Of course genealogy is not unproblematic. The genealogist must twist the expressions of power that form the material upon which genealogy operates, counter power with a "relentless erudition," make the organization of knowledge cry out under a harsh interrogation. As such, genealogy is a technique that endangers by implicating the genealogist in the nihilism he or she wishes to diagnose; the deconstruction of meaning comes about by the infliction of pain upon the body of language.[8]

Genealogy is dangerous in this sense, but it is also dangerous in that it is a technique for stripping selves of protection, for removing subjects from the field of protection. Genealogy's intent is cautionary. It opens up secrets, strips modern subjects of their shields. By focusing on the multiple relationships of reciprocal danger, genealogy suggests ways out of domination that do not depend upon the transcendence of truth with new truth, or, as Habermas has put it, "the fuller realization of reason in the world."[9] Such a dependence is ultimately futile, according to genealogy's notions concerning how the materiality of existence proceeds. Even worse, such dependence threatens the continuation of existence on a larger scale, for the trajectory of reason has been a trajectory of control, of the rationalization of life to the point of its total disallowance.[10]

Genealogy, when used to investigate such a moral phenomenon as liberal democracy, which pretends no history but that of reason and yet which implicitly recognizes a history to reason, can present two critiques. First, genealogy addresses the history of reason as the history of progress, the seemingly relentless moral advancement that accompanies the assertion of freedom by individuals. By tracing the contingencies underlying progress, genealogy strips away the pretense of the heroic individual, and reveals that individual's more fundamental reliance upon history, understood as necessity. When genealogy critiques necessity, a more fundamental conflict is expressed concerning being and nothingness, or, more prosaically, the artfulness of life, which is denied by those who can only keep their noses to the grindstone and their eyes resolutely fixed to the horizon necessity draws for them.

### The Critique of Progress

It is somewhat ironical that traditional historians of social institutions such as David Rothman have condemned Foucault for what they have perceived to be his Marxian tendencies, arguing that he focuses too much on the service that discipline performs for the system of production under capitalism. From Rothman's perspective, Foucault is unable to see devisiveness and incoherence underlying the development of penal policies in industrializing societies. Foucault, he asserts, mistakenly sees a conspiracy of class at work in the development of discipline. For Rothman, the controversies that have accompanied the movements of penal reform, the incompleteness with which reform has been accomplished, and the continuing reassessment of the values of particular penal policies indicate the naivety, and sometimes the venality, of particular actors, but hardly represent the work of a hidden hand of totalitarianism. Moreover, Rothman suggests, a translation of penal discipline to American society at large has never really occurred, for the United States is a free society.

Rothman's recent two volumes on the institutional evolution of asylums and prison is perhaps the most well known study of the American carceral, and it is from the platform of the introductions to these two works that he launches his attack on Foucault.[11] It is worth noting, then, that he uses as his foil Foucault's studies of the creation of madness (*Madness and Civilization*) and of the penitentiary (*Discipline and Punish*). Rothman characterizes Foucault's argument as a critique of Enlightenment reason: "Foucault deals with ideas alone, almost never connecting them to events."[12] Rothman asserts that this detachment from historical reality renders Foucault's study meaningless.

> The prison did not descend once and for all from some capitalist spirit. The more one understands the alterations within the system, the more one explores motives, designs, and alliances, the less an air of inevitability hangs over the practice of punishment and the less compelling arguments of economic determinism become. Choices were made, decisions reached, and to appreciate the dynamic is to be able to recognize the opportunity to affect it. . . .
>
> It is one thing to claim that the goal of surveillance dominated the *theory* of punishment, quite another to examine what actually happened when programs were translated into *practice*. . . . In Foucault's world, the fit between a capitalist society and the prison is tight, as

though rationality dominated throughout. In fact, the fit was much looser and procedure less systematic. . . . There is much more room for maneuver than a Foucault could ever imagine or allow.[13]

Rothman understands the gap between ideas and practices to be significant enough so that the relationship between the two is tenuous at best. Foucault's analysis, for Rothman, does not enrich an understanding of how the development of the penitentiary and other asylums reflects particular concerns expressed by "society" as a whole; rather, it is a one-dimensional, ideological attack on the history of ideas combined with an attack against class domination. In his view, either of these attacks would do much to weaken a study of the history of institutions. The practices, as far as he can tell, simply do not support Foucault's larger claims.

The stress that Foucault placed on the leading role of what Rothman refers to as "ideas" is, in fact, crucial to understanding Foucault's intent. Moreover, there is a particular sense in which Foucault tried to demonstrate that there is a fundamental relationship between the establishment of discipline and the emergence of capitalism. However, Rothman's depiction is grossly reductionist; Foucault emerges as either a mechanical neo-Weberian or a mere historian of ideas, both roles that Foucault, in the corpus of his writings, was always at pains to disavow.

Part of Rothman's difficulty, I think, is a result of the fact that Foucault's project not only opposed Rothman's, but undermined the value of the work Rothman does. Rothman argues that those who concerned themselves with the development of the asylum were attempting to preserve older notions of community that had dominated colonial-era social relationships throughout much of what was to become the United States. Under the pressure of change—political, but also demographic—the older form of community simply was falling apart at the close of the Revolutionary War. By redrawing the lines between stranger and friend, the new institutions were designed both to monitor the movement of marginal characters in society and to protect existing communities from too many incursions on their part. This effort failed, Rothman argues, as it was bound to fail, in the face of inexorable forces of modernization. But the more important question, he claims, is why these institutions persisted even after they went into decline, after public attention wavered, and after they demonstrably failed to produce the reforms that they initially claimed to be able to produce. The failure of these institutions to produce such reforms undermines Foucault's argument, in Rothman's view, because, instead of establishing discipline over criminals and mad people, these places became custodial institutions, marginalized.[14]

The emphasis Foucault placed upon these failed institutions is thus wrongheaded, according to Rothman. But this argument works only to the extent that Rothman is able to demonstrate that the purposes of these institutions were thwarted. In fact, he must look more deeply into the realm of ideas that he discounts, if he is to understand those purposes. Mere inertia of policy does not explain persistent concern with policy consequences.

In contrast to Rothman, Foucault explained this consistent concern as the result of an epistemological revolution that found its first realization in the invention of these institutions. The creation of the penitentiary was important because it provided a model for disciplinary strategies that could be disseminated throughout society. Thus, its functions as a site of behavioral reformation was important, but so were the specific failures of that institution once established. They served to spur on further elaborations, fine tunings, and expansions of the system.

Foucault's famous example of Jeremy Bentham's Panopticon is often cited as evidence of his totalistic bent. But the Panopticon is depicted by him as the ideal of a universal machine for subjugating bodies, not realized in practice. It provided a model for all subsequent attempts to shape bodies into disciplinary subjects.

> The domain of panopticism is . . . that whole lower region, that region of irregular bodies, with their details, their multiple movements, their heterogeneous forces, their spatial relations; what are required are mechanisms that analyze distributions, gaps, series, combinations, and which render visible, record, differentiate, and compare: a physics of a relational and multiple power, which has its maximum intensity not in the person of the king, but in the bodies that can be individualized by these relations.[15]

Panopticism not only brings order to a disorderly domain, but establishes the terms of disorder's definition. In other words, in establishing a domain of panoptic relationships, policymakers contributed to the creation and perpetuation of a realm of artificial disorder over which it would establish strategies of containment. Panopticism unified and established coherence over the disorder that was also a product of its definitions.

After elaborating upon how these separate principles came to constitute a unified series of practices, Foucault speculated about why panopticism has been overlooked by historians and everyone else.

> There were many reasons why it received little praise; the most obvious is that the discourses to which it gave rise rarely acquired, except in the academic classifications, the status of sciences; but the real reason no doubt is that the power that it operates and which it augments is a direct, physical power that men exercise upon one another. An inglorious culmination had an origin that could be only grudgingly acknowledged.[16]

In sum, it is not a history of ideas Foucault describes, it is the emergence of the social sciences, it is a genealogy of practices for inscribing bodies, brutal and crude in origin, secretive and subtle in result.

It should be clear that one need not claim that the social sciences have ever been successful as autonomous forms of knowledge in order to claim that they have dominated thinking about humankind, provided rationales for the development and extension of practical methods of social control, in short, shaped the constitutive foundations of modern social policies.[17] This does not mean that they have been successful in enforcing a "rigid and unvarying discipline," as Rothman claims Foucault asserted. The modes of discipline have undergone radical shifts and changes, strange continuities and discontinuities. Indeed, Foucault pointed out these disruptions more dramatically than anyone before him.[18] Nor does it mean that technologists have controlled everything, that social scientists have really been the modern sovereign. All who labor in the disciplines (probably including those who are reading this) know how little power rests in the hands of social scientists *as such*. Foucault was not making such an argument. He in fact argued against such understandings of direct agency.

Rothman, however, does not hesitate to make an argument in favor of some general and direct form of agency in order to legitimate his own theses. For him, there is a backdrop of "the times," and of "Americans," both of which are enlisted in the service of his argument. Hence, Americans were concerned with preserving community at one point in time, and with individualizing punishment at another. The categories and systems of social knowledge that influence the ways in which people come to think and act in regard to those "others" on the margins of society, in fact, the very conceptualizing of those margins, ultimately are only matters of background for him. Rothman does not demonstrate a different kind of pluralism of power in the emergence of social sciences that might refute Foucault's depiction of the gridlike function of the Panopticon. Implicit in the operations of reform, or at least in the detachment from and control over subjects, is this power. But Rothman pretends that ideas are irrelevant, and focuses on intentions. Good intentions go bad. There are unintended consequences. History becomes an accident.

From the point of view of Foucault, moreover, Rothman retrospectively reads the political strategies of the present into the very political matrix that was responsible for allowing the present to emerge. By simply attributing the same sort of political struggles over constituencies, the same notions of political corruption, and, in fact, the same ideas of bureaucratic failure that dominate contemporary understanding of the terms of political discourse to a situation in which the possibilities for the establishment of these modes of conflict were only then being created, Rothman distorts the meaning of the development of the penitentiary, both specifically in the United States and, more generally, in what Foucault called "Western society." History, in this view, ultimately becomes one damned thing after another, monotonous repetitions of the victories and defeats of particular actors, or the glacial movement of some posited and artificially created "society."

Hubert Dreyfus and Paul Rabinow argue that Foucault's presentation of the genealogy of disciplinary society is designed to illuminate the tendency of rational practices toward repressiveness. The analysis of "exemplary institutions" that Foucault undertook in his study of the development of discipline is not supposed to demonstrate that the modern organization of everything leads inevitably to a closed society. In fact, a major point of Foucault's work is to show, albeit with great irony, how categories of deviance, criminality, and illness in large part created the very possibility of an ordered society. Dreyfus and Rabinow note:

> The spread of normalization operates through the creation of abnormalities which it must treat and reform. . . . This effectively transforms into a technical problem—and thence into a field of expanding power—what might otherwise be construed as a failure of the whole system of operation.[19]

Hence, the struggle to establish more effective categories for classifying the behaviors of criminals, and the sporadic efforts of reform movements, both of which Rothman cites as evidence against Foucault, can be turned against him. The sense of urgency on the part of reformers, the periodic eruptions of public concern for the operations of these "marginal" institutions, and the continual refinement of categories of deviance and criminality can be read as forms of evidence of the ongoing operations of disciplinary strategies. While Rothman describes these phenomena as specific problems that arose as the result of unintended consequences and public neglect, the more general role they played, reflecting and contributing toward the elaboration of the modern individual subject, completely escapes his analysis. He might argue that historians should not undertake such a task, but the argument Foucault made compels them, if only because it attempts to explain so much more than such a history can. Moreover, policy incoherence, if that is indeed what Rothman wishes to argue characterized the realm of prison policy, also is only observed, not explained, by him. Such explanations as he does tentatively advance suggests only that neglect of the policy area, a product of its relative unimportance, caused such problems. But why, if one accepts his description, have criminal punishment decisions and the policies underlying them been so controversial during the past two centuries? Why does the plea of every generation echo the plea of the one before it, that attention be paid to this area of policy? One might guess that attention has been paid, that the incoherence is less than observers such as Rothman believe it to be.

But the reading Rothman gives to the history of these institutions is shared by many others who then attempt to explain further the alleged incoherence of punishment policies. Relevant in this regard is the argument advanced by Richard Sparks and reenforced by John Langbein.[20] Langbein, following Sparks, argues that the enforcement of criminal law is a marginal activity that has little to do with the day-to-day maintenance of the social order. Laws of contract, within the realm of the law proper, do much more by framing the content of regular activities. "From the standpoint of the rulers," Langbein suggests, "the criminal justice system occupies a place not much more central than the garbage collection system. True, if the garbage is not collected the society cannot operate and ruling-class goals will be frustrated, but that does not turn garbage collection into a ruling-class conspiracy."[21] One might add that if criminal justice is so unimportant, it might provide a ready explanation for the alleged neglect of prisons on the part of the citizenry and policymakers.

The argument that Langbein advances is explicitly intended as a refutation of a Marxist position, but for my purpose here, Foucault is just as accountable. Why, after all, make such a big deal of the criminal justice system? One response would be to point to Foucault's massive output concerning so many other shifts in institutional strategies during this era, to show that he is "really" criticizing Enlightenment thought, not any specific instance of public policy. That path, however, ignores one of the most important points that Foucault has to make in regard to the modern era, that it is in fact the product of a series of highly specific practices that are woven into the social fabric at a deep level. In other words, I want to suggest that Foucault's case does indeed depend upon a kind of facticity that is brought to bear on the problem of understanding the development of the penitentiary. Bluntly, either Langbein and others who support the argument that punishment is not important are right, and Foucault is wrong, or vice versa. For them to be found wrong, penal discipline, implemented on the margins of social relations, must be much more closely related to the more ordinary activities of everyday life than Langbein understands them to be.

To make this argument it is necessary to outline the connections between the specific practices of penal discipline and the more general development of discipline. The penitentiary did not come into being until the close of the eighteenth century. Foucault traced its emergence in the following way:

1. As armies grew in size and started recruiting from the ranks of vagabonds, practices were designed to create docile bodies. Medical authorities as well started recognizing the value of separation as a means of controlling the spread of contagion. In education, the secular use of the techniques of monastic asceticism, cellular in nature, constituted another disciplinary practice. These techniques were, at first, local in impact, unconnected to each other.

2. These practices developed into more general rules and procedures, such as hierarchical observation, normalizing judgment, and examinations. In separate fields of operation, these practices for the organization and patterning of bodily functions established particular divisions of labor, provided rationales for schemes of public hygiene, and presented aesthetics of orderliness, thus establishing the grounding for the development of a series of more general rules of discipline.

3. These techniques came together at the end of the eighteenth century

in the Panopticon model, panopticism expressing the general principle of a political anatomy that moves away from relations of sovereignty toward relations of discipline. "At this point," Foucault wrote,

> the disciplines crossed a "technological" threshold. First the hospital, then the school, then, later, the workshop were not simply "reordered" by the disciplines; they became, thanks to them, apparatuses such that any mechanism of objectification could be used in them as an instrument of subjection, and any growth of power could give rise in them to possible branches of knowledge; it was this link, proper to the technological systems, that made possible within the disciplinary element the formation of clinical medicine, psychiatry, child psychology, educational psychology, the rationalization of labour. It is a double process, then: an epistemological "thaw" through a refinement of power relations; a multiplication of the effects of power through the formation and accumulation of new forms of knowledge.[22]

In short, the penitentiary arose at the transition from a social system in which juridical/sovereign relationships determined the limits of a common political reality to one in which power/knowledge does.[23] It exists as a conduit through which the reordering of relationships along the lines of a disciplinary society is funneled, through which dangerous relationships are given their initial expression in the modern era. If its influence was not always direct, then it was indirect, by virtue of the penitentiary's exemplary status, its fit with and constitutive role in the emergent "micro-physics of power."

This is the "causal" role that Foucault assigned to the prison. To read criminal punishment as garbage collection is to miss completely the importance of the practice of discipline and the contributing role that penal practices played in its development. Foucault's study of prisons, it must be remembered, is an exercise in understanding the development of a new theory and new practice of power, disciplinary power:

> The automatic functioning of power, mechanical operation is absolutely not the thesis of *Discipline and Punish*. Rather, it is the idea, in the eighteenth century, that such a form of power is possible and desirable. It is the theoretical and practical search for such mechanisms, the will, constantly attested, to organize this kind of mechanism which constitutes the object of this analysis.[24]

The fetters that Rothman reads into Foucault are the epistemological limits defined by discipline. Rothman confuses those limits with an argument for historical determinism. But they are not the same. From Foucault's perspective, an argument such as Rothman's not only misses the point, but by missing the point perpetuates a secret of the practical exercise and, ironically, the most dangerous effects of modern power. The challenge such a history presents to its readers is to discover the role it plays in perpetuating secrets of danger.

In *Discipline and Punish,* Foucault wrote what he called a "history of the present," a history of the subjection of the body as disciplinary object. He wanted to identify the mechanisms through which the effects of modern power are realized. That these mechanisms have a history to them, that they are in large part responsible for the ways modern subjects are able to think about their selves, others, and the relationships that they create with each other, are what Foucault did not assert so much as attempted to uncover. In this sense, his work is incommensurable with those studies that take the individual as given, that ground the study of social control in such ways as to fail to take into account the establishment of the object that is to be controlled. This is the reason why criticisms such as Rothman's fail; they do not question the ground upon which they themselves have been built. It is also why Foucault's project directly confronts the normative basis of liberal democratic political theory.

If genealogy is understood as serious play, play devoted to understanding the limitlessness of the will to knowledge and to pointing out the dangers that inhere in that will, then the painstaking care with which the genealogist reads the "field of entangled and confused parchments . . . documents that have been scratched over and recopied many times," can be understood to be directed toward a radical rejection of origin and the establishment instead of broken fields of knowledge.[25] But why? Out of a sense of perversity, as so many people claim?

I sense a different reason for the strategy of the genealogist. If one accepts the metaphor that modern authority is a structure built upon the epistemological foundations of instrumental reason, and then accepts, for the moment, that these foundations have been crumbling under the weight of the structure they were designed to bear, then the demolition tactics of the genealogist are more understandable. For then one is also accepting the idea that modern authority exists without true justification, that knowledge is constantly uncertain, and that no one ever becomes normal despite perpetual struggles. Rather than try to shore up the structure of authority, the genealogist instead works to complete the removal of the underlying foundation.

But many thinkers are frightened at the prospects of uncertainty entailed in the abandonment of the foundation that instrumental reason provided. *Dangerous* relationships appeal to them as a viable alternative to the elimination of the idea of rational authority, regardless of their realization of the invalidity of instrumental reason. In a sense, they need to shore up what they oppose, if only to have the comfort of enemies. Genealogy warns against that sort of comfort, warns that any teleological reasoning is foundational and that foundations protect at too great a cost. Genealogy is a cautionary exercise. It opposes history, even critical history, because it knows that the lessons history has to teach are always illusory when thought of as being "the lessons of history." Instead of understanding human struggle in terms of progress and enlightenment, genealogists understand it in terms of power and the effects of power. Realizing that truth is an artifact of the struggle over power, and that the construction of new truths depends less upon discovery than upon the transformation of one regime to another, constitutes the first step in uncovering the politics of dangerous relationships.

Such was Foucault's attempt to move political theory beyond the study of state sovereignty, or as he put it, to "cut off the King's head."[26] The existence of that head, the representation of power as a negative and prohibiting power, is permitted and sustained by a multiplicity of very specific, carefully developed positive powers. Genealogical interpretation of the history of the relationships between these different practices of power takes on "the form of a war rather than that of language: relations of power, not relations of meaning."[27] To move the study of power beyond sovereignty, then, genealogy must move beyond any substitutes for a sovereign. Foucault thus extended the warning to all teleologies, all totalities. All can be dissolved.

### The Critique of Necessity

In a recent study that reasserts the primacy of history as the ground for interpretation, Fredric Jameson argues that Foucault, along with many other poststructuralist thinkers, has misplaced the attack on hermeneutics by posing his critique in antihistorical terms. Hence, Foucault's attack on totalizing discourses ironically has only a specifically historical and culturally limited validity. Jameson also argues implicitly that Foucault's genealogy is reactionary, in the sense that it is a direct response to the totalizing tendencies to be found in French culture and political institutions. While that reaction might be appropriate in the French political context, he argues, it does not translate well to American society. "In the United States," he argues, ". . . it is precisely the intensity of social fragmentation of this latter kind that has made it historically difficult to unify the Left or 'antisystemic' forces in any durable and effective organizational way."[28] The translation of the genealogical critique to the level of political action, Jameson seems to be saying, indicates the cultural affinities and specific limitations underlying the critique of totalizing discourse. Yet ultimately, he seems to argue, one cannot deconstruct history.[29] The implications of such a riposte for projects such as Foucault's are clear. Attempts to historicize radically such phenomena as the constitution of subjectivity, when pursued without the recognition of some ultimate ground of necessity, are bound to "eat their feet,"[30] that is, they lead to positions that are nihilistic, in the sense of providing no grounds for the assertion of any truth claims. Foucault's discourse, because it rejects standards of truth, must also reject standards of justice. In Jameson's view, such a position ultimately is antipolitical, and hence irresponsible.

One need not rely only on Jameson in order to get a sense of the direction Marxian critiques of Foucault might take. Genealogy, as a deconstructive enterprise, plants major doubts concerning the validity of such constructs as the base/superstructure model of society, the idea of species being, the concept of class itself, and the role of ideology in the formation of consciousness. But all of these radical doubts presented by genealogical analysis do not necessarily lead one to the conclusion that genealogy is consistently incompatible with Marxian analysis. What they have in common is not claims to truth, but an affinity for the importance of history in relationship to knowledge. There is a parallel here between the affinities of Derridean deconstruction to the negative dialectics of Adorno, and those of Foucault's genealogy to the more traditional understanding of ideology and production presented in Marxian thought.

Writing of the relationship between Derrida and Adorno, Michael Ryan points to the parallels and distinctions between the forms of immanent criticism pursued by both. The closest affinity between these thinkers, he claims, and the source of their most important difference, lie in their critiques of identity, critiques which are at the core of the teleological (metaphysical) approaches to truth. Both thinkers, Ryan argues, attack metaphysics, but ultimately in different ways.

> All philosophical concepts lose what they seem to retain. On the basis of this insight, Derrida calls for a nonconceptual concept of the concept. I am immediately reminded of Adorno's notion of "the preponderance of the object." Derrida will speak in an analogous way of the necessity of the world as a prephilosophic "already there," a necessity that detracts from idealism's pretensions to constitutive spontaneity and primordial originarity. The world, Derrida points out, is primordially implied in transcendence; the major difference is that the critical lever for Derrida is logical (or philosophical-historical), whereas for Adorno, the lever is social. The next item on the agenda of the critique of identity is the principle of exchange, and at this point, Adorno and Derrida part company. Exchange implies equivalence, that is, a principle whereby different things are made equal and opposites are established as equivalent, antithetical poles. The homogeneity of opposition and equivalence allows exchange. Adorno sees a heterogeneity at work within the homogeneous system of equivalence, pointing toward a utopia of nondomination. Yet he distrusts action, and he provides no method for practically realizing that utopia. Derrida, in contrast, does provide a method for unbalancing the metaphysical system of equivalences. Deconstruction is an aggressive act of reading which subverts the grounds of metaphysics in general and of idealism in particular. And the kingpin of those grounds is the principle of exchange whereby difference is reduced to identity.[31]

Adorno and Derrida both have recognized the danger that lies in hoping that transcendental truths might inhere within systems of thought and action. For Ryan, Derrida moves further toward preventing the reconstruction of such metaphysical idealisms than did Adorno, who ultimately refused to move far enough away from the binary of identity/nonidentity. This binary, which lies at the root of dialectic method, itself is deconstructible, can be further dissolved into a multiplicity of spun-off partialities, providing "a more radical dissymetry, heterogeneity, or alterity—supplementarity, differentiation, trace—which includes as one of its determined orientations the metaphysical conceptual system Adorno attacks."[32]

For Ryan, some kind of critical Marxism might emerge from deconstruction, one which would no longer retain or attempt to regain its hope of eventual utopian unity, an end to conflict through the final reconciliation of identity with nonidentity. Yet the philosophical battle that rages on in regard to the dialectics of an open-ended struggle nonetheless can be trivial in the worst sense. Ryan admits to the potential problems that inhere within Derridean-style deconstruction, how its privileging of texts and textuality (even broadly understood), and its implicit elitism (which it shares with negative dialectics), might result in an endless discussion of texts for their own sake, or might even close down discussion by way of imposing a radical skepticism upon all discourse.[33] Reasonable people might even end up saying patently silly things—for example: "After Derrida, it's hard to take 'logocentrism' seriously."[34] But to admit these problems, even if one accepts the broader understandings of textual analysis and rejects the notion that criticism of "common sense" constitutes a snubbing of the intelligence of ordinary people, is to trade in one set of worries for another. The practices associated with both deconstruction and negative dialectics have so often centered exclusively on the reading of literary texts that one might wonder what the political import of this revolution in theory is. One is reminded of Marx's caustic rebuke of the young Hegelians, how he pointed to the bankruptcy of a revolution that "is supposed to have taken place in the realm of pure thought."[35]

The differences between Adorno and Derrida are played out at a more concrete level when one examines genealogy in relationship to the dialectical materialism of Marx.[36] Both Derrida and Foucault try to open up dialectics, and through their incitements try to make the critical analysis of the modern era multidimensional. Even given the notion that genealogy is designed to keep open a radical interrogation of practices, it nonetheless, as a critique of practices and as a descriptive analysis of practices, shares a common discursive field with Marxian analysis and hence observes and describes the same things. This is clear when one looks at some of the most potent passages of *Discipline and Punish*. In them, Foucault embraces one of the most important conceptual assumptions advanced by Marx, that *production* is the single most important organizing category of experience under modern capitalism. Modern punishment emerges for Foucault as a "political technology of the body," which has as its object the normalization and regulation of the activities of large numbers of people.[37] Force is replaced by control. Power becomes positive, where once it could be treated only as a negative force. Because it is positive it is multiple.

We must cease once and for all to describe the effects of power in negative terms: it "excludes," it "represses," it "censors," it "abstracts," it "masks," it "conceals." In fact, power produces; it produces reality; it produces domains of objects and rituals of truth. The individual and the knowledge that may be gained of him belong to this production.[38]

At this level Foucault's argument has links to Marx. But Foucault conflated power and productive power into a single entity. Production is the function of power. Foucault wished to suggest that power is the source of production, just as Marx wished to argue that production is the source of all value. In genealogy, power is not a concept but a variety of specific practices inhering in a variety of contexts, and so is not amenable to deconstructive strategies. Instead, techniques of exposing the secrets of power practices enable a richer understanding of the contingencies of power than that of dialectical critique (seeking the play of opposites). While informed by deconstruction, genealogy sees the play of language to be but one "trick" of discursive power. Thus, genealogy might be said to operate in the political/philosophical gap between Derridean deconstructive strategies and the more socially oriented critique provided by theorists such as Adorno.

There are a variety of highly specific practices through which production is realized as an effect of power. In his attempt to examine these practices and evaluate them, Foucault described in great detail the extent to which the institutional arrangements that enabled the development of particular relationships contributed to the establishment of new modes of production, and vice versa. Significantly, he established no ultimate causative agency.

If the economic take-off of the West began with the techniques that made possible the accumulation of capital, it might perhaps be said that the methods for administering the accumulation of men made possible a political take-off in relation to the traditional, ritual, costly, violent forms of power, which soon fell into disuse and were superseded by a subtle, calculated technology of subjection. In fact, the two processes—the accumulation of men and the accumulation of capital—cannot be separated; it would not have been possible to solve the problem of the accumulation of men without the growth of an apparatus of production capable of both sustaining them and using them; conversely, the techniques that made the cumulative multiplicity of men useful accelerated the accumulation of capital. At a less general level, the technological mutations of the apparatus of production, the division of labour and the elaboration of the disciplinary techniques sustained an ensemble of very close relations (cf. Marx, *Capital*, Vol. I, Chapter XIII and the very interesting analysis in Guerry and Deleule). . . . Let us say that discipline is the unitary technique by which the body is reduced as a political force at the least cost and maximized as a useful force.[39]

Foucault referred to the chapter from *Capital* on variable and constant capital. Variable capital is that which is present in labor power, and is dependent upon the interaction between the laborer and the organization of labor. That interaction is in turn dependent upon the techniques brought to bear on the specific productive process under consideration. Marx emphasized the close practical relationship between the two kinds of capital.[40] But while Marx took great pains to emphasize that there is indeed a central logic of concentration of productive power under capitalism that determines the specific relationships that develop in different capitalist societies,[41] Foucault made no such assertion. Instead, he asserted that any transformations that might occur in such relationships are as likely to be the source of change as they are to be the product of change at a "higher" or "deeper" level. In that sense, the "micro" can be the ultimate source of change.

Foucault in *Discipline and Punish* thus decentered Marx, rearranging the order of the relationship between Marx's most fundamental categories of value and production. This rearrangement was designed to show the importance of production in regard to power and knowledge, even as it asserted that Marx was mistaken to make the struggle between labor and capital so central. That opposition is but one of several oppositions for Foucault, and is not always or necessarily even most often the most important one. What thus emerges, at least in this reading of *Discipline and Punish*, is a remarkably specific analysis of the operations of power at a level below that recognized by Marxist politics. These operations are compatible with but different from those of Marxist exploitation.

Such is the domain of dangerous relationships, which exists in the space between specific institutional expressions of exploitation or repression. Dangerous relationships are most likely to arise when subjects need the continual protection of authority. This need in turn is the result of conflicts inherent in the coincident exercises of repression and exploitation. When

Foucault discussed the failure of the old form of punishment in the eighteenth century and the need for the creation of discipline, it was this clash that he was discussing. Describing the birth of the prison, i.e., the creation of the modern soul as the prison of the body, he was describing as well the transforming power of capitalism, which, in Marx's words, "must nestle everywhere, settle everywhere, establish connections everywhere."[42] But his terms are not readily acceptable by or easily absorbed into Marxian discourse.

He used incompatible terms because he was challenging not only the dialectic but also the teleology of Marxism. Foucault ultimately came to understand teleology as being the greatest threat that humanitarian thought poses to humankind. Foucault's critique of the will to knowledge, found not only in *Discipline and Punish* but in all of his work, confounds those Marxian thinkers who have feared that his project may have been no more than an irrational attack on the grounds of all reason, and therefore especially on the "true" science of historical materialism. Foucault argued in response to the Marxist critique that he was engaged in the study of the history of problems, by which he meant that he was not concerned with the intrinsic truth claims of Marxism, or of any teleological system of thought, so much as with the specific problems that always are generated by such thought systems. Asserting the radical conventionality of moral assertions and applying a continuing critique to appeals to truth are major weapons of the genealogist, weapons which the genealogist uses to gain leverage over and distance from the never-ending war of words. Power inheres in the relationships established and continued during the course of this war, and those who assert that they can end it only add one more weapon to their rhetorical repertoire. Thus, Marxian politics presents itself to the genealogist as more culpable than other humanitarian strategies, if only because it has within it the critical elements that might enable its practitioners to avoid the trap imposed by its telos, yet nonetheless continues to assert truth claims.

This concern with truth and its relationship to totality, which dominates Western Marxism, has resulted in the clearest and most important attack on genealogy.[43] Habermas hinted at his later critique of Foucault in his discussion of Nietzsche at the end of *Knowledge and Human Interests*.[44] Nietzsche proceeded, Habermas argues, first by assessing the damage that critical science does in its destruction of science: "The process of enlightenment made possible by the sciences is critical, but the critical dissolution of dogmas produces not liberation but indifference. It is not emancipatory but nihilistic."[45] For Habermas, though, Nietzsche accepted as given the positivist concept of knowledge, and despaired of it, knowing that it was only a "sovereign ignorance." Paradoxically, Habermas argued, Nietzsche could reach such a stage of the denial of critical knowledge only through the exercise of critical self-reflection. He was "a virtuoso of reflection that denies itself."[46]

A positivism which leads to either a desperately pessimistic or a frighteningly blasé moral relativism is what Habermas thus sees as the Foucauldian inheritance from Nietzsche. "Young Conservatives," he called the poststructuralists, and argued,

> To instrumental reason, they juxtapose in manichean fashion a principle only accessible through evocation, be it the will to power or sovereignty, being or the dionysiac force of the poetical. In France this line leads from Bataille via Foucault to Derrida.[47]

Hence, while Habermas values the relentlessly critical insights of Foucault for demonstrating the tendencies in instrumental reason toward repression, he rejects as positivism any argument which seeks to characterize as repressive the elements of discourse he himself has privileged as liberatory. (His own theory of communicative action is based on the notion of the possible systematizing of that which is outside of instrumental reason.) The "emancipatory" moments of communication, the "substantive" elements of rationality, will thus lend themselves to "completing the project of modernity."[48]

Foucault's response to such a treatment was to concede first, in biographical terms, that the critical discourse which moved from Weber through the Frankfurt School to Habermas was ignored by French thought in the postwar era, and that from the Frankfurt School especially he might have learned to avoid "many of the detours which I made while trying to pursue my own humble path."[49] More important, he directly challenged Habermas's accusations concerning the nature of genealogical criticism. First, he recapitulated the organization of Habermas's argument but, in what might be termed a genealogical tactic, rendered the familiar argument slightly foreign.

> I think that the blackmail which has very often been at work in every critique of reason or every critical inquiry into the history of rationality

(either you accept rationality or you fall prey to the irrational) operates as though a rational critique of rationality, or as though a rational history of all the ramifications and all the bifurcations, a contingent history of reason, were impossible. . . . I think, since Max Weber, in the Frankfurt School and anyhow for many students of science since Cangiulhem, it was a question of isolating the form of rationality presented as dominant, and endowed with the status of the one-and-only reason, in order to show that it is only *one* possible form among others.[50]

Foucault's response to Habermas, then, might be thought of as the rejection of a gambit, the refusal to concede that a "contingent history of reason," one which need not be grounded in one "side" of reason to attack the other, is impossible. In short, Foucault rejected *the* dialectic of Enlightenment, substituting for it multiplicities.

True, I would not speak about *one* bifurcation of reason but more about an endless, multiple bifurcation—a kind of abundant ramification. I do not address the point at which reason became instrumental. . . . [W]hat led the *techne* of self to develop . . . everything propitious to the development of a technology of the self can be very well analyzed, I think, and situated as an historical phenomenon—which does not constitute *the* bifurcation of reason. In this abundance of branchings, ramifications, breaks and ruptures, it was an important event, or episode; it had considerable consequences, but it was not a *unique* phenomenon.[51]

In short, Habermas's idea that a rectification or balancing out of reason can be made a "project" is symptomatic of seeking a transcendence which is impossible on the face of it—the "abundance of branchings, ramifications, breaks and ruptures" ensures against the success of such a project, a project which may well be emancipatory in intent but which is authoritarian (at least) in its implied singularity of purpose and its hopes of encorporating *all* interests in its judgments.

This conflict between critical Marxism and genealogy can be seen as well in Foucault's own various attempts to articulate the themes that surround ideas of truth in the modern age. In an essay he wrote shortly before his death, Foucault presented a contemporary response to the question answered by Immanuel Kant at the end of the eighteenth century, "What Is Enlightenment?"[52]

This essay has been used by Habermas to claim that Foucault ends up caught within the circle he had attempted to escape through his life's work, that of critical philosophy.[53] Habermas realizes that the critical philosophy of "What Is Enlightenment?" is not that of the three *Critiques*. In the text that Foucault chose to analyze, Kant was engaged, in Foucault's terms, "at the crossroads of critical reflection and reflection on history. It is a reflection by Kant on the contemporary status of his own enterprise," or, to use Habermas's phrase, Kant (like Foucault) was "taking aim at the heart of the present."[54] For both Foucault and Habermas, Kant's attempt to see the Enlightenment as a moment—as a constantly present moment—is itself a pivotal moment in philosophical discourse, because it signals the turning of the philosophical enterprise from the esoteric comparison of the ancients with the moderns to the interrogation of modernity from within the lived experience of modernity itself. For Habermas, the key to Foucault's reading of Kant lies in Foucault's realization of the irony that the consciousness of the contemporaneous expresses itself most sharply through the personalization of philosophical discourse.

On the basis of this analysis of Foucault's interpretation of Kant, Habermas interrogates the interrogator:

> If this is even a paraphrase of Foucault's own train of thought, the question arises: how does such a singularly affirmative understanding of modern philosophizing, always directed to our own actuality and imprinted in the here-and-now, fit with Foucault's own unyielding criticism of modernity? How can Foucault's self-understanding as a thinker in the tradition of the Enlightenment be compatible with his unmistakeable criticism of this very form of knowledge of modernity?[55]

Again, Habermas asks the question concerning Nietzsche, the question about self-reflection, and, again for Habermas, the answer is clear. Foucault was unable to sustain the "contradictions" presented by his own critique of modernity. As a result, his work presents the reader with a set of valuable insights regarding the paradoxes that the modern age presents to human-kind, but also, owing to its relentless pessimism, it fails to provide any ways out of this paradoxical situation, this exitless version of modernity.

Leaving aside Habermas's own problematic formulation of the paradoxes presented by late capitalism (capitalism surely being the greatest and most problematic expression of the modern age), there is nonetheless a major difficulty with this critique of Foucault. It takes as a useful contradiction what is instead an analysis of separate dimensions of enlightenment. Because Habermas understands Foucault to be no more than a critic of the will to truth, because he does not see any possibility of the existence of a counterontology, that is, of a position from which Foucault might be able to affirm without surrendering to the telos of necessity, he sees only the trap in which Foucault allegedly caught himself. But in Foucault's essay, he took care to separate *enlightenment* from *humanism*, and understood enlightenment, not in terms of truth, but in terms of a particular attitude or aesthetic that underlies the experience of modernity. If the spirit of Kant moved Foucault, it was in this regard. And it is this distinction, closely related to the critique of teleology, that is minimized by Habermas and overlooked completely by Jameson.[56]

Foucault's view on the question of Enlightenment is better characterized, I think, as concerned with the artful attitude made available through modern experience. Foucault discussed the experience of the modern by evoking Baudelaire's study of the artist (in a manner eerily reminiscent of Walter Benjamin).[57] The artist who is engaged in the work of transfiguring the world in the moment when it seems to be just falling asleep is, in Foucault's reading, the modern artist. "His transfiguration does not entail an annulling of reality, but a difficult interplay between the truth of what is real and the exercise of freedom; 'natural' things become 'more than natural,' 'beautiful' things become 'more than beautiful,' and individual objects appear 'endowed with an impulsive life like the soul of [their] creator.' "[58] Such artists apparently only watch and collect the present, but actually they imagine it. They are not *flaneurs*, the dandies who wear the modern age as danger, but something else again.

> For the attitude of modernity, the high value of the present is indissociable from a desperate eagerness to imagine it, to imagine it otherwise than it is, and to transform it not by destroying it but by grasping it in what it is. Baudelairean modernity is an exercise in which extreme attention to what is real is confronted with the practice of a liberty that simultaneously respects this reality and violates it.[59]

The modern liberty sought by Foucault is the liberty to imagine. Imagination, freed of the trap of the gaze, was at the core of his search for a counterontology, and fundamentally informed the trajectory his work. From the analysis of Bosch's *Ship of Fools* in *Madness and Civilization*, to his startling rendering of Velazquez's *Las Meninas* in *The Order of Things*, through his horrific analysis of the medicalization of vision and the establishment of the inverted democracy of surveillance in his later works, Foucault concerned himself with trying to figure out ways in which Western civilizations might be able to see without cursing sight. In his short study of Magritte (*This Is Not a Pipe*) Foucault concluded with a chapter entitled "To Paint Is Not to Affirm."[60] The canvas upon which such a life is to be painted is never blank, and thus any stroke one might make is a gesture of resistance against some already existing reality. There is no mere life, no mere facticity; that which already exists does so as the result of the artfulness of those who have already done their play. Layer upon layer builds up; artists modify, renovate, demolish. Such plasticity does not exist in the realm of discourse as it is now constituted, because in that realm play is work, and art production. Nor did it exist in Classical painting, which, Foucault argued, reintroduced a linguistic element of affirmation into a realm from which it had once been rigorously excluded. Now, at the end of the modern era, the process of respecting reality and violating it seems to require that art-creating subjects move out of that epistemological space in which the war of words is fought (or into a realm where imagination is allowed free play).

Foucault thus moved beyond the aesthetic position advocated by the most aesthetically sensitive critical theorist of all, Walter Benjamin, in his own, very radical, "Theses on the Philosophy of History."[61] While both men shared a common set of concerns in their sustained criticism of modern domination, Benjamin's bleak view, most densely articulated in his "Theses," clung to a strange, materialistic mysticism as the last hope of humankind. Foucault, while constantly appealing to examples culled from his reading of alternate epistemes in order to outline his hope for change, never resorted to theology, or, for that matter, to idealism of any sort. But for Benjamin, an angel of history is blown forward against its will, its back to the wind, its wings caught in the storm blowing from paradise, as it is driven further and further away from it. The events that humans might see as discrete, the angel sees as the wreckage, the fragments, of a single history, which he would love to reconstruct, but the storm of progress drives him further and further away from them. This imaginary reconstruction of Paul Klee's painting *Angelus Novus* is absolutely desolating in its perspective, full of regret, beyond the subject's capacity to mourn. Disaster piles up at the angel's feet. His face is turned toward the past. Ultimately, however, the potential for a utopian redemptive moment appears, a small gate through which some messianic salvation may occur, and for Benjamin this redemptive potential exists in every moment.

In opposition to Benjamin, Foucault turned toward the present. Benjamin celebrated the *flaneur* who strolls through the arcades as a draped object, as a work of art in a sense, but one who wears authority in the dangerous manner prescribed by modern times. Benjamin celebrated the collector, too, who lives as an owner, ownership being the most intimate relationship one can have with objects. "Not that they come alive in him; it is he who lives in them."[62] Foucault celebrated the artist, in opposition to the *flaneur*, and exposed rather than simply or complexly collected texts. (Ironically, Foucault may have achieved a goal of Benjamin in assembling the story of Alexina Herculine Barbin, a hermaphrodite of the nineteenth century, who told her story and had her story told. Benjamin ultimately wanted to write a book composed of nothing but quotes from other sources.)[63] In so doing, Foucault was not simply exploring another avenue untaken by others, but expressing hope.

**Conclusion**

Either progress or necessity has defined the horizons of political thinking throughout the modern era, representing the expression of *doubling* that is at the decentered core of modern discourse. If the history of humankind until now has been the history of class conflict, it has also been a history of war at all levels of existence. There is no escaping such wars, yet there is no way to imagine, within the boundaries of necessity and progress, fighting without endangering.

Foucault was at times apocalytic in his vision of the future of politics, understanding nuclear war as the ultimate expression of a "bio-power" which gradually disallows life, numbing people so that the final political wager on the life of the species is quietly accepted.[64] It may be, as Alexander Hooke has suggested, that Foucault advocated a form of "anonymous individualism."[65] But it might be better to remember that any understanding of the individual needs to move through and beyond these two horizons, to think through but then beyond the implications of class as it expresses itself in the political economy of capitalism, and to recognize the imagination of individuality as well as acknowledge the unbreakable costs associated with its modern sustenance.

If one wishes, one can employ the rubric of *danger* as a way of following the establishment of disciplines as they have moved the horizons provided by these ways of thinking. Regardless, the remaining chapters document certain moments in which attention was paid to orders, and subjects were made into well-behaved citizens.

The conclusion of this book returns to the theme of danger with which I began. There I assess the extent to which discipline informs the politics of life in the United States. There as well I discuss the role that fear, as a countermemory to danger, might play in the betrayal of the writing that informs such a politics. I do not argue that I have *demonstrated* this argument, only to claim that I have found a way out of danger. Instead, in acknowledging my failure, and in the hopes of opening up a field as yet not cleared, I perhaps may be able to argue something else: that an honest acknowledgment of such a failure is the beginning of a new understanding.

# 3

## Friendly Persuasion:
## The Prehistory of the Penitentiary

In 1682, the council of the proprietary government of the Commonwealth of Pennsylvania approved a charter law. While this law was to undergo various amendments during the thirty-six years of proprietary rule, none of the amendments altered two of the law's provisions, that concerning toleration and that concerning the penal code.[1] Yet at the end of that era, these two laws were considered to be the source of all the troubles afflicting the colony, and the English Privy Council struck down the entire government in order to try to have them both removed. A battle was joined concerning not only the extent to which government should rule, but what its techniques of rule should be. The Quakers of Pennsylvania lost this battle, but in losing can be said to have contributed to altering permanently the terms of discourse concerning the nature of government in relationship to its subjects. A modern government, one that could administer modern subjects, made its first, albeit brief, appearance, and then disappeared again from sight.

At the core of the Quaker project was an effort to establish an order in which the exercise of coercion would be displaced by what might be called an exercise of persuasion. Central to the Quaker mission was a radical modification of the system of criminal punishment. Through their criminal laws, they attempted to establish institutions which would redeem rather than torture. They wanted to reconcile the conflict between freedom of conscience and the exercise of power. This attempt was to lead, ironically, to a rudimentary establishment of dangerous domination.

The Quaker experience in Pennsylvania during the period of proprietary rule coincided with and was in many ways an extension of the political conflicts of the Glorious Revolution in England. An issue that provided a catalyst for the ascent of William and Mary to the English throne was the demonstrated intolerance of James II, who was Catholic. Regardless of that monarch's munificence to William Penn, the Quakers had engaged for decades in a struggle to make toleration a policy of sovereign authority. In fact, the Quakers shared a deep elective affinity with the pamphleteer of the Glorious Revolution John Locke, who had no small part in the eventual downfall of James. During the course of his long and fruitful life, Locke was as interested in questions concerning toleration as he was in the construction of government. For the Quakers, toleration not only complemented proper government; as a principle of rule it preceded the establishment of any and all institutions of government.

In light of the Quaker experience, Louis Hartz's famous claim that Lockean liberalism leads to conformitarianism needs further elaboration: it was not the natural law component of Locke's thought that was conformitarianism's source, but toleration.[2] The Quakers enshrined toleration not only as a principle, but as a policy. More specifically, the separation between inner belief and outer work, established by Lockean liberals as a means of protecting the freedom of religious belief, also enabled authorities to influence the actions of subjects and, more fundamentally, actually to construct those subjects as liberal individuals. The doctrine of toleration was directed against the use of coercion by the state in regard to matters of belief, but the separation of inner from outer contributed to a new correspondence between public and private that was to greatly enhance the capacity of civil society generally, and government as a servant of civil society, to exert social control. In the setting of Quaker Pennsylvania, where the personal was political in a comprehensive and clearly articulated sense, regulatory mechanisms, or friendly persuasion, supplanted mechanisms of physical coercion as the predominant means through which this control would be imposed. If the means by which authority might be exercised became gentle physically, they also became qualitatively more extensive, contributing to the simultaneous creation and violation of what, following Foucault (and Tocqueville), can be called the modern "soul."[3]

### Lockean Toleration and Inner Light

Locke's theory of toleration was formulated in response to an upheaval in the politics of English society. Underlying Locke's immediate political concerns, however, were more deep-seated politico-epistemological ones. Politics and knowledge interweave throughout most of his texts, even in his most rigorously abstract work, *An Essay concerning Human Understanding*. There, his primary question was to what extent knowledge is possible and to what extent humans must rely upon faith in order to act. By establishing an initial distinction between knowledge and ideas, Locke created an opening for the development of what he was to refer to as moral science.

The order of relationships which connects politics to knowledge and which calls for the establishment of such a science is as follows. Knowledge is containable within the wider realm of ideas.[4] Knowledge, while limited, nonetheless is able to "know" the relationships of ideas to ideas. Especially, it is possible for subjects to discern the extent to which ideas agree or disagree with each other.[5] An accurate comparison of agreement of ideas with each other can aid in the establishment of a moral science, since a firmer knowledge of ideas would grow from their agreement. But such a science remains incomplete because knowledge of ideas is less than belief in them. For belief, faith is necessary, and in fact constitutes the second founding principle of any moral science. Without faith, belief in ideas is impossible. And for Locke, all faith must ultimately be synonymous with faith in God.[6]

It follows that two premises must be accepted if a moral science is to be established: first, that a rational comparison of ideas is possible, and second, that God exists.[7] Convincing people of God's existence during this era was easier than persuading them to accept principles of rationality. The latter was difficult because of what Locke understood to be a paradox involving rationality itself. To accept rationality could, and often does, run counter to one's short-term interests. Just as Rousseau was to argue that men must be forced to be free, Locke argued that men must be forced to be free to be rational. Thus it was necessary to end the monopoly of power of those who perpetuate irrational beliefs, namely, the bishops, the papists, and anyone else who would conspire to keep people in ignorance to serve their own ends. He asked,

> But whilst the parties of men cram their tenets down all men's throats whom they can get in their power, without permitting them to examine their truth or falsehood; and will not let truth have its fair play in the world, nor men the liberty to search after it; what improvement can

we hope for of this kind? What greater light can be hoped for in the moral sciences?[8]

It followed that the establishment of the moral sciences depended on the protection of the moral scientist from political pressure.

The power of those who "cram their tenets down all men's throats" was to be circumscribed through the establishment of a policy of toleration. In *A Letter concerning Toleration,* Locke explicitly developed a political strategy for the realization of the moral sciences by establishing distinctions between inner and outer things. While his later works would emphasize the connections between rationality and Christianity by showing how a religious pedagogy could underscore revelation and reason together in support of Christian belief,[9] in this *Letter* the political differences were stressed. The distinction between inner and outer corresponded to a distinction between persuasion and coercion. He argued that the use of force needed to be reserved for only those matters that are vital to the public good. If this distinction and the practice that emerged from it were not established, morality would become dangerously dependent on the whims of those holding public offices. "We must acknowledge," he wrote,

> that the Church . . . is for the most part more apt to be influenced by the Court than the Court by the Church. . . . To conclude, it is the same thing whether a king prescribes laws to another man's religion, pretend to do it by his own judgment, or by the ecclesiastical authority and advice of others.[10]

In any case, such an intervention distorts the proper functions of both religion and the state.

Locke argued that people should come to know and acknowledge political authority only in relation to "outer things," such as defining and protecting property, and establishing and protecting the public goods of the commonwealth.[11] Religious values are "inner things" over which the state should have no power. Only when inner belief leads directly to outer works that threaten the existence of the commonwealth itself can the exercise of state power over inner things be validated. State power should thus be circumscribed, and exercised only as a prohibition.[12] When and how the state applies coercion should be guided by a knowledge of ideas provided by the moral sciences, which under the protective umbrella of toleration would establish the necessary criteria for judgment, the understanding essential for reasonable rule. Sins against God, to cite the central case, could not in and of themselves be judged to strike at the political order. Religious and political authority might overlap, but the judgments rendered by political authority would serve one standard of judgment, and those of ecclesiastical authority another. "Nay, even the sins of lying and perjury are nowhere punishable by law; unless in certain cases, in which the real turpitude of the thing and of the offense against God are not considered but only the injury done unto men's neighbors and the commonwealth."[13] The separation advocated by Locke thus had as its explicit purpose the clarification of the boundary separating public and private actions. Such a clarification was designed to limit the authority of the state.

The minimal state Locke developed in his *Two Treatises of Government* served just such a separation. Although toleration is never explicitly mentioned in that work, Locke's mechanisms of government established in the second treatise perpetuated the division between coercion and persuasion. Protection of the private rights of the citizenry implicitly informs the framework of governmental authority, which relies upon civil society for its continuing legitimacy. Locke's separation of civil and ecclesiastical authorities thus fit into a broader, more comprehensive theory, in which the division is made more general; between private and public, persuasion and coercion, and belief and action.[14]

With few modifications, the separation advocated by Locke fit into the Quaker experiment in Pennsylvania. At first glance, such a separation seems to contradict the Quaker theology of Inner Light, because the reception of Inner Light (God's grace) is directly dependent on the way in which one behaves in the world. Yet the specific practices of the Quakers, especially the way in which they bridged the gap between outer action and Inner Light, enabled them to embrace Locke's parallel distinctions between persuasion and force, and thus between private and public actions.

The Quaker ethos was at once perfectionist and egalitarian, individualistic and communitarian, and anti-authoritarian and orderly. Inner Light, as a doctrine of grace, emphasized the presence of Christ in all people and the importance of respecting the autonomy of individuals in their efforts to move from the state of sin toward perfection. In England, the stress that the Quakers placed on individual autonomy had brought them into direct conflict with existing political authorities, because those authorities could not and would not permit the range of freedom that accompanied Quaker practices. Initially forced by circumstances into their advocacy of pacifism,[15] the Quakers soon found that their withdrawal from politics enabled them to refine their moral practices. Indeed, until they established their own colony, the Quakers can be said to have had the luxury of opposing authority when it conflicted with their beliefs. During the early years of their existence they pursued that opposition vigorously, but following their losses in politics and the systematic persecution that followed, they increasingly devoted their efforts to the project of developing individual autonomy through techniques which would encourage the establishment of self-discipline.

Such internal discipline, necessary for the reception of Inner Light, was to be shaped through prayer and silent meditation. The external discipline that magistries were capable of imposing through coercion was not capable of touching the inner self. Grace was to be received freely, or not at all. Violence on the part of ecclesiastical authorities, regardless of whether they were being used by the state or were using the state, was especially repugnant to the Quakers, and they mocked their persecutors for what they perceived to be a fundamental weakness in their position. As Penn once stated polemically, "[The Church of England] says she is afraid of Popery because of its violence, and yet uses force to compel it; Is not this resisting Popery with Popery?"[16]

Although people were not to be compelled to obey, they could, under Quaker doctrine, be subjected to techniques of persuasion. The duty of all good Christians was to do what they could to convince others of the existence of God's grace, and to show them how to seek it.[17] The vehicles through which the propagation of faith could best be advanced were those of neither church nor state, as those institutions had agendas that were both forceful in method and too narrowly conceived. A way needed to be found to reach people at the level of their daily lives if they were to be made free. The institution of the meeting served just that purpose.

In the Quaker community the meeting was the center, spiritually, intellectually, and economically. It included a library and a school. Disputes of whatever nature were settled in the business sessions of the meetings. The poor were looked after, moral delinquents dealt with, and marriages approved or performed. There was little need for

court or police force or officials of any kind, except for a few whose
function it was to transfer property and perform similar legal duties.[18]

Authority, here exercised in what is now usually referred to as the private
sphere, was extensive and thorough. It was precisely in this realm of social
activity that the doctrine of toleration was developed, to protect religious
authorities from the incursions of the state.

Not surprisingly, most of the problems that the Quakers faced when they
acquired their own colony resulted from their reluctance to exercise the
kind of authority that most people at the time recognized as compelling
obedience. Until the acquisition of Pennsylvania, the only political activity
that had engaged the Quakers since the Restoration had centered on achieving toleration, a struggle that was accurately seen by them as crucial to
their very survival as a group. When the principle of toleration was initially
translated into policy, even most of the Quaker inhabitants of Pennsylvania
(there were others, as well) had trouble adjusting.

Pennsylvania was characterized from its founding by both extraordinary
economic success and political chaos. The former can be explained in part
by the class background of the Quaker settlers. Penn was only one of a
group of Quakers from the wealthy bourgeoisie who had converted during
the second decade of the sect's existence, as George Fox, the movement's
founder, attempted to broaden the base of support for the movement and
to give it an aura of respectability.[19] This "second generation" of Quakers
provided the colony with a group of wealthy and experienced business
people who organized the economy of the colony with great acumen. Their
skill in enterprise was a result of their politically marginal position in
England. In business, aware of the suspicions that many others had of
them, they traded largely with each other, and were scrupulous in their
adherence to the promises of contracts.[20] They gained a reputation for
being honest, shrewd, and thrifty.[21] Despite the personal bankruptcy of
Penn, Pennsylvania eventually came to be considered the most spectacular
economic success of the American colonies.[22]

Politically, the problems associated with setting up a doctrine of rule
were compounded by the fact that the Quakers were unaccustomed to
participation in public affairs. The Quakers' reliance on the meeting was
in part a result of their lack of experience with and antagonism toward the
ordinary politics of faction that they had turned away from in England.
Constant deadlock between merchant and landholding interests resulted

from a lack of understanding of the role of compromise in ordinary political exchange.[23] This problem was a manifestation of a deeper problem concerning authority. The Quakers' inability to establish institutions that would command respect and yet remain consistent with their anti-authoritarian political stance was to contribute to continued tension among the colonists through the years of proprietary rule.

But at the founding of Pennsylvania the elements necessary for the emergence of what might be called a Lockean society were in place. A minimal state guaranteed contracts and protected private property. Freedom of conscience was the first principle of government. Moreover, the inhabitants of Pennsylvania were prepared in the main to accept the most important elements of Lockean liberalism in regard to economics, politics, and, most important, morality. If the realization of Locke's moral science depended upon faith in God and in acceptance of reason as a human characteristic, its achievement seemed more likely in Pennsylvania than anywhere else. Indeed, the Quakers were so passionately convinced that friendly persuasion could lead all people to enlightenment that it underlay even their most difficult task of rule, punishing criminals.

## Punishment Prior to the Quakers

Before discussing how the Quakers applied techniques of persuasion to the punishment of criminals, it is necessary to note the function of criminal punishment in English society prior to and during the time of the Quaker experiments. In so doing, I wish to dramatize the role that criminal punishment played in maintaining late feudal relationships of authority and to lay a groundwork for understanding the expanded role that the milder form of punishment was to play after that older social system broke down. Key to the reordering of society during this period was that a system of punishment characterized by a simple relationship of criminal to sovereign was supplanted by a complex system in which a set of standards and judgments not only came to determine the guilt and innocence of criminals but helped to constitute the criminal as a subject.[24]

When one examines the statutes of the English Criminal Code during the late seventeenth and early eighteenth centuries and reviews the history of their implementation, one gets some sense of the peculiarities of this earlier system of punishment in legitimating authority.[25] The code itself was full of harsh penalties. But it also included many implicit escape clauses through which punishments would be dramatically reduced, such as the ordinary use of "pleaing clergy," or, more directly, the liberal use of the pardoning power of the sovereign.[26] When exercised, punishment remained severe, but it was often reduced or eliminated through the ameliorating effects of these provisos.

Nonetheless, one still might reasonably conclude that punishment was used by authorities as a means of deterrence during this era. The point is that the primary role of punishment was still retributive. Punishment focused much more on the reestablishment of a moral balance between ruler and ruled than on whether or not future crimes were to be discouraged. In contrast, the Quakers were to be concerned with the relationship between punishment and the moral reform of the criminal as a potential recipient of Inner Light. Criminals received no such individual attention by a monarch, who paid attention to a criminal only when the crime appeared to be so heinous as to constitute a direct challenge to sovereign authority, and then there was no concern at all about the reformability of the criminal, except in those cases when the crime concerned direct political opposition. Interestingly, political prisoners were for the most part the only criminals sentenced to spend time in prison. These sentences to imprisonment for political opposition were most often a result of the sovereign's attempt to preserve alliances, rather than a sign of mercy, but they served as a way of attempting to convince opponents to change their positions.

For the most part, punishment not only eliminated the offender as a threat to the power of the king, but also served a ritual function in which the obedient subjects of sovereign authority were put in awe of the sovereign's power. Sentences were publicly executed to guarantee an audience for the demonstration of the terrible justice of retribution. At a general level, a deterrence was achieved, a raw and prohibitory form of deterrence.[27] The subjects of authority were, in brief, terrorized.[28]

In this context, a pardon demonstrated the power of the sovereign as much as did the execution of sentence, for offenders were diminished in importance by virtue of being granted the forgiveness of the ruler. In fact, one might gauge the decline of the power of the late feudal order by tracing the rise of the rate of execution of sentence in proportion to the granting of pardons and pleas of clergy.[29] The harshness of the English Criminal Code at the end of the seventeenth and beginning of the eighteenth century can be accounted for by the lack of confidence that the emerging bourgeois order had in its own legitimacy. Without having yet achieved enough confidence to forgive, and fearful of the loss of the power they were starting to exercise, the bourgeoisie enforced criminal law with a greater rigidity than had the nobility which preceded it.

The Great Law of Pennsylvania can be understood in this context as an early attempt on the part of a vanguard of the bourgeoisie to create a new mechanism for the legitimation of authority. It was not a utopian experiment in the humane treatment of God's fallen children, but a well-conceived if poorly executed policy designed to establish a new method of control over the rapidly developing individual subject. Conflicts entailed in the transfer of power from the monarchy to the parliamentary elite, as well as continued countryside resistance to the inscriptions of the new authority, hampered the development of such mechanisms in England. The Quakers were free to advance these new mechanisms, confident that their views would not be so strongly challenged, representing as they did the most basic extensions of their fundamental principle of rule, toleration.[30] They did not fear a loss of power in a struggle against the monarchy, having long since been excluded from the traditional arenas in which such power struggles occurred. Indeed, they viewed the Glorious Revolution itself with some ambivalence, for they resented the brutality of the Puritans who shared their class position and felt some sympathy for a monarch who had protected their right to dissenting beliefs.[31] In short, the experiment the Quakers were to undertake in criminal punishment was in part the product of their social cohesiveness. They did not fear social disintegration, but instead projected confidence in the capacity of their social system to prevent such a disintegration. In a sense, the Quakers were in the position of a strong monarch, able to grant clemency as a sign of strength. More than this, however, the new penal code was to encourage the cultivation of a new kind of person, a new subject, one whose inner discipline would be encouraged by the imposition of the fetters of friendly persuasion.

### The Great Law and Toleration

Through the centuries, the Great Law has been described by sympathetic readers as a utopian blueprint of society that anticipated both the democratic and the liberal impulses which would later inform the American Revolution.[32] Yet as a sustained vision of relationships between government and citizenry, it was not an unusually democratic document, even within the context of the times, and even though it provided for representative assemblies. The Great Law is unique, however, if one keeps in mind the prohibiting function of government that dominated thinking about the state in the late seventeenth century: the Great Law stands out for the positive role it assigned government in its interventions into society.

The Great Law emerged out of several compacts: the Charter Agreement between William Penn and Charles II, the Frame of Government, and the Law Agreed Upon in England, all of which preceded and shaped the Great Law approved by the colonists after their arrival in Pennsylvania. As the proprietor of the colony, Penn was largely responsible for drafting the law, although there were substantial restrictions placed upon his authority by Charles. Nonetheless, Charles gave Penn a broad range of powers, including the power to make law, execute law, appoint judges and other necessary officials, organize counties and incorporate towns, license importers and exporters, and protect colonists from direct taxation of the crown.[33] The primary check Charles placed on Penn was that every arrangement of the proprietary government be "consistent with English Law."[34] This check did not limit the Great Law as much as one would suspect, largely because there were many areas of legislative authority, particularly the area of the penal code, which English law failed to address. Within these silent spaces some of the Great Law's most important innovations were to appear.[35] Only later, when they fell from favor and the consequences of some of their policies were questioned, were these laws challenged by the Privy Council.

The Frame of Government, which with one major change became the Law Agreed Upon in England, was the first draft of the Great Law. In some respects, this document was more radical than the Great Law proper.[36] It outlined in detail both the political theory on which the Great Law was to be based and the specific institutions of representation and governance that were to be established to fulfill the requirements of that theory. Perhaps more than any other single document, it explains the linkages between the Quaker theology of Inner Light and positive, interventionist government.

The preamble of the Frame starts from fairly conventional premises and draws radical conclusions. Government, it states, was created because people are imperfect, and it serves to control the evils that result from imperfection. Thus government is a kind of religious institution, although because it is primarily concerned with earthly matters it is less exalted than religion itself. Because of its unique status as a semireligious, semisecular institution, government has a dual role: "first, to *terrify* evildoers; secondly, to cherish those who do well."[37] This second role of government receives extraordinary emphasis in the Great Law, enough to make it a radical departure from previous legal codes.

> They weakly err, who think that there is no other use of government than correction, which is the coarsest part of it. Daily experience tells us, that the care and regulation of many other affairs, more soft and daily necessary, make up the greatest part of government.[38]

This assertion provided the rationale for the establishment of an interventionist government, one which would play a positive role in the development of its citizenry. Seen in this light, Penn's most famous statement, which followed this one in the preamble, "Let men be good, and the government cannot be bad," becomes clear. Penn was not advocating disinterest in the form that government might take, as so many have interpreted him. To the contrary, he was arguing for the establishment of governmental institutions that would compel goodness on the part of the citizenry.[39]

This concern is reflected in various provisions to be found in the Frame. The scheme of representation was to include all classes.[40] Representation was not an end in itself, but was designed to involve all members of society in governance so as to encourage responsibility. Pennsylvania was unusual for the amount of power the proprietor gave up to property holders. Penn himself abandoned the absolute veto of the proprietor. He later had much cause to regret his decision, since the representative assembly rarely cooperated with him, and in fact rendered some decisions that contributed to his personal bankruptcy.[41] Other principles of government, made explicit in the Law Agreed Upon in England, reiterated the encouragement of individual responsibility and rights by establishing principles of free justice and due process.[42]

Overriding all other concerns, however, was the importance of toleration, which implicitly informed these other provisions. The very first chapter of the Great Law guaranteed all Christian colonists freedom of conscience.

> *Be it enacted by the Authority aforesaid*, That no person, now, or at any time hereafter, living in this Province, who shall confess and acknowledge one Almighty God to be the Creator, Upholder and Ruler of the World, and who professes himself or herself Obliged by Conscience to live peacefully under the civil government, shall in any case be molested or prejudiced for his, or her Conscientious persuasion or practice.

All were to "fully enjoy his or her Christian religion."[43] Limiting freedom of conscience to Christians was fully consistent with Locke's argument in *The Reasonableness of Christianity*, in which Christianity was so deeply identified with reason as to make the profession of any other faith "unconscientious."[44] Within the prescribed boundaries, all were to enjoy this inner freedom, though the importance of Christianity was underlined in the second chapter of the Great Law, which declared that all officers of the commonwealth were to be Christians.[45]

Toleration was emphasized even more in a later chapter of the Great Law, which declared toleration the fundamental law of the colony, not to be abrogated by any later amendment.[46] It is interesting to note, especially in light of the tenacity with which the Quakers were later to defend their penal code, that the guarantee of nonabrogation which applied to toleration was not applied as well to the laws which outlined the underlying principles and the institutions of criminal punishment. It may well have been that Quakers believed that criminal punishment was so closely associated with toleration that the protection of the latter would guarantee the former. Such, however, was not to be the case, as will be seen below.

### The New Punishment

It was but a small jump from the declaration of principles of toleration to the codification of new penal laws. The Quaker concern with toleration was a result of their experience as victims of intolerance. One form of their persecution for adhering to dissenting beliefs had been display on the stocks, and, as political criminals, some of them, including Penn, had suffered imprisonment.[47] The abuses of corporal punishment were, in their minds, inextricably connected to intolerance. They believed that the solution to the problem of punishment of criminals lay in the same ethics that encouraged goodness in the world. Hence, they prescribed a criminal code that would clearly establish the sphere of life over which criminal statutes would apply, minimize the physical suffering of the convicted person, and maximize the free play of techniques of moral suasion. Criminals would be given the chance to be redeemed as Christians. It would be assumed that by virtue of their very existence as human beings they would be potentially redeemable. God's Inner Light could shine on all; as all are sinners so all might be saved.[48]

Ironically, the punishment that the Quakers proposed for criminals paralleled in milder form one important technique of the punishment the Quakers had suffered at the hands of political authorities in England. Imprisonment, previously reserved for political crimes, was to be the most important feature of their new code. Imprisonment preserved the life of the convict while allowing the convict to consider the wrongness of the deed. The notion of individual autonomy to which the Quakers adhered was not inimical to imprisonment itself. Their understanding of the role that contemplation played in salvation was no doubt reenforced through the prison experience, which provided many hours of quiet, regardless of what else it did. The contemplation that such empty time provided was used by Penn himself for self-improvement. To make this contemplation available to regular criminals was, in a sense, to privilege them as political actors, because they would be treated as dissenters were treated, with the same opportunity for seeking Inner Light.

More immediately important, imprisonment was to provide a technique for encouraging the development of a selfhood responsive to friendly persuasion. Criminals were to be taught to respond to the social pressure that encouraged good Christian behavior. They would be given new *selves* so they might be saved.[49] Although terrorization was not to be totally absent from the Great Law's criminal statutes, the bias of its provisions was overwhelmingly on the side of correction, rather than punishment. Thus the reclamation project of the Quakers can be understood as a constructive project, an initiation of the criminal to the terms of self-responsibility. A nineteenth-century biographer of Penn was to put it this clearly: "He saw . . . the wickedness of exterminating, when it was undoubtedly to deter, or prevent others from the commission of crime; but on the other hand, it was the great object of the Christian religion to reclaim."[50]

Many features of the criminal code of the Great Law distinguish it from the English Criminal Code. The English Code listed some two hundred capital offenses; the Great Law listed one, willful murder.[51] The English Code provided for corporal punishment and banishment as the major penalties for noncapital offenses; the Great Law substituted fines and confinement at hard labor.[52] Perhaps of most lasting significance, the Quakers used a scale of punishment intended to correspond with both the seriousness of the crime and the degree of responsibility of the offender.[53] This scale was an early attempt in the history of the penal reform to use punishment as an instrument of individuation.[54] Finally, the Quaker code was more encompassing than was the English Code. Clarification of the law did not imply simplification. Indeed, the Quakers involved government in the details of everyday life to an unprecedented extent. Private affairs were exposed to the judgment of the community. They established penalties for behavior as mundane as cursing and as kinky as bestiality, providing for a minor fine in the first instance and a major fine, imprisonment, and the destruction of the animal in question in the latter case.[55]

The comprehensive nature of the code served the purpose of establishing firm guidelines for the administration of justice in the absence of lawyers and judges trained in common law. Any responsible person serving in the capacity of judge could render a decision by relying on the code. Although Quakers might well find themselves tried in the public courts, depending upon the severity of the crime, the meeting was the more frequent site of law enforcement.[56] This organization of authority, in which the meeting existed parallel to the public forums of justice, increased the sphere of social life over which the Quakers had control. It also led to a more widespread appreciation of and respect for the laws themselves, especially among the Quaker constituency. In relying upon their religious institutions, the Quakers were not so different from the religious authorities of the other colonies. But the Quaker experiment was distinct because they were acutely aware of the need for forums of justice other than the meeting for those who were not members of the Society of Friends and even for those who were. The distinctions they rendered were less between public and private than between those who had developed an appreciation of the meaning of Inner Light and those who had not.

If imprisonment was to be a pedagogy, designed to teach criminals the difference between right and wrong so that they might reach salvation, so was the codification of specific violations of the public morality designed to be a similar guide to correct behavior. Two provisions of the Quaker code illustrate how they expected prisoners to achieve a state of genuine repentance for their sins. First, as I have already mentioned, prisons were to be the primary site of punishment. This was an innovation which had few if any precedents.

> *Be it enacted by the Authority aforesaid,* That all Prisons shall be work-houses for felons, Thiefs, Vagrants, and Loose, abusive, and Idle persons, whereof one shall be in every county.[57]

The workhouse was an institution that had been used in several European nations as a means of controlling poor people. Particularly successful in the Netherlands, it had recently been used experimentally in the Dutch administration of justice, but not as a primary means of punishment.[58] In England, the workhouse, also known as the bridewell, was designed to impress upon poor people work habits that would lead to their acceptance of employment in textile mills, which were coming to play a major role in the English economy by the mid-seventeenth century.[59] Throughout the more advanced mercantile countries, workhouses were being used to supply labor for manufactories of all sorts.[60] While the Quakers themselves suffered from acute labor shortages during the proprietary period, and they had a large number of indentured servants whom they needed to control,[61] the workhouse represented primarily a means of eliminating torture, not of controlling the poor.[62]

The elimination of torture as a technique of punishment also meant that the execution of punishment would no longer be public. The simple act of removal to prison was to privatize punishment, to make it intimate and anonymous. Public order was not to be disturbed by the acts of individuals. In the context of a highly personalized society such as Pennsylvania, where one's identity was shaped under the constant exposure of the meeting, such removal had all the impact of an external banishment. Convicts were banished to the interior spaces of the prison, where they would work to exculpate their sins, and then rejoin the community. A justice of restraint was to serve to reform, rather than deform.

The Quakers were also aware of the conditions that obtained within most of the workhouses of England, and sought means to prevent their prisons from slipping into the conditions of those in Europe.[63] Their solution went far beyond the minimal needs of sanitation:

> *Be it enacted by the Authority aforesaid,* That gaolers shall not oppress their prisoners, and that prisons shall be free as to Room, and all prisoners shall have liberty to provide themselves bedding, food, and other necessaries, during their imprisonment. Except such as whose punishment by law, will not admit of that liberty.[64]

The ordinary administration of jails until then had been structured so that prisoners had to pay the jailer. Jailers were contracted by municipalities to hold prisoners in return for the fees they could extract from them.[65] Under such a system, prisoners would have to buy their food from the jailer. Of course, until the prison was made into a site of punishment, rather than a holding place for those accused of crimes who could not post bail, there was less concern about the status of those held.[66] But when the prison became a central object in the administration of justice, more attention followed. Hence, what seems at first glance to be a step backward (prisoners being responsible for providing their own necessaries) was part of the process of neutralizing the corruption inherent in having the imprisoned totally dependent on the jailer. Other provisions in the law established fees that the government would pay to jailers, further removing their interest in exploiting prisoners.[67] A bottom line was established, then, at least in law. Prisoners, regardless of their economic status, would have free room in jail.

The administration of justice was carried out in a more haphazard manner. The first task was to build the prisons mandated by the Great Law. Counties often found themselves faced with lack of revenues as a result of the continuing battles waged among the colonists concerning taxation. In most counties, if prisons were built at all, they were usually nothing more than log cabins.[68] Only in Philadelphia was the spirit as well as the letter of the law adhered to. There, a rudimentary prison was constructed in 1685. Prisoners were put to work grinding meal and breaking stones; oversight of the prison was provided by a board of governors.[69] Despite the lack of solid prisons in most counties, by the turn of the century imprisonment was the established sentence for the majority of serious felonies in Philadelphia and Chester counties, the two most densely populated counties of the commonwealth.[70]

The penitentiary did not appear at this time. While the Quakers clearly understood that the route to salvation was the path of contemplation and solitude, their workhouses did not provide for solitary confinement, a feature which was to distinguish the first penitentiary from earlier reforms.[71] There was no cell system. Instead, the architectural model followed was that of the colonial home. Sometimes, in fact, the jailer's family would live with the jailer and the prisoners in the prison itself.[72] But even though there was not the total isolation required for solitary confinement, the rudimentary prisons of the Quakers did provide for the sexual segregation of prisoners, and the separation of prisoners into different age groups as well. All in all, the extent to which the Quakers departed from previous practices represented a formidable accomplishment.

### The Failure of the Law and the Preservation of Toleration

Judging from the perceptions of British policymakers at the time, the code and its implementation succeeded only in making Pennsylvania a haven for smugglers and other criminals. By the time of the close of proprietary rule, most colonists and, more important, most members of the Privy Council thought that the criminal code was too lenient, responsible for high crime rates. As early as 1701, complaints from the Privy Council concerning smuggling led to a modification of the code.[73] This smuggling, much of it implicitly encouraged by the Quaker merchants themselves to avoid internal tariffs in their exchanges with other Quaker merchants in the East Indies, led to a direct challenge on the part of the Privy Council to continued proprietary rule in Pennsylvania, once Philadelphia emerged as a premier center of trade in the American colonies.[74]

Subsequently, the criminal code was abandoned when Pennsylvania became a royal colony in 1718. The Great Law was for the most part dismantled. Only the provision that guaranteed toleration remained. The transition period is worthy of note, for it reveals the extent to which the colonists understood the importance of toleration for the development of liberal society.

In 1711, Parliament passed what was called the Occasional Conformity Act, a law which directly prohibited the right that Quakers asserted in their affirmation law, not to swear oaths.[75] While the Pennsylvania Quakers (as opposed to those still in England) had successfully sought exemption from previous restrictions on the right to affirm, the political climate in both England and Pennsylvania had evolved to the point where they no longer could make such a bargain. The Anglican presence in Pennsylvania had grown to the point where hostilities with the Quakers had become overt. Anglicans in Philadelphia both encouraged the passage of the Occasional Conformity Act and attempted to use it to drive Quakers out of office. After seven years of increasingly futile negotiations between the Quakers and the Privy Council, all affirmation laws of Pennsylvania were disallowed.[76]

The Quakers then boycotted all public affairs, including civil and criminal court proceedings.[77] The administration of public affairs could cease without too much damage to the Quaker community, even twenty-six years after they became responsible for governance. For the non-Quaker population, which at this time constituted a majority of the colonists, matters were not so easily handled. The colony's administration became more and more chaotic. Into the breach stepped William Keith, governor of the colony, who, realizing that there could not be a complete return to the Great Law, bargained with the Privy Council for the preservation of affirmation laws in return for the abandonment of the Quaker criminal reforms. The Privy Council quickly agreed to Keith's compromise.[78] Thus ended Pennsylvania's first experiment in penal reform.

One legal historian has remarked that this bargain was in essence a betrayal of the Quaker's most fundamental principles, because the preservation of a symbolic right (the right to affirm rather than swear oaths) was achieved at the expense of Pennsylvania's most important social innovation.[79] Such an argument obviously fails to understand the order of Quaker priorities. In 1718 it was by no means clear to the inhabitants of Pennsylvania that the penal code they had established as part of the Great Law contributed to effective rule. The doubts they may have had concerning the Great Law itself were veiled, but what one historian has called a more general "politics of disaffection" served to undermine the already weak confidence that many colonists had in the public institutions under which they were governed.[80] Moreover, by 1718 the solidarity of the Quaker community itself had weakened as the conflicts between merchant and landed factions became exaggerated, and as the stratification of all colonists into different economic classes, with conflicting economic interests, accelerated.[81] Indeed, much of the immediate political turmoil of early-eighteenth-century politics in Pennsylvania was a result of class resentments, which were then exploited by politicians such as David Lloyd in their attacks on Penn and proprietary rule.[82]

Ultimately, the choice of affirmations over the preservation of a criminal code that no longer seemed to work (if it ever had) can be understood as simply the result of the success of the colony. As emigration from England (and Ireland) increased, as more and more non-Quakers entered the colony, the bonds that once had held the community together no longer held. The newer colonists were not for the most part members of the Quaker community. Separation from society may have been sufficient punishment when criminals were composed only of Quakers; it may have been effective in transforming recalcitrant Quaker criminals into genuine enlightened Christians. But as time went by, it was not a society of Quakers that the penal code served. The code presumed too much of those who were its new constituency.

### Toleration and the Prehistory of the Penitentiary

Toward the close of British rule over the North American colonies, William Bradford explained that Pennsylvania had long suffered under the yoke of a criminal code that was foreign to the values of Pennsylvanians: "the severity of our criminal laws is an exotic plant, and not the growth of Pennsylvania. It has endured, but, I believe, has never been a favorite."[83] By the 1770s, the enduring image of the Quaker founders of Pennsylvania was firmly in place. Christian compassion, moral rectitude, an understanding of the capacity of all people to achieve God's grace, became the touchstones for generation after generation of penal reformers who were to interpret their own tinkering with the machinery of punishment as following in the footsteps of the Quakers.

Perhaps the Quaker vision appealed to these reformers because it so unambiguously expressed both liberal and democratic values. For the Quakers, all could be saved, yet all were to achieve salvation as individuals. Of course, the Quaker vision was hardly laissez-faire. It did not preclude the imposition of a rigorous discipline on those who failed to achieve their standards of goodness. The very specificity of their legal code, more than the specific content, reflected their belief that the state can and should be intimately involved in the development of the character of the members of society. That they turned to government at all is an irony of the highest order, given that a brief thirty years earlier they had been considered one of the most anarchic religious sects on the island of Britain. But the manner in which they used government to advance their goal of a society of reasonable Christians undermined distinctions between public and private even as they enshrined that difference as the means through which toleration could develop. Civil society was to be the source of social control, not by directly establishing the underlying mores, the common sense which when violated would provoke rebuke, but indirectly, through the mediation of legal codes. These codes, which had no force other than that granted from the social realm, would by their very specificity, their very regularity, establish the modern, liberal democratic person.

For it was this task that the Quakers undertook in their trip across the ocean. They knew enough of other errands in the wilderness of North America to recognize that their journey too was a new beginning.[84] Their preparation for that trip consisted of sermons and petitions, charters and laws, the encoding of their moral framework into a set of comprehensive documents, as well as the loading of ships, the recruitment of servants, a gathering together of the loose ends of lives that had been rich in the experience of marginality. To lose that marginality they crossed an ocean. But they were not unburdened by that passage, nor did they want to be.

A prison was inscribed in the Quakers' unspoken attempt to preserve a sense of distance from the political by subordinating it to the goodness of Inner Light.

"Penitentiary" entered the English language as an adjective before it became a noun; the word conveyed an attitude before it came to mean a place to go and do penance. The modern penal project was to encompass much more than even the ambitious vision of the Quakers. (To this day the Society of Friends attempts to work toward exculpating their original sin.) But the invention of a place to go and do penance, the modern penal project, fit well with the plans of the Quakers to establish conditions which would encourage silent contemplation, places where they might prepare themselves to receive God's Inner Light. The simple prison of the Quakers, then, might be considered a preparatory institution, designed as a vestibule through which the future might be glimpsed, the beginning of the history of the present, a prehistory of the genealogy of the modern soul.[85] In the late seventeenth and early eighteenth centuries, the gentle folk of the Society of Friends were busy in preparation. Friendly persuasion was an early attempt to move to the kind of regime in which the soul, as the prison of the body, becomes the battleground of power, a regime in which people are made into individuals so that they might learn to behave themselves.[86]

What was to be tolerated by the Quakers, what was to be tolerated and protected by generation after generation of Lockean liberals, was precisely this process of subjugation. A strange mix of public and private was established, leading to what in retrospect appears to be the inevitable dissolution of the distinctions that might exist between them. The restructuring of criminal statutes and techniques of punishment gathered momentum, after setbacks and delays, to form a major policy (policing)[87] initiative, one that sprung directly out of Lockean concerns with the source and end of knowledge. Once the yoke of British rule was lifted from the colonies, the newly freed states of North America began to build their model prisons, to show their Quaker ancestors how to proceed into the modern age of inscribed bodies. By then, friendly persuasion would not exist to protect a fragile, as yet underdeveloped individual. Instead, it would provide the inspiration for the new mechanisms of rule, ones that built upon the old even as they elaborated and furthered the progress of the modern prison.

It may have been possible to construct a more autonomous individual out of the materials at hand, or to have gone in the other direction and more explicitly established the domination of the social over the individual. But the Lockean paradox lies in the attempt to have it both ways, to interiorize social discipline, to make individuals who are neither meaningfully social nor autonomous. This tension introduced a remarkable subplot in the subsequent development of American society. Overt concerns that the state not exert too strong a control over the people were to be accompanied by covert debates concerning how the people were to be made into proper subjects. A weak state paradoxically would require subjects who would be weak as well.

The American Revolution was to clear the way, not only for the establishment of a democratic republic which would balance interests against each other, but for the constitution of the techniques which would establish those interests, which would develop more firmly the realm of danger. For the subjects of authority were to need more protection than ever before, as new demands were placed upon them, as new threats to their existence appeared, as the republic of bees gathered into its first swarming in the United States.[88] The range of the social was to become more and more complex, and people would need to know even better how to behave themselves.

# 4

## Republican Machines:
## The Emergence of the Penitentiary

The American Revolution was not only the successful separation of the North American colonies from their colonial masters, but also the "bursting asunder" of the fetters that bound them to the old regime.[1] Such moments in history can extend for many years, and the destruction of the old order and the establishment of the new often coincide. But the American Revolution cannot be reduced to the simple replacement of feudal relationships with capitalist ones. The variety of institutional and social relationships that mark the emergence of the United States are the result of processes through which some of the customs and principles that had governed the colonists' previous lives were purged, while many of the structures upon which those previous lives had been constructed were preserved.[2] From these processes new institutions emerged: a system of constitutional rule; new educational institutions and pedagogic practices; a reconceptualized property law; an economy reoriented to encourage frontier development. This is just a partial listing of the changes that contributed to the constitution of the United States.[3]

Many American historians have explored such dimensions of the American Revolution, employing a variety of perspectives; almost all have emphasized the depth and breadth of the change that occurred in a brief period of time.[4] But these historians have underestimated one of the crucial components in the reordering of the ideological universe that occurred during this period: the transformation in the system of criminal punishment during the years immediately following independence from Britain.[5]

The penitentiary became a primary institution through which a new set of techniques of pedagogy developed. These techniques, by which the action of citizens might be assessed, managed, and controlled, became an integral part of the process of creating a constitutional republic. Derived from medical science, religion, and positive legal principles, they were woven into a fabric of authority that underpinned the principles embodied in the Constitution, providing a foundation for the legitimacy of republican rule. The transfer of authority to the freed colonists, in brief, was completed not through the establishment of constitutional rule, but through a complete transformation in the use of repressive power.

In this chapter, I describe what I think are the most exemplary, rather than most "representative," texts concerning the initial establishment of the "soul" that was to entrap the citizens of the United States. I remain enmeshed in the history of Pennsylvania because of its exemplary status—site of the American Enlightenment, engine to the political machinations that resulted in the establishment of that new soul. But the focus and order are arbitrary; the narrative that follows, I again remind the reader, should be understood as such, though I hope as well that it also demonstrates a certain regimentation of truth.

Knowledge of Benjamin Rush's work is crucial if one wishes to understand the development of the U.S. penitentiary system. He argued that along with the establishment of constitutional rule, there needed also to be the creation of what he called "republican machines," citizens who would fit the demands required by such a form of government. Not only did he assert this, he devoted his life to the development of means through which such a production could take place. The first attempt to apply the principles articulated by Rush to the system of punishment in the United States occurred through the good offices of the Philadelphia Society for Alleviating the Miseries of the Public Prisons. In this chapter, I document their efforts to make the Walnut Street Jail of Philadelphia the first penitentiary in the world. I examine their lobbying efforts with the Pennsylvania legislature, and the basic system of discipline they set up in the Philadelphia prison. The failure of the Walnut Street experiment meant the eventual triumph (in Pennsylvania) of a mature system of solitary confinement as the major means of discipline for the achievement of reform of criminals. This chapter thus sketches the emergence of the first modern system of punishment in the United States, and presents its relationship to the development of an idea of citizenship that was very much a part of the revolutionary vision. That vision was captured in Rush's notion of the creation of republican machines.

## Benjamin Rush and the Mechanics of Moral Health

In the years that followed the War of Independence, and even during that war, political leaders of the new states devoted much time and effort to establishing governments which would remove vestiges of British rule from the law at least, and which in some cases would radically restructure the system of representation, the extent of power, and scope of activity of government.[6] Yet even as this prodigious effort in the realm of constitution building was taking place, many of the same leaders were devoting their energies to creating the kind of citizen who would fit into the new governmental structures being built. One need look no further than to Tom Paine's call to arms, *Common Sense,* in order to find evidence that the concerns of revolutionary leaders extended to the reordering of subjects. In his essay, Paine developed the metaphor of the youth going out into the world on his own, leaving the security, but also the dissolute values, of his parents behind. His immaturity placed the youth in great danger. Yet it also presented a great opportunity, for the youth would be unencumbered by the bad habits that he would inevitably have picked up from his parents had he remained with them.[7]

The central point of *Common Sense* was to persuade the colonists that it was time to leave the dissolute values of a corrupt and obsolete political system behind. The British monarchy represented the worst in their parent nation. The colonies were at that point developed enough to find their own way, but not so developed as to have replicated the bad habits of the parent nation. However, should the North American colonies delay, the ties that bound them to Britain would tighten. Though the colonies might continue to grow stronger, they would lose their innocence, and become as corrupt as the nation from which they sprang, losing the desire to separate. "Youth is the seed-time of good habits in nations as well as in individuals," Paine argued.[8] "From errors of other nations let us learn wisdom, and lay hold of the present opportunity—*to begin government at its right end*" (italics mine).[9]

Society as individual writ large has been an enduring metaphor in the history of political thought, but Paine and other revolutionists of the day understood the formulation he presented in literal terms. They believed that the new order they wished to establish, if it were to have any chance of success, must inculcate in its citizens a new set of habits.[10] The idea that government should begin "at its right end" was a call for a government that would not only reflect the radical liberalism of individualism, but also play an active role in establishing the values of that liberal telos among the citizenry. The people of the United States were to be the subjects of a great experiment in self-rule, but the selves were to be ruled as much as they were to rule. The famous set of checks and balances, designed to limit the encroachments of majorities against minorities, was to extend its machinery into the "souls" of individuals.

This goal was in keeping with the mission of the Revolution, which was not merely to achieve a separation from England, but to reform American society. Benjamin Rush reminded the former colonists of this larger purpose in an essay written following the peace with England.

> The American War is over: but this is far from being the case with the American Revolution. . . . It remains yet to establish and perfect new forms of government; and prepare the principles, morals, and manners of our citizens, for these forms of government, after they are established and brought to perfection.[11]

For Rush, the people of the United States needed to be made into what he called "republican machines," who would recognize and respond to the correct cues provided them by their government.[12] "This must be done, if we expect them to do their parts properly in the great machine of the government of the state."[13]

Rush devoted most of his life to understanding human behavior. While his involvement in the creation of the penitentiary was not as deep as that of some other prominent reformers, his writings informed every aspect of the theory and practice of punishment in the reformed system. Rush wrote about government, education, morality, physical and mental illness, as well as about the development of a new model of punishment. Indeed, for him, all of his projects were related to the same end—the establishment of a moral community.[14] He was, aside from being a founding member of the Philadelphia Society for Alleviating the Miseries of the Public Prisons, a member of the American Philosophical Association, a signer of the Declaration of Independence, founder of the first modern insane asylum in the United States, military surgeon of the Continental Army during the War of Independence, and, in his later years, treasurer of the National Mint. His acquaintances and intimate friends included Thomas Jefferson and, until a falling-out over the publication of the atheistic *The Age of Reason*,

Tom Paine, who originally wrote *Common Sense* at the urging of Rush. In short, Rush was one of the intellectual leaders of the Revolutionary era.[15]

It is not surprising that Rush had clear and deeply held opinions about the goals of the American Revolution. What is remarkable is the way in which he reconciled science with religion in his specific formulations concerning how that revolution was to be completed.[16] This reconciliation was important, for there was no escaping the religious impulses that informed, and well may have been the catalyst of, the Revolution.[17] The proper training of citizens for their roles in the great machine of government was indeed to be accomplished in those institutions where morality was traditionally formed, namely, the church, home, and school. Rush recognized the importance of these institutions, and suggested ways in which they could be strengthened, calling, for instance, for a system of universal and free education.[18] But when these institutions failed—and in the disruptive circumstances of the revolutionary era they were bound to fail from time to time[19]—others were needed to inculcate those internal checks and balances.

Rush was so confident that science enabled the social reformer to engage in the reconstruction of human beings that at one point he developed a treatment for turning the skin of black people white, solving in theory what he discerned to be the most crucial social problem facing the United States.[20] Regardless of the defect that afflicted the individual, if it could be accurately diagnosed, then a cure could be effected. Both diagnosis and cure, however, depended upon the ability of the physician to control the activity of the patient. The flow of blood, the flow of digestion, the flow of heat and cold, the flow of various vaguely identified lymphatic fluids, all needed to come under the control of the physician if the proper balance of the internal actions of the patient, and hence the patient's health, were to be established. Disease was an imbalance; the imbalance might be the result of a trauma, the invasion of a "humour," or immoderate habits in eating, drinking, smoking, sexual activity, or sleeping.[21] In some cases, of course, a body might be defective in its original construction, making the establishment of a balance impossible through existing techniques. But the discovery and cure of the imbalances that afflicted the patient depended upon establishing a controlled environment in which the patient's motions could be accurately monitored.

All diseases were thus considered the results of defective interactions with the surrounding environment, except those rarer cases in which there was an original defect in the body itself. Mental diseases were caused by such imbalances, just as were physical diseases. Indeed, for Rush there was no clear line of demarcation between the two.[22] Madness, according to Rush's mechanistic model, was the result of a variety of imbalances at the site of the moral faculty, the brain. The direct cause of these imbalances varied according to the type of symptoms patients might exhibit. The theory established not only a variety of types of madness but, more important, a variety of causes of madness, so that the patient would not necessarily be exonerated for his or her immoral behavior.[23] Pressure on the brain might be the result of physical causes over which the patient had little or no control, but alternatively pressures might be the consequence of some morally degenerate habit. In some cases the first cause of the disease was clear, in other cases ambiguous. But one could always trace the etiology of the disease to a site within the body.

> All the operations in the mind are the effects of motions previously excited in the brain, and every idea and thought appears to depend upon a motion peculiar to itself. In a sound state of mind these motions are regular, and succeed impressions upon the brain with the same certainty and uniformity that perceptions succeed impressions upon the senses of the mind.[24]

It followed that the correct procedure for curing the diseases of the mind first involved isolating the specific stimuli that affected the various mental faculties. For Rush, such faculties were of two types, those governing intellect and those governing morality. If the sensual stimuli that have effect on these faculties were controlled, the defects that resulted from the over-stimulation or understimulation of particular faculties could be cured. In the worst cases, control of the whole variety of stimuli that might affect the patient's behavior could be achieved only in the controlled environment of the asylum.[25]

In Rush's notes concerning the derangement of the moral faculty is a model of treatment that is tied to issues of legal and moral culpability. His formula for the assignment of responsibility for actions applies alike to the criminal and to the insane; thus the structure of punishment and the treatment of the insane followed parallel and explicitly related paths. Rush argued that total derangement was most probably caused by "an original defective organization of those parts of the body, which are occupied by the moral faculties of the mind."[26] Rush then considered the issue of guilt and innocence.

> How far the persons whose diseases have been mentioned, should be considered as responsible to human or divine laws for their actions, and where the line should be drawn that divides free agency from necessity, I am unable to determine. In whatever manner these questions may be settled, it will readily be admitted that such persons are, in a pre-eminent degree, objects of compassion, *and that it is the business of medicine to aid both religion and law, in preventing and curing their moral alienation of mind.* We are encouraged to undertake this enterprise to humanity, *by the sameness of the laws that govern the body and the moral faculties of man.* (Emphasis mine)[27]

The way in which Rush anticipated what was to become a major legal issue in the twentieth century—the insanity plea—is not as important as his introduction of science as an aid to justice and morality. Rush never considered, and in fact explicitly rejected, the use of his techniques for determining guilt and innocence. Following such a determination, however, the forces of science were to be allowed full play.

In the realm of punishment after conviction, Rush deployed the disciplines of medicine, law, and religion. How is vice to be cured? Rush mentioned an entire arsenal of weapons, all arising from the diagnosed causes of the debility. Vice caused by indolence has its cure in employment. Vice caused by "stimulus of vicious motives": remove the debilitated mind from the influence of bad company. Vice as a result of the undue excitement of passions and will: regularize and moderate the stimuli of the overexcited mind. "Wear down" the "excessive morbid excitement" of this disease through labor. Such drastic actions on the part of the attending physician may seem, at first glance, excessive and harmful, but while

> the first impressions of confinement and bodily pain generally produce a vicious fretfulness and sometimes impious expressions and immoral conduct . . . these effects of those moral remedies are generally very transient. When continued long enough they never fail of producing a change in the moral temper of the mind.[28]

These practices were the techniques of the asylum. They were also the techniques of the penitentiary.

Rush concluded his study of the diseases of the mind with a peroration on the virtues of the newly established penitentiary of Pennsylvania.

> The abolition of the punishment of death, and of cropping, branding, and public whipping, and substituting for them, confinement, labor, simple diet, cleanliness, and affectionate treatment, as a means of reformation and forgiveness, have produced . . . moral effects on the jail of Philadelphia. If this original and humane institution, *in which science and religion have blended their resources together,* has not been attended with uniform success, it must be ascribed wholly to the imperfect manner in which the principles that suggested it have been carried into effect. They have been rendered abortive, chiefly, by the criminals sleeping in the same room, and by the facility and frequency with which pardons are obtained for them. (Emphasis mine)[29]

The control of vice could be achieved only by the perfection of an institution in which the common demands of religious and scientific reformative practices would be met, a place of quiet contemplation and order. Once the judicial system had made its decision, the scientific and religious apparatuses must be allowed to perform their tasks without further interference. A division of moral labor would thus be established.

For Rush the penitentiary was no more and no less than a particular kind of asylum, one that addressed the kind of moral debilitation that resulted in criminal actions on the part of the convict/patient. Regardless of the extent of individual culpability for the acts that brought the inmate to the door of the asylum, within its confines all inmates could be made subjects of the same diagnostic and curative processes. The environment would be controlled, the inmates would be controlled, and reform would follow from control.

It must be understood that Rush's advocacy of the asylum was not a speculative theory, but a defense of an existing set of institutions. He was defending these institutions, moreover, not from attacks that they were inimical to the values of the Revolution, but only from attacks concerning their effectiveness and expense. The implicit assumption that lay behind the creation of the new system—that the state possesses the right to deprive autonomous individuals of their physical freedom—was not questioned by anyone. Indeed, the denial of freedom was a particularly appropriate form of punishment for a society that emphasized freedom as an important political right, and made it an attractive institution in other capitalist countries as well.[30]

Inside the walls of the penitentiary, the absence of freedom had the ironic effect of establishing the conditions necessary for the reconciliation of liberal and democratic assumptions about the behavior of men. The penitentiary was already liberal and was to become democratic. It was liberal because the entire force of its operations was designed to reconstruct the psychology of individual persons. It was to be democratic because the same operations applied to each individual. All were to be made into republican machines through the use of the same technique. And the technique was derived from Rush's work.

This technique concerned the mechanics of moral health, but the model is more general. The regularity that was to be so important to the success of Rush's scheme was ultimately tied to the mechanics of the universe. There is a tendency, noted well by Garry Wills, to dismiss the scientism that permeated political discourse during this era.[31] Yet that scientism belied the empiricism, not only of Rush, but of every major figure who played a role in the American Revolution.

*On the Diseases of the Mind* was published in 1812, but was a summation of the work in which Rush had been engaged for the previous twenty years. While it is true that Rush's primary concern was the treatment of the patients in his asylum (the Philadelphia Dispensary), he considered the asylum model to be applicable to the treatment of criminals, and, as will be seen below, it was indeed used by those more directly involved in the administration of the early penitentiary. Thus there can be little doubt that the penitentiary was a form of asylum. Yet this direct connection has been overlooked in the most prominent study of the U.S. penitentiary and asylum during the founding period that has been published in recent years, Rothman's *The Discovery of the Asylum*.[32] Rothman argues that in the early years of the new republic, the focus of the criminal reform movement was on the law itself, rather than on the reform of criminals in the manner of the asylum. The former colonists, he argues, believed that crime was largely to be accounted for by the severity of the English Criminal Code, and most revolutionary leaders felt that a revision of the law itself, as it applied to the definition of crimes, would largely solve the problem of crime in the new states.[33] The revision of punishment came about only when the implementation of the new laws failed to result in the expected reduction of crime.[34]

In a limited sense, Rothman's argument is accurate, in that many of the former colonies failed to do more than simply revise their laws. But in Pennsylvania, the penitentiary's establishment was practically simultaneous with the revision of the criminal statutes. Other states eventually were to look at the Pennsylvania system as the model for their reform, even New York, which was later to develop a system which would challenge the penitentiary of Pennsylvania. The priority of Pennsylvania in this movement is important, because Pennsylvania was also at the forefront of the continuing revolutionary movement. The laws that were passed in Pennsylvania before the close of the eighteenth century determined the general direction of all subsequent reform. This initial establishment of the policy of imprisonment, as much as the particular techniques carried out within the prisons, was to result in the general abandonment of nonimprisonment alternatives in the field of punishment. The policy agenda can be said to have been captured early by the advocates of the penitentiary, which resulted in a shutting off of debate about alternatives to imprisonment. Such debate would have had to appear inconsistent with the goals of the Revolution, a return to the spirit of the discredited English Code.[35] Those who concerned themselves most with the problem of crime moved beyond the simple revision of the law from the start.

Rothman tacitly acknowledges the essential unity of the asylum and the penitentiary, understanding them as institutions that were created in response to the destabilizing effects of "new and changing circumstances" in U.S. society.[36] Yet the penitentiary was not simply a reactionary invention. Certainly there was widespread fear that the release of the U.S. marketplace from the constraints imposed by the British would have destabilizing social effects, and fear of moral degeneration was at the core of the Revolution itself. But it was the opportunity to establish a new order, as Paine put it, that lay at the heart of the penal reform movement. The preservation of "community,"[37] as Rothman describes the later efforts of the reformers, may well have been reactionary, but it was a reaction that was in response to later events.

But what were the specifics of the penal institution that was constructed? How was its history related to the theoretical assertions of Rush? In what ways and to what extent did it adhere to the goal of creating republican machines? In order to answer these questions, it is necessary to describe in some detail the genesis and early development of the penitentiary in Philadelphia.

## Walnut Street Jail in the 1790s

The first revision of the penal code in the independent commonwealth of Pennsylvania was made in September of 1786. When independence had first been declared in 1776, a new constitution for the state was created, and one of its provisions required that the criminal code be revised as soon as the contingencies of the war made it feasible to do so.[38] The 1786 code was the first in a series of legislative actions taken to meet this constitutional requirement. When passed, it was considered to be the completion of the reform, but its flaws led to its immediate reevaluation. It had as its chief object the establishment of a system of proportional punishment, designed to replace the system of capital and corporal punishment that constituted the core of the English Code.[39] Capital punishment was relegated to the crime of murder; hard labor and confinement in the Walnut Street Jail served as the substitute punishment. The use of a standard measure of punishment, in the form of length of time confined, was designed to ensure proportionality and uniformity in the distribution of sentences.[40]

This seemingly simple reform of the penal code was consistent with the most enlightened penal theory of the day as propagated by European reformers. Such figures as Beccaria and Howard had been demanding that punishment must be consistently applied to all, predictable in severity, and certain in application.[41] While consistent with the goal of justice as formulated by these reformers, the new punishment, when implemented, revealed itself to be inconsistent with the image of justice held by the ideologists of the Revolution. It contained too many elements of the punishment that had existed under the old regime. Traditionally, as in the punishment of the pillory, the role of the public in the execution of punishment had been to participate in the public humiliation of the convict. Through such participation, the pedagogic function of punishment was explicitly carried out. Those who committed crimes were, in this model, outcast from society by society itself, and the general public, as a corporate body, absorbed a clear and unambiguous lesson about the consequences of crime.[42] The social retribution that was an integral part of the old system of punishment, however, was not important, and indeed could be counterproductive, to the goal of just punishment as defined by Beccaria, because the measure of punishment could vary greatly depending upon the mood of the public.[43] In Philadelphia, the citizenry responded to the spectacle of chain gangs dressed in ragged clothing, working under armed guards in the streets, in the manner prescribed by tradition; they harassed and taunted them, sometimes threw stones and vegetables at them, and generally made sport of them in an attempt to humiliate them. It has been recorded that at times a prisoner would manage to break free and assault his tormentors, sometimes using his ball and chain to strike passersby.[44]

The new law, which became known as the "wheelbarrow law," since prisoners pushed wheelbarrows about the streets as they cleaned them,[45] immediately attracted the negative attention of the leading citizens of the city. While the law had been designed to lessen the harshness of the penal code, convicted criminals were in some respects treated with greater cruelty after the law's passage than before. Under the old code, while the sentences were harsh, they were rarely carried out to their final conclusion, particularly those providing for capital punishment. In all cases, sentences, while painful and dangerous to the convicts, were not extended through time but swiftly, if cruelly, executed. But because the new law demanded a length of time in confinement as a part of the sentence, and because the punishment was public, the overall effect was merely to make the English Code apply to a broader category of convicts than before.[46]

Nonetheless, the adoption of the new law marked the starting point of meaningful reform in the United States. The very passage of the law was representative of the efforts that were being made to rid the state of the influences of English law. But more important, for the first time in the United States, a code that emphasized the deprivation of freedom as a central component of criminal punishment was put into effect. Punishment of the body was for the first time displaced by a punishment of the soul.

Part of the irony of the law was that its very failure attracted attention to the problem of criminal justice. Before the passage of the law, the conditions of the prisons of Philadelphia had been the concern of but a small elite group of reformers who had not yet even organized themselves into a reform society. Jails, prior to the passage of the wheelbarrow law, had been only holding places for those awaiting sentence. Debtors' prisons, while miserable places, allowed a considerable degree of freedom to the inmates who often only lived near, not in them.[47] But with the reform of the law, the attention of the public was focused on the conditions of the prisoners; the results of their treatment could be observed on the streets of the city every day. It was this publicity surrounding the first law that led to the organization of the first major prison reform group in the United States, the Philadelphia Society for Alleviating the Miseries of the Public Prisons, which would later become the Pennsylvania Prison Society.[48]

The society was composed of the civic elite of Philadelphia, including prominent clergy, lawyers, and businessmen. Some of its members had participated in the creation of the wheelbarrow law.[49] All of them considered themselves to be enlightened, sophisticated citizens, and had been active supporters of the Revolution. Some had been involved in earlier prison aid associations that had visited the jails and debtors' prisons in the period prior to the Revolution. But their purpose in coming together was to establish a more effective system of punishment.

The preamble of the prison society charter stated that "such degrees and modes of punishment may be discovered and suggested, as may, instead of continuing habits of vice, become the means of restoring our fellow creatures to virtue and happiness."[50] This goal did not vary from that expressed earlier by the Quaker founders of Pennsylvania, but the reform program developed and subsequently implemented by the society departed substantially from the Quaker tradition. At a general level, both the Great Law and the system constructed at the end of the eighteenth century made prison the primary site of punishment, and in both systems the reform of prisoners was to be achieved through the inmates' penitence. The wheelbarrow law did not move beyond the Great Law in that regard. But subsequent reforms to the wheelbarrow law introduced the principle of separation, or solitary confinement, and hence moved far beyond the practice and theory of the old system. This movement reflected the radical changes that had occurred in the understanding of the motives and behavior of individuals since the Quakers had first postulated the idea that all were potentially redeemable.

Rush's studies had made redemption and science compatible. This enabled the prison society to develop strategies for active intervention into the habits of inmates without violating their autonomy as individuals. This qualification was important, for it enabled the reformers to avoid the sort of conflict that had split the European prison reform movement. In England especially, home of John Howard and Jeremy Bentham, the conflict between religious reclamation and behavioral reform was great. In a study of the English penitentiary system during this period, Michael Ignatieff notes that

> Howard and Bentham both denied criminal incorrigibility, but from diametrically opposed positions—one accepting the idea of original sin, the other denying it. One insisted on the universality of guilt, the other on the universality of reason. Materialists like Bentham and

Priestley asserted that men could be improved by correctly socializing their instincts for pleasure. Howard believed that men could be changed by awakening their consciousness of sin.[51]

The prison society did not see any such conflict. The reconciliation of science and religion in the service of reform was to be one of the most important features of the punishment system of the United States.

The prison society presented its argument to the Pennsylvania legislature in a series of "memorials," a device through which organizations and individuals could petition the legislature for changes in or passage of new legislation.[52] From their first memorial, it seems clear that they were firmly committed to, if not yet fully prepared to address the implications of, the system of solitary confinement. In that memorial the one firm recommendation they made was for the immediate establishment of "*more private or even solitary labour*" than was provided for by the wheelbarrow law.[53] But this initial memorial was only the beginning of their efforts. At the request of the legislature, they prepared a more comprehensive memorial describing conditions in the prison of Philadelphia and a series of specific recommendations for its improvement, which they delivered on December 15, 1788.

That second memorial systematically described the barriers to criminal reform in the Pennsylvania prison system. As a result of lack of separation with respect to sex and type of inmate, women engaged in prostitution and felons intimidated debtors. At the request of the society's visiting committee, jailers had removed women from the general population, but the mingling of prisoners in common spaces was still a major problem.[54] The second major problem was that all prisoners had access to "spirituous liquors." "To obtain money to purchase spirits," the report stated, "great irregularities, and even outrages, are committed by the prisoners, by not only selling their own clothes, but forcibly stripping others on their first admission in jail."[55] While these abuses were already prohibited by the existing penal laws, the committee noted that the laws on alcohol were universally avoided, and those calling for separation of debtors from felons were impossible to enforce given the structure of the jail. The most serious problem had to do with the effects of the mixing of debtors and felons: "debtors . . . have formed connections which ultimately lead to their being convicts themselves."[56] This problem extended itself to the families who often accompanied debtors to the jail," whereby they are initiated, in early life, to scenes of debauchery, dishonesty, and wickedness of every kind."[57]

The administration of charity was frustrated by the corrupt conditions in the jails. "Clothing distributed by the society to apparently the most destitute has, in many instances, been quickly exchanged for rum."[58] Efforts to provide supplements to the meager fare provided by the law were frustrated as well, for there was no equitable system of food distribution for any but those who were in the work gangs. The society could do absolutely nothing to amend these problems, having neither the resources nor the right to take the necessary actions, which involved a restructuring of the administration of the jail in a comprehensive manner. Hence, their petition to the legislature.

On the basis of these observations, the society made its recommendations for reform. Yet they also noted that they were guided by theory as well as by their observations of the jail. "The committee think it their duty to declare, that from a long and steady attention to the real practical state, as well as the theory of prisons, they are unanimously of the opinion that *solitary confinement to hard labour*, and a total abstinence from spirituous liquors, will prove the most effectual means of reforming these unhappy creatures."[59] While the theory of prisons they espoused was indebted in some degree to Howard, the central principle of solitary confinement that was to be the core of the new system was developed and first practiced as a means of behavioral reform by Benjamin Rush. Their denunciations of the chaotic conditions in the jails clearly paralleled the denunciations Rush made of the conditions that supposedly led to the overstimulation of morally deranged patients. The recommendations that were to be incorporated into the law subsequently drawn up by the Pennsylvania legislature (and written by the prison society) were to contain the same provisions for controlling stimuli that were implemented in Rush's asylum; the control over diet, housing, cleaning, scheduling, and social interaction were to reform the prisoner, just as the same measures reformed the insane patient.[60]

The key to all of the controls was the provision of solitary confinement. There would be an ongoing controversy over the use of hard labor, especially when it conflicted with the principle of solitary confinement. Diet, cleaning, and schedules, the society concluded, could best be controlled by solitary confinement. Because of this coupling of solitary confinement with an entire arsenal of reforms, the insistence of the society on solitary confinement was also the insistence on a totally new system of punishmment.

The second memorial presented by the society resulted in the legislature's recommendation that the society prepare a law which would provide for the reconstruction of the state penal system, and systematically revise the criminal code.[61] The new law, when passed in April of 1790, contained all the provisions necessary for the establishment of the first mature penitentiary.

The preamble to the act (section 1) noted that "the laws heretofore made for the purpose of carrying the said provisions of the constitution into effect have in some degree failed of success, from the exposure of offenders employed at hard labour to public view, and from the communication with each other not being sufficiently restrained within the places of confinement."[62] The next six sections established a common punishment for all felonies except murder, substituting for corporal punishment confinement at hard labor.[63] The remainder of the law, some thirty sections in all, described in detail how the jail at Walnut Street in Philadelphia was to be transformed into a penitentiary for the Commonwealth of Pennsylvania.

The first of these sections called for the construction of cells "six feet in width, eight feet in length, and nine feet in height, . . . separated from the common yard by walls of such height, as, without unnecessary exclusion of light and air, will prevent all external communication, for the purpose of confining therein the more hardened and atrocious offenders, who . . . have been sentenced to hard labour for a term of years."[64] The society did not get all that it wanted; the following two sections both specified the amount of money that was to be spent for the construction of the cells and indicated what provisions were to be made for all of those who would not fit into the cells and would instead remain in the common spaces of the jail. These prisoners were to be "kept separate and apart from each other, as much as the convenience of the building will admit, and . . . be subject to the visitation and superintendence of the Inspectors."[65] The assembly hoped that regular inspection would compensate for the lack of strict separation. This provision would later be cited as one of the inadequacies in the law when discipline broke down at the Walnut Street Jail.[66]

The next two provisions concerned specific directions for ensuring the health and welfare of the inmates, as well as for the sort of labor in which they were to be employed. All who were confined to labor were to be initially confined alone, cleansed, and observed until examined by a physician who would certify the inmate as healthy; the clothes of the incoming inmate were to be burned or fumigated; the new inmate was to be supplied with the standard garb of the prison; and all male prisoners were to be shaved, both beard and head, once a week (presumably to discourage the outbreak of lice). This initial isolation was to become an important means through which the prisoner would start the process of reform.[67] Diet was to be coarse and simple, consisting mainly of starches. The diet that was actually implemented in the Walnut Street Jail during the first years of its existence was later recorded by one of the first inspectors. It is notable for what it tells about the regularity of the life that was imposed upon the prisoners.

Sunday—one pound of bread, and one pound of coarse meat made into a broth

Monday—one pound of bread and one quart of potatoes

Tuesday—one quart of Indian meal made into mush

Wednesday—one pound of bread and one quart of potatoes

Thursday—one quart of Indian meal made into mush

Friday—one pound of bread and one quart of potatoes

Saturday—one quart of Indian meal made into mush

A half-pint of molasses to every four prisoners on Tuesday, Thursday and Saturday.[68]

The establishment of a clear and unambiguous work schedule was mandated in the next section of the law, which calibrated the hours to be worked to the seasons and set aside standard times for breakfast, dinner, and supper. No work was to be done on Sundays. All work was to be of the "hardest and most servile kind, which work is least liable to be spoiled by ignorance, neglect or obstinacy, and where the materials are not easily embezzled or destroyed." Workers were also to be separated from each other as much as possible. But again, owing to the contingencies of money and space, the assembly did not totally prohibit contact between them, another point of the law that would be later criticized by the prison society.[69]

The confinement of prisoners, within the constraints imposed by the assembly, was to be more absolute than in any previous system. One later section (section 18) underlined the importance of isolation, as well as the role that exposure to the proper authorities should play in the new system. Prisoners who only months before were on public display were now to be completely sequestered, not only from the public, but from each other as well.

No person whatever, except the keeper, his deputies, servants or as-

sistants, the said Inspectors, officers and ministers of Justice, Coun-
sellors or Attornies at law, employed by a prisoner, ministers of the
gospel, or persons producing a written license signed by two of the
said Inspectors, shall be permitted to enter within the walls where
such offenders shall be confined; and . . . the doors of all the lodging
rooms and cells in the said gaol shall be locked, and all light therein
extinguished at the hour of nine, and one or more watchmen shall
patrol the said gaol at least twice in every hour, from that time, until
the return of the time of labour in the morning of the next day.[70]

This provision, a security measure, was also a regulatory measure. It
extended the control that was to be exercised over prisoners to those who
were to watch the prisoners. It meant that only those who were approved
by the penal authorities could participate in reform. In a later era, with the
establishment of parole and probation, this idea would germinate in the
prohibition of association with "known criminal elements."[71] But for the
early system, the most important task was to establish the control within
the walls of the prison itself.

Coupled with the restructuring of the jail itself was the restructuring of
administration, staffing, and supervision. A board of twelve inspectors was
to examine and inspect the jail on a weekly basis and to supervise the
management of jailers. These inspectors were recruited from the member-
ship of the prison society itself. They were charged with making the
regulations and orders that would "carry this act into execution."[72] In short,
they were to establish the program they advocated, constrained only by
the legislation they had written, and continually to evaluate themselves.

While this conflict of interest contained the seeds of future abuse, the
inspectors provided a strong external check on the abuses of the jailers,
who had been notorious for their participation in the extortion of prisoners.
Jailer's fees, which had provided the jailkeeper with his sole source of
income, were replaced by a salary; as a result, the incentive for corruption
was reduced.[73] Because jailers were to be hired and fired by the inspectors,
they needed at least to pretend to share the goals of the reformers, and in
one case, that of Caleb Lownes, the jailkeeper was in fact a reformer
himself.[74]

In summary, the law of 1790 embodied the most advanced principles of
penology of the day. Isolation; labor; control of diet, hygiene, and rest; and
the rationalization of administration were all provided for in the new law.

The physical structure of the penitentiary may have lacked completion owing to inadequate funding, but the organizational structure was complete. Indeed, by embracing the principles of Rush's political psychology of control, penal reform became more than organizational reform; it became a new philosophy of punishment. The Walnut Street Jail was soon overcrowded, decrepit, and dysfunctional. Yet it was also the model for, and cornerstone of, all subsequent prison reform. For the second time (the failure of the wheelbarrow law being the first), but hardly for the last, the inability of a specific penitentiary to maintain the standards for which it had been built was to lead the reformers, not to reject the penitentiary, but to expand it. The movement of reform was to acquire a breathtaking pace in the next three decades, as Pennsylvania and other states expanded and elaborated upon the penal model of the Walnut Street Jail. It is useful to examine that system, which became known as the Pennsylvania system, to illustrate just what kind of republican machine it produced. As it turns out, that machine was to be rejected by U.S. civil authorities and the citizenry at large, but it nevertheless established as viable the idea that changing the behavior of criminals is possible and necessary. All subsequent models of punishment had to contain prescriptions for the kind of machine they would create.

### The Pennsylvania System

The 1790s witnessed the rise and fall of the Walnut Street Jail. From the time of the initiation of penitentiary discipline at Walnut Street, members of the Philadelphia society had been worried about the inadequate execution of their plan. As more felons were accepted from outlying counties, the capacity of the prison was overreached, to the point that by the end of the decade all semblance of separation of felons was abandoned.[75] Although laborers were no longer seen on the streets of the city, by 1810 it could be said that the intent of the 1790 legislation had been effectively frustrated.[76] Inmates lived in common, work standards were relaxed, dietary standards diminished, and maintenance of standards of hygiene disintegrated.[77] While the original inspectors were still active in the oversight of the prison, thus preventing rampant corruption of guards and overseers, there was little they could do to prevent the decline of the conditions of the jail. The funds needed to create a system of solitary confinement were simply greater than had been anticipated.

This problem was not rectified until the early 1820s, when legislation was introduced and passed in the Pennsylvania Assembly for the construction of a second penitentiary near Pittsburgh, and of a new penitentiary at Cherry Hill to replace the Walnut Street Jail.[78] The approval of these projects represented a major commitment on the part of the Commonwealth of Pennsylvania. They were the largest public works projects undertaken by the state government up to that time.[79]

When one compares the costs of the Walnut Street Jail with those of the two penitentiaries constructed during the 1820s, it becomes understandable why the Pennsylvania legislature hesitated for so long. The Walnut Street Jail's original and supplemental costs (for the construction of cells) totaled approximately $30,000. By 1821 it held approximately 570 prisoners (more than it was designed for), at a cost per prisoner in construction of about $104. The Pittsburgh and Cherry Hill prisons cost a total of $618,000. In Pittsburgh, where not all the cells were for solitary confinement, the per prisoner cost was about $908. At Cherry Hill, the most complete system of solitary confinement, it was an astronomical $1,648.[80] Combined, the Cherry Hill and Pittsburgh prisons were designed to hold about the same number of prisoners as were being held in the Walnut Street Jail.[81]

Proponents of the Pennsylvania system argued that while the initial costs were high, the efficiency of the new prisons—in terms of decreased maintenance, reduced needs for staff, and the use of prisoner labor to produce goods—would result in long-term savings.[82] In 1831, Cherry Hill Penitentiary (or Eastern Penitentiary, as it was officially known) managed to pay for itself, except for the salary of its officers. Continued success of such a program depended, of course, on the market for the goods that the prisoners, working individually, could produce. In the 1840s, the costs of yearly maintenance of the Pennsylvania penitentiaries skyrocketed as the labor of the system ceased to be competitive on the open market. The economic forces that were making slave labor less viable were hurting the penal systems as well.[83]

Costs and arguments over the possible long-term efficiency of the penitentiary were not at the core of the decision to build the new prisons, even though such arguments were real and may have swayed some doubters. Pennsylvania was but one of several states that went ahead with plans to build during the 1820s. The reason lies in the changes that were occurring in these states. As early as 1797, New York and New Jersey had adopted penal laws similar to those in force in Pennsylvania. In 1804, Maryland established its first penitentiary in Baltimore. By the time of Beaumont and Tocqueville's visit in 1831, penitentiary systems of either the Pennsylvania or Auburn type existed in nine of the twenty-four states.[84] Every one of those states had experienced a radical increase in population during the years between 1790 and 1830. All of them had significantly sized cities where none or few had existed before. In the Northeast, where penitentiaries proliferated most rapidly, the growth of population was the greatest. As Rothman observes, "In 1790, no American city had more than fifty thousand residents. By 1830, almost half a million people lived in urban centers larger than that." To pick but three states in which prison reform was most ardently pursued, for the forty-year period Rothman discusses, the population of Massachusetts doubled, Pennsylvania's tripled, and New York's increased five times.[85]

While demography reflects social changes more often than it directly causes change, the pressures caused by the growth of population on what had been a highly rural society were immense. Growth, in this instance, was a result of migration. The attractiveness of the new republic was considerable to European immigrants during this era, as it was to be for so many succeeding generations. Yet at a time when the country was relatively unpopulated, especially if one excludes the American Indian population, the impact of the first migration was disproportionate to the raw numbers.[86] Whether crime increased as a result of this migration is not clear, but what is clear is that a disproportionate number of inmates in the prisons of the United States during the 1820s and 1830s were foreign born or first-generation U.S. citizens.[87] If one of the purposes of penal discipline was to reach those who had escaped the socializing effects of free public education, as Rush had earlier suggested, then the constituency the penitentiaries served during this period was the appropriate one.

What was the penitentiary of Pennsylvania to teach these immigrants that they did not already know? It is possible that the first lesson they learned was a confirmation of the reasons that they had come to the new republic in the first place. Compared with the prisons and forms of punishment that still prevailed in Europe, the new prisons of the United States were as different as night from day.[88] With that acknowledgment, however, it must be pointed out that they were hardly mild. The terrors of severe corporal punishment did not present a threat in the penitentiaries of Pennsylvania, but the basic instrument of the Pennsylvania system, solitary confinement, was a certain and constant instrument of punishment.

A prisoner who entered the prison at Cherry Hill was immediately placed in the strictest of solitary confinement, with no relief in the form of any contact with anyone. During the first two weeks of confinement, even contact with the guards and inspectors was limited. This initial period of introspection was designed to break the prisoner from his (or her)[89] immediate past in as clear and radical a way as possible. In isolation, the prisoner would be forced to do nothing but think. Sleep during the day was not permitted; reading materials were prohibited. In effect, a form of what might now be called "sensory deprivation" was applied to the new prisoner. (Erving Goffman, in *Asylums*, has noted the importance of such orientation procedures for the establishment of control over inmates in mental hospitals and prisons.)[90] Thoroughly disoriented by the end of the two-week period, the prisoner would then be visited on a regular basis by guards and inspectors, would be given reading material, usually religious in content, and would be put to work. The work most often consisted of spinning and weaving, the kind of work that did not depend upon the use of too many tools, and which could be done in isolation.[91] The prisoner would exercise daily in a small yard that adjoined his cell. That cell yard also guaranteed enough light and air for health.[92] Meals were taken in the prisoner's cell. At most, a prisoner could receive one visitor a year from the outside. As a matter of general policy, however, no visitors except the prisoner's attorney would ever be allowed to visit. Mail from the outside was more often than not forbidden; even when it was allowed, it was usually limited to one letter a year. All mail was subject to censorship.[93]

Under such constraints, an inmate in the Eastern Penitentiary disappeared from the face of the earth. He would not know the circumstances or conditions of any associates from the outside world, including members of his family. The connection they had with him, it was hoped, would be discouraged as well. The inmate, completely cut off from the past, his future in suspension, would live only in the immediate time of his penitentiary sentence. The new habits and attitudes which would result would, it was hoped, enable him upon his release to assume his place in the community as a regular member. Because no one would know him, and because so few cared about the past, he would meet with no opposition.

What was the effect of this system on the inmate? A series of interviews conducted by visitors to the Eastern Penitentiary reveals the depth of the impact that this system had. In interview after interview, prisoners reported the same general experience.

QUES. Do you believe you could live without labour?

ANS. Labour seems to me absolutely necessary for existence; I believe I should die without it . . .

QUES. Do you think labour an alleviation to your situation?

ANS. It would be impossible to live here without labour. Sunday is such a long day, I assure you.[94]

One of the chief intents of the system was to establish in the inmate the desire to work. Out of a sense of frustration and boredom, the inmates were anxious to work, at least while still in the confines of the prison. But did they understand why work was valuable?

If the interviews are to be believed, and there is good reason to trust them,[95] inmates did indeed understand what they were being trained to do and why. The contrast between the system of labor in which inmates are forced to work, and the Pennsylvania system, in which if they did not wish to work they were not forced to, resulted in a contrast in attitude:

QUES. You work here without reluctance: you have said to me that this is not the case in other prisons, in which you have been imprisoned; what is the cause of this difference?

ANS. Labour here is a pleasure; it would be a great aggravation of our evils, should we ever be deprived of it. I believe, however, that forced to do it, I might dispense with it.[96]

What was worse than work, so much worse that inmates understood the conditions under which they accepted work as a positive benefit and still enjoyed their employment? It was the solitude that the prison imposed on them.

The effects of solitary confinement on inmates were deep. Again, from the interviews:

Solitary confinement seems to have made a profound impression upon this young man. He speaks of the first time of his imprisonment with horror; the remembrance makes him weep. During two months, he says, he was in despair; but time has alleviated his situation. At present, he is resigned to his fate, however austere it may be. He was allowed to do nothing; but idleness is so horrid, that he nevertheless is always at work. . . . He ended the conversation by saying: Solitary confinement is very painful, but I nevertheless consider it as an institution eminently useful for society.[97]

In the deprived environment of the solitary cell, any stimulus was dramatic for the prisoner. One prisoner described his relationship with insects: "This summer, a cricket entered my yard; it looked to me like a companion. If a butterfly, or any other animal enters my cell, I never do it any harm."[98] The point is clear. Even as short a period as a week in solitude had its impact.

> No. 00.—Age forty years; has been in the penitentiary but eight days. We found him reading the Bible. He seemed calm and almost contented. He said, that during the first days, solitude seemed insufferable to him. He was neither allowed to read nor to work.
>
> But the day before we saw him, books had been given to him; and since then, he found the condition entirely changed. He showed us that he had read already the whole volume which contains the four Gospels. This perusal furnished him with several moral and religious reflections. He could not conceive that he had not made them sooner.[99]

The imposition of solitary confinement eventually would come to be considered by the prisoners as an advantage rather than as a punishment. The longer they lived in solitude, the more accustomed to it they became. Ideally, it would lead them to enjoy the fruits of solitude. A highly educated prisoner put the matter clearly: "For a well educated man, it is better to live in absolute solitude than to be thrown together with wretches of all kinds. For all, isolation favours reflection, and is conducive to reformation."[100] While not all of the prisoners were enthusiastic about solitary confinement, it was accepted more readily than one might expect given the amount of mental anguish it caused initially.

There was one other important effect of solitary confinement. A lengthy interview revealed the tale of a criminal who had "gone straight" and learned a trade while in prison for a previous offense. Upon release he had gained employment in a tailor shop in Philadelphia. He married, and "began to gain easily my sustenance." Eventually, however, he was discovered by two former inmates, who threatened to tell his employer of his past. He moved to Baltimore, where word of his past caught up with him, and soon he was unemployed, sickly, and bitter. He returned to a life of crime. He favored the Pennsylvania system. "If I leave in nine years this prison," he claimed, "no one will know me again in this world; no one will have known me in the prison; I shall have made no dangerous acquaintance."[101] For the good inmate, separation from others was desirable, not only because they were likely to corrupt him, but because they posed a threat to his reentry into society. The inmate wanted no one to know him. Solitary confinement provided that anonymity.

Did the Pennsylvania system of punishment work? An answer to that question depends upon what one means by it. The most obvious criterion one might use—were the prisoners truly "reformed," as measured in rates of recidivism—is unworkable because the records are nonexistent. But that criterion is not the only one, and in terms of this study is hardly the appropriate one. Instead, one must ask to what extent the Pennsylvania system corresponded with the emergence of other components then shaping the discursive universe of liberal-democracy in the United States during the 1820s and 1830s.

The answer to that question is lengthy, and is best deferred until the outlines of the "other" penitentiary system, the Auburn system of congregate punishment, have been described. But if nothing else, the Pennsylvania system of punishment can at least be remembered as the system from which its subjects would emerge to say, "No one will know me again in this world. I have made no dangerous acquaintance."

In its maturity, then, the Pennsylvania system of punishment represented the completion of Rush's revolutionary vision. As Rush had hoped, a method for achieving total control over the behavior of subjects was quite possible and useful for effecting change in their character. If they failed to be reformed—in the sense of receiving the blessings of Inner Light—at least the prisoners in the Pennsylvania system would learn one fundamental lesson, that they were alone in the world. Perhaps they would learn that solitude was the condition of all members of society.

These isolated subjects could be joined together by the machinery of republican government. Once set in motion by the dynamics of attraction and repulsion, heat and cold, flux and calm, the moderated passions of the citizenry would be harnessed to the never-ending project of self-adjustment.

Republican machines were products of the American Enlightenment, the practical achievement of an empirical knowledge, a knowledge enabled and advanced by the scientific (and simultaneously moral) philosophers of the time. It was a knowledge that was to unify diverse fields of inquiry into a general mechanics. The symbol of that mechanics is the clockwork of David Rittenhouse's orrery. The American orrery, the most advanced of its day, bringing its inventor a fame equal to that of Franklin and Washington, synchronized the time of the earth to the times of the sun, moon, and planets. In his study of Thomas Jefferson, Garry Wills has emphasized the mechanics that informed this thought of synchronicity:

> Jefferson saw in the self-taught Rittenhouse a proof that Nature can speak directly to her student, without priestly or professorial intermediary. . . . He felt that Newton was best deciphered in the wilderness, where Rittenhouse repeated his experiments and put them to new uses. It was the attitude of Defoe's *Crusoe:* "So I went to work; and here I must needs observe that as reason is the substance and original of the mathematics, so by stating and squaring everything by reason, and by making the most rational judgment of things, every man may be in time master of every mechanic art" ("I Build My Fortress").[102]

Robinson Crusoe is the liberal man of nature, in nature yet dominating it, and eventually, through "his man" Friday, developing a rudimentary life for himself. Rittenhouse, Jefferson, Rush, all could accept a federal republic, but on terms that would allow that republican machine, the liberal man, to be alone.

The proposition that all are fundamentally alone is the most extremely liberal aspect of what was designed as a liberal institution. Upon the discovery of that fundamental loneliness, however, the subjects of the penitentiary were to be confronted with another truth—that loneliness was to be a shared condition. The Pennsylvania system, as innovative as it was, did not and could not shape its subjects to cope with this essentially democratic discovery. Even as its elements finally fell into place, and as it was accorded the praise of reformers from around the world, it was being superseded by another system of punishment which, while using the principle of isolation as its starting point, made that isolation a shared experience, thus fundamentally changing the lessons that punishment could provide. That system of punishment would complete the first cycle in the establishment of modern danger in the United States; it would present the citizenry with a model institution, an orrery of behavioral mechanics, from which more lessons about the dangerous relationship between rulers and ruled might be learned.

# 5

## The Woof of Time:
## The Penitentiary as a Democratic Institution

In the summer of 1831 two young French noblemen embarked on a trip to the United States on a commission from the French government. Their official mission was to make a study of the U.S. penitentiary system in order to determine whether it was suitable for transplantation to France. Beaumont and Tocqueville were also deeply interested in studying the effects of democratic institutions on the lives of Americans, and the limits imposed on the realization of democracy by other cultural institutions. In their correspondence, but especially in Tocqueville's *Democracy in America,* this broader mission found its realization.

A rich literature has accumulated over the one hundred and fifty years since Beaumont and Tocqueville made their visit, most of which has focused on the famous analysis of democracy contained in *Democracy in America.* Ironic note has been made from time to time of their original commission to study the prison system.[1] And within the discipline of criminology the study they ultimately wrote for their government has been recognized as a classic in descriptive analysis.[2] The relationship between their study of prisons and their studies of democracy, however, has in the main been neglected by social theorists and political scientists.[3] While it is true that what Beaumont and Tocqueville observed during their visit was the effect of democracy on all institutions, it was the penitentiary that they devoted the most time to. Moreover, at the time of their visit, it was the penitentiary that was the social cause extraordinaire, an issue that ranked, in its own way, with the controversy over the U.S. Bank for defining the political values of the country.[4]

Surrounding the controversy over the way in which criminals should be

113

punished was a set of questions concerning the nature of democratic citizenship in the United States. Yet the relationship between punishment and democracy, while taken as a serious problem by those policymakers and administrators who determined what punishment policy should be, was eventually seen by Tocqueville himself as having been an ephemeral and temporary concern. The last edition of *Democracy in America* makes no explicit statement concerning the relationship between punishment and democratic values. Indeed, in that edition, Tocqueville pointed to the excitement over the competing new models of punishment during the 1830s as an example of the shallowness of the enthusiasms of democratic people. Rather than concern themselves with existing prisons, citizens in the United States simply built new ones beside the old ones.

> This double effect is easily understood: the majority, preoccupied with the idea of founding a new establishment, had forgotten the already existing ones. Everybody's attention was turned away from the matter that no longer held their master's, and supervision ceased. The salutory bonds of discipline were first stretched and then soon broken. And beside some prison that stood as a durable monument to the gentleness and enlightenment of our age, there was a dungeon recalling the barbarities of the Middle Ages.[5]

By the early 1850s, the attention of U.S. citizens was diverted to an issue that was hardly of passing interest: the continued existence of slave labor in a political economy that was increasingly becoming reliant on free labor.[6] The prelude to the Civil War was bound to divert attention from other issues. Indeed, this diversion of attention could have illustrated the ability of U.S. citizens to concentrate on fundamental issues. One can note that following the resolution of the Civil War, penal reform was again to become a high-visibility issue.

One cannot, however, deny the importance of Tocqueville's argument. A fundamental problem investigated in *Democracy in America* concerns the effects of democracy on the concept of social order. For Tocqueville, the United States was a highly disorganized society on the surface. In fact, the complexity and detail of *Democracy in America* resulted from Tocqueville's understanding of this chaos: in order to understand common underlying principles of democracy, Tocqueville felt it necessary to trace the impact of democratic values in almost all dimensions of life. To take but one example of this complexity, Tocqueville's description of individualism roots it in time, the family, and in the nature of the U.S. economy.

> New families continually rise from nothing, while others fall, and nobody's position is quite stable. *The woof of time is ever being broken and the track of past generations being lost.* Those who have gone before are easily forgotten, and no one gives a thought to those who will follow. All a man's interests are limited to those near himself. . . . Aristocracy links everybody, from peasant to king, in one long chain. Democracy breaks the chain and frees each link. . . . [N]ot only does democracy make men forget their ancestors, but also clouds their view of their descendants and isolates them from their contemporaries. Each man is forever thrown back on himself alone, and there is danger he may be shut up in the solitude of his own heart. (Emphasis mine)[7]

How can a people so lost outside of time and place give sustained attention to any common concern? For Tocqueville the answer is clear. They cannot. Ironically, however, this self-absorption was for Tocqueville the key to understanding the mechanisms that bound them together. How and why those mechanisms worked, and the role that penal discipline played in their development, are the hidden dimension of democracy in America.

It cannot be the primary purpose here to present a complete analysis of Tocqueville's theory of democracy. However, a major element of that theory, Tocqueville's explanation of democratic despotism, can be shown to have been derived from Beaumont and Tocqueville's study of the penitentiary system. The relationship between the kind of reform advocated by such policymakers as Elam Lynds, warden of Sing-Sing, and the emergence of Jacksonian democracy illuminates the larger questions about how citizens of the United States could be disciplined.

Throughout this chapter, I use Beaumont and Tocqueville's *On the Penitentiary System of the United States and Its Application in France* as a primary source of information on the controversy between the Pennsylvania system of penal discipline and the Auburn system.[8] Supplemented by other sources, it provides clear insight into the associated problems of penal discipline and democratic values and sheds new light on the system of authority that emerged during the Jacksonian era. That system, while based on the fundamental principles of control first articulated by Rush, took a new direction as the breakup of the old feudal chain was completed and a society of unconnected citizens emerged. For Tocqueville, the only constant in the life of democratic America, besides the principle of the accumulation and circulation of money, was the chain forged in the American penitentiary.[9]

### The Auburn System: All That Society Has a Right to Expect

Tocqueville and Beaumont found themselves confronted by two exemplars of penitentiary discipline when they visited the United States. During the 1820s, New York had advanced a modified model of the system of complete isolation that prevailed in Pennsylvania. While in Pennsylvania the failure of the Walnut Street Jail led to the construction of a more elaborate system based on the same principles, the initial failure of the prison at Auburn, New York, resulted instead in the reevaluation of the idea of continual and constant isolation.

Isolation was a failure at Auburn because the construction of the prison was faulty. The cells at the Eastern Penitentiary of Pennsylvania had adequate ventilation, and even included individual yards in back so that the prisoners would be able to get at least a minimal amount of exercise.[10] The cells at Auburn, however, did not include such yards. Moreover, they were stacked on top of each other in the interior of the penitentiary building for the convenience of the inspectors. Finally, they were so small that the prisoners barely had room to turn around in them, much less exercise.[11] When the first group of prisoners was incarcerated in the new wing of the prison in 1821,[12] five of the original eighty were dead within six months, and over half of the remaining inmates were considered unhealthy enough, emotionally or physically, to be in danger of losing their lives.[13]

In the face of this failure, the inspectors of the Auburn system initiated the removal of inmates from their cells during the day. Only at night would they return to their cells. Through daytime surveillance of the prisoners as they worked in common rooms, and the prohibition of conversation (soon to become famous as the "silent" system), they hoped to overcome the sanitary and health problems without diminishing the practical benefits of isolation.[14] Eventually, the innovation was elaborated into a complete theory of punishment that varied from, and came to compete with, the Pennsylvania system.[15]

The major elements of this system consisted of surveillance as a substitute for walls, the use of the whip to enforce silence, and labor in workshops under the supervision of guards and wardens. While each of these techniques was designed to achieve the reformation of criminals in a manner that was not dissimilar to that of the Pennsylvania system, the difference in technique implied a difference in the ends of punishment. The administrators of the Auburn system were less concerned with moral reclamation than with the actions of the prisoners upon release from prison. They were not concerned about the harshness of their punishment just so long as there was no evidence that the harshness resulted in recidivism on the part of released inmates.

Every policy initiated under the new plan had its own rationale. Surveillance during the day was understood to provide two benefits. First, it lessened the costs of prison construction, because cells could be less elaborate when prisoners were confined only at night.[16] In the controversy that erupted over the prisons, this factor was to be a major consideration for those states that had not yet adopted one plan or the other. Second, surveillance itself was understood to provide positive benefits for the inmates. While working in common, inmates would be subject to the constant temptation to communicate with each other. This temptation was understood by advocates of the Auburn system to parallel those that inmates would confront in society upon their release. Thus they would learn how to withstand such temptations.[17] Enforced by the spur of the whip, the silent rule was designed to create habits of obedience. It did not matter that the motivation to obey came from fear of pain; the results were what interested the advocates of the Auburn system.

Constant surveillance also ensured that the convicts would continue their labor uninterrupted. Silence and diligence were to be engrained in the prisoners as habits. While the results might not be internal enlightenment and reform, the released inmate would, it was hoped, become a useful and productive citizen. As Elam Lynds described the situation,

> I do not put great faith in the sanctity of those who leave the prison; I do not believe that the counsels of the chaplain, or the meditations of the prisoner, make a good Christian of him. But my opinion is, that a great number of old convicts do not commit new crimes, and that they even become useful citizens, having learned in prison a useful art, and contracted habits of constant labour. This is the only reform which I ever have expected to produce, and I believe that it is the only one that society has a right to expect.[18]

In the Auburn system, then, in contrast to the Pennsylvania system, the goal was simply to attempt to prevent future crimes on the part of inmates, as opposed to salvaging their souls.

Surveillance, which was the principal means of control in the Auburn system, had another dimension that was a source of enthusiasm among its supporters. Not only were the prisoners themselves subject to constant watching, so were the guards who presided over them. Lynds explained, "The point is, to maintain uninterrupted silence and uninterrupted labour; to obtain this, it is equally necessary to watch incessantly the keepers, as well as the prisoners; to be at once inflexible and just."[19] The Auburn system thus established a complete hierarchy of surveillance, with a single person (in the case of Auburn, and later Sing-Sing, Elam Lynds) at the top. This innovation was an important departure from the Pennsylvania system because it helped demonstrate to the inmates the inevitability and consistency of the enforcement of authority within the prison.[20] With authority understood in such terms by the prisoners, they would, upon their release, seek out and find other such structures in employment situations and in their day-to-day existence.

The Auburn system also presented a clear demonstration of the relationship between power and communication. The ability of the wardens to communicate with each other was the primary source of the power they had over the inmates. This power was illustrated by their ability to control the inmates in the absence of any confinement. Sing-Sing was built with convict labor. During its construction, thirty guards were all that was required to control nine hundred prisoners. Beaumont and Tocqueville noted that it was "the power of association" that led to such a remarkable degree of control.[21] Correlative to this power of the warden and the guards under him was the powerlessness of the prisoner, which was derived almost exclusively from his inability to communicate with his associates.

One reformer of the day was so struck by this "power of association" that he made a parallel between its use in prison and its use in society. That commentary is useful for what it demonstrates concerning the level at which reformers understood their mission during the 1830s.

The question, so often made, why does history exhibit so many instances of whole nations allowing themselves to be tyrannized over by a few . . . cannot be answered in a clearer way than . . . because the rulers have the "power of association," and the oppressed are "isolated." Separate the interests of the officers of your government from that of the people, establish easy and rapid communications between the former, and destroy as much as possible free intercourse among the latter, deprive them of all opportunities of association, and you may rule with an iron sceptre as long as you maintain the order of things.[22]

Implicit in this statement (the commentator was an advocate of the Pennsylvania system of punishment) was a critique of the Auburn system, an argument that the tyranny it imposed was too close to the potential conditions of society itself.[23] Nonetheless, the very depth of the critique reveals the power of the Auburn system not only to preserve a specific structure of communication that was intrinsic to its design, but to demonstrate the power of that design to the interested observer.

In short, the discipline that was imposed in the Auburn system had as its goal the reshaping of the actions of its subjects. It was not designed to reconstitute the inner self of the inmate. Scant attention was paid to the individual prisoner. The role of the chaplain was circumscribed as was the role of the various guards and inspectors. Little concern was demonstrated for the moral conversion of prisoners, because the results of moral conversion were irrelevant to the achievement of the penitentiary's purpose. While such conversion might be admirable, it was cheaper and more effective simply to change the habits of criminals. Habit thus was decoupled from the inner self of the prisoner. The prisoner was free to have an inner life, so long as the actions did not deviate from the law. Conformity with the law was all that "society has a right to expect."

What sort of prisoner emerged from this system? It was hoped that the ex-convict would, in the face of the choices that would confront him upon his departure from prison, rely on the prison experience as a guide to his behavior. Beaumont and Tocqueville summarized the hoped-for results:

Perhaps, leaving the prison he is not an honest man; but he has contracted honest habits. He was an idler; now he knows how to work. His ignorance prevented him from pursuing a useful occupation; now he knows how to read and write; and the trade he has learnt in the prison, furnishes him the means of existence which formerly he had not. Without loving virtue, he may detest the crime of which he has suffered the cruel consequences; and if he is not more virtuous, he has become at least more judicious; his morality is not honour, but interest. His religious faith is neither lively nor deep; but even supposing that religion has not touched his heart, his mind has contracted habits of order, and he possesses rules for his conduct in life; without having a powerful religious conviction, he has acquired a taste for moral principles which religion affords; finally, if he has not become in truth better, he is at least more obedient to the laws, and that is all which society has the right to demand.[24]

A diligent, literate laborer. A moderate, self-interested citizen. In short, the released inmate was to be a member of the great middle class that was, at that point, emerging as a dominating force of public life in the United States.

The diminished expectations presented by the advocates of the Auburn system, in contrast to those of the supporters of the Pennsylvania system, represented neither a sense of despair over the status of reform in the penitentiary, nor an overwhelming optimism regarding the eventual perfection of society. Beaumont and Tocqueville echoed Elam Lynds almost precisely: simple obedience is "all which society has the right to demand."

Such a shift in the agenda of the penitentiary seems, at first glance, to severely diminish the importance of its role in regard to shaping the relationships between rulers and ruled. Yet the controversy that system aroused, and the debate that ensued, indicate that it was perceived to pose a serious threat to the earlier vision of a republican government. That earlier vision was one of liberal freedom. The new vision was of democratic equality. "All which society has the right to demand" struck the opponents of the new system as far too much. To understand why, it is useful to turn to the debate itself.

### What Kind of Citizen: The Struggle over the Souls of Men

A phrase of Tocqueville captures the tone of the debate that ensued between advocates of the Auburn and Pennsylvania systems of punishment during the early 1830s: the idea of the "indefinite perfectability of man."[25] Recognition of the failures of the past had not led to despair among advocates of the Pennsylvania system, nor had the mistakes of the original Auburn penitentiary prevented the development of the Auburn system. Instead, failure provided a spur which encouraged further innovation. This phenomenon was characteristic of reformers in the United States, Beaumont and Tocqueville observed. In the United States, which has neither troublesome neighbors, who disturb it from without, nor internal dissensions which disturb it from within, nothing more is necessary, in order to excite public attention to the highest degree, than an essay on some principle of social economy. As the existence of society is not put in jeopardy, the question is not how to live, but how to improve.[26]

The concern in regard to the manner in which criminals should be punished, then, was the result not of an overriding fear of crime so much as of the hope that the failures of the past could lead to improvements in the future. Part of the continuity in the reform of punishment can be ascribed to this attitude. Rothman has remarked that, judged from the perspective of the twentieth century, the intensity of the debate between the advocates of the Auburn and Pennsylvania systems is puzzling. But what seems a minor difference—whether all prisoners should be put together during the day or whether they should remain in constant isolation—takes on the aspect of a major controversy when the hidden dimension of the debate is understood: it involved the proper way to effect improvement of character, and the improvement of character was directly connected to and identified with the improvement of society.

At the core of the controversy was the principle of isolation. Isolation was the foundation upon which the entire edifice of punishment had been built in Pennsylvania, the one irreplaceable element in the theoretical structure built by Rush and the Philadelphia prison society. Further experience with the Pennsylvania system, especially at the Eastern Penitentiary, had confirmed for these reformers their belief that isolation afforded the strongest means of reform. Why, they asked, tamper with a successful system?

Beaumont and Tocqueville, who temporarily sided with the advocates of the Auburn system, were quick to admit that the Pennsylvania system, as a theory, "undoubtedly belongs to the highest philosophy," by which they meant that it was more analytically and functionally consistent than the Auburn system, and more likely to truly reform the convict.[27] "The Philadelphia system being also that which produces the deepest impressions upon the soul of the convict, must effect more reformation than that of Auburn."[28] But at the time of their report they also believed that the Auburn system was effective on *more* inmates. "The [Auburn system]," they argued, "is perhaps more conformable to the habits of men in society, and on this account effects a greater number of reformations, which might be called 'legal,' in as much as they produce the external fulfillment of social obligations."[29]

In Beaumont and Tocqueville's evaluation, the Auburn system was better because it corresponded more closely to the conditions of the real world. In the penitentiaries of Pennsylvania, the prisoner "was dead to the world, and after a loss of several years, he re-appears in society, to which, it is true, he brings good resolutions, but also perhaps, passions, the more impetuous, from their being longer repressed."[30] This separation from the life of society, which was seen by the advocates of the Pennsylvania system as one of the primary benefits of solitary confinement, thus was understood as one of the problems. In the real world, citizens are not isolated from each other, nor is it desirable that they should be. If prisons fail to have some correspondence to the real world, the inmates that emerge from them cannot be expected to adjust to their new circumstances. In this argument, of course, everything hinges upon what are considered to be the circumstances of the "real world."

Advocates of the Pennsylvania system were quick to point this problem out. Roberts Vaux, for example, a major figure in the Pennsylvania Prison Society, argued that if the standards of citizenship had dropped to the level of the requirements imposed by the Auburn system, then there could be little doubt that society was deteriorating.[31] In response, Elam Lynds argued that the standards held by the Pennsylvania system advocates were themselves unrealistic. After all, how can anyone realistically understand or expect to understand the internal motives of the criminal, let alone know when the criminal has truly ceased to be criminal and converted to the values of good citizenship?

> I would even say that the prisoner who conducts himself well, will probably return to his former habits, when set free. I have always observed, that the worst subjects made excellent prisoners. They have generally more skill and intelligence than the others; they perceive much more quickly, and much more thoroughly, that the only way to render their situation less oppressive, is to avoid painful and repeated punishments . . . they therefore behave well, without being the better for it.[32]

Ironically, the prisoners described by Lynds are precisely the ones who are most likely to benefit from the solitary discipline imposed by the Pennsylvania system. All they lack is the necessary moral sensibility, but Lynds was doubtful concerning the ability of the prison to teach this.

QUES. The system, however, which you attack is that of all theorists?

ANS. In this, as in many other points, they deceive themselves, because they have little knowledge of whom they speak. If Mr. Livingstone, for instance [a proponent of the Pennsylvania system], should be ordered to apply his theories of penitentiaries to people born like himself, in a class of society in which much intelligence and moral sensibility existed, I believe that he would arrive at excellent results; but prisons, on the contrary, are filled with coarse beings, who have had no education, and who perceive with difficulty ideas, and often even sensations. It is this point which he always forgets.[33]

In a sense, Lynds was arguing that the Pennsylvania system, quite nobly, but also quite futilely, required that inmates have a philosophical turn of mind.[34]

The Auburn system had no such requirement. Indeed, Lynds's comment that "the worst subjects made excellent prisoners" suggests that more intelligent criminals, the type who would seem most susceptible to the kind of discipline imposed by the Pennsylvania system, actually would be least likely to be reformed by it. But because reform in the Auburn system was achieved through forced conformity to rules, no inquiry into the minds of the inmates was needed. The question of internal reform became irrelevant. A prisoner emerging from the Auburn system needed to undergo not a change of heart but only a change in "habit." It is interesting to note the transformation of the term *habit* by the 1830s. For the generation of Rush and Paine, *habit* indicated the moral orientation of the nation as expressed through the behavior of its citizens. To argue, as advocates of the Auburn system did, that changing the habits of inmates was separate from changing their moral orientation to the world suggested that the initial vision of the Revolution had been lost. Even though the techniques for inculcating new habits did not vary in the two systems—both relied on hard labor, both maintained rigorous schedules, and both carefully regulated the diets of the prisoners—the Auburn system advocates, by presenting their argument in terms of habits, clearly separated their approach from that of the Pennsylvanians.

Implied in the debate between the advocates of the Auburn and Pennsylvania systems was a struggle to define the meaning of good citizenship.

Tocqueville in *Democracy in America* and Beaumont and Tocqueville in the earlier *The Penitentiary System of the United States* can be interpreted as having used that debate in order to sharpen and develop their understanding of the substantive content of citizenship in the United States. Their ruminations on a variety of phenomena fundamentally connected with the problem of crime and punishment were also explorations into the problem of how the formal characteristics of subjects of the United States were established.

In the preface to *The Penitentiary System*, Beaumont and Tocqueville briefly addressed what they understood to be the causes of crime. For them, there were only two; poverty, which results in the corruption of character of the working classes and leads them to crime; and "the progress of intellectual improvement," which results in an energy in the minds of men "which knows not where to find an object," thus disrupting society.[35] For Beaumont and Tocqueville, the United States was a much more law-abiding society than was France.

> There is a spirit of obedience to the law, so generally diffused in the United States, that we meet with this characteristic trait even within the prisons: without being obliged to indicate here the political reasons for this fact, we only state it as such; but the spirit of submission to the established order does not exist in the same degree with us.[36]

Tocqueville explored the governmental reasons for the fact of obedience in *Democracy in America*. But he also looked for factors that might, at the source of criminality, reduce the level of crime.

What were the U.S. equivalents of the causes of crime in France? Poverty in the United States was quite different from poverty in France.[37] Tocqueville and Beaumont mentioned two million paupers in France, a level of poverty that made the situation there qualitatively different than it was in the United States.[38] While the poor in the United States tended toward criminality as they did in France, pauperism was practically nonexistent. Indeed, part of Tocqueville's fascination with the United States had to do with why this was so. In *Democracy in America* he noted that the pursuit of money pervaded the "mores" of the people to such an extent that "one usually finds that money is either the chief or a secondary motive at the bottom of everything the Americans do."[39] Criminals in the United States shared a common characteristic, poverty, but it was not a result of the same social forces that existed in the more explicitly class-structured society of

France. When poverty and criminality correlated in the United States, it was because the criminals had somehow avoided being "socialized" into the money values of society. To be sure, few criminals lacked interest in money itself. The problem lay in their inability or unwillingness to strive for it in the manner prescribed by society.

The intellectual fervors of France (which Tocqueville was eventually to describe in detail in *The Old Regime*) had their equivalent, not in the speculation of reformers, but in the almost anti-intellectual drive for conquest, which was in itself tied to the desire to acquire money. This drive was a result of a combination of fortuitous circumstances that faced the settlers of North America; the vast land holdings, the need for trade, and the Protestant work ethic.[40] The constant movement of settlers into the United States and through it was one of the most striking aspects of the new country for Tocqueville. "Nothing," he claimed, "in history is comparable to this continuous movement of mankind, except perhaps that which followed the fall of the Roman Empire."[41] Tocqueville linked this movement directly to the desire to make money.

> Millions of men are all marching together toward the same point in the horizon; their languages, religions, and mores are different, but they have one common aim. They have been told that fortune is to be found somewhere to the west, and they hasten to seek it.[42]

Such is the U.S. citizen depicted by Tocqueville. Marvin Meyers, in a study of the dominant ideologies of the Jacksonian era, called such people "venturous conservatives."[43] Such people are the fitting members of a society in which "nothing changes but everything differs," where "the names of the actors is all that changes, the play being always the same."[44] There is constant flux, but it is, within bounds, predictable. The citizen lives on the edge of a precipice, knowing that he might fall at any time, but also knowing that his experience is shared by others, who take the same risk. The rewards promised were considerable.

Underlying the conditions that existed by the time Tocqueville made his analysis of the U.S. citizen was a history of policies designed to encourage risk taking. The period between 1790 and 1830 had seen the destruction of traditional means through which the social dislocations and upheavals caused by economic expansion had been ameliorated. Such means included primogeniture and entail as controls over the exchange of land property, harsh penalties for bankruptcy, and the national bank as a (relative) control over the capitalization of enterprise.[45] By the early 1830s, all of these institutions, which had served to check the economic flow, were either abolished or soon to be abolished. During this period, what Lawrence Friedman has called the "society of bees" emerged; an unprecedented scramble for wealth through speculation and industry.[46] The new flexibility of property, especially of land, contributed to its wide-scale distribution, as did the distribution of public lands in the west by a national government eager to raise revenues and, more important, to settle populations in isolated and vulnerable areas.[47]

Tocqueville noted a double effect of this liberation of property from its traditional confines. The first effect, the creation of a universal interest in making money, has already been noted. But the underside of this interest was the anxiety of the speculator. Stability of society depended on a government that could uphold property rights, especially when property was distributed widely. The creation of a "great middle class" of property owners reinforced the legitimacy of a government that could protect their property.[48]

By definition the propertyless were excluded from this mutuality of interests. While there were devices to placate them—for instance, including them in the voting franchise[49]—relatively little was done during that period to control them, except for the creation of the penitentiary. For the penitentiary was not only a means of keeping track of and controlling the movement of criminals.[50] More important was the way in which it attempted to instill in the propertyless the same interests as informed the behavior of the propertied, without providing them with property. It was designed to replicate in criminals the values of the "venturous conservative," for during this period, political leaders still assumed that there was or could be enough property for all. But penal discipline was not to be dependent upon that assumption.[51] By recreating the tensions that informed the behavior of those of the "great middle class," the penitentiary would become a means of reinforcing the relationships that bound the citizenry and political authority together.

The penitentiary was thus in an important strategic position. Its high visibility reflected its ideological importance. Its task was to form behavior compatible with the new property arrangements; thus it was part of the process through which a new form of control was to be exercised over that citizenry. The penitentiary system took care of those not bound by property.

But it was not a mere reflection of the new principle of property. The penitentiary demonstrated during this period that it could shift the content of what it taught without severely modifying its techniques; thus it demonstrated that it could be adapted to the requirements of any regime, could shape the behavioral requirements for any political authority. Even as the original liberal principles of republicanism were being superseded by those of mass democracy, the epistemological assumptions of liberalism were being confirmed; the focus on the individual as the object of reform persevered. So while the struggle between the Auburn and Pennsylvania systems of punishment was a struggle over ends, it nonetheless did not really touch the means through which authority would be reinforced. The arguments between the two systems were fought at the level of tactics, not at the level of basic assumptions. The Pennsylvania advocates wished to move the debate to that level in support of their system, but the Auburn advocates successfully refuted their claims, arguing that their system was indeed no departure from original penal principles, but only their fulfillment.

Beaumont and Tocqueville compared the two systems in regard to what they considered to be the three most important criteria of reform, and discovered that both systems addressed all three elements to a greater or lesser degree. The Pennsylvania system was more likely to prevent the mutual corruption of prisoners, and more likely to produce a "radical reformation" of its inmates, that is, a "true" conversion from bad to good. The Auburn system produced a greater "probability of contracting habits of obedience and industry, which render [prisoners] useful citizens."[52] "If [our investigation] be so," they concluded, "the Philadelphia system produces more honest men, and that of New York more obedient citizens."[53]

By 1835, only Pennsylvania, and to a lesser extent New Jersey, continued to maintain the separate system as the model of punishment. Every other state that had upgraded its system of punishment chose the Auburn model of congregate punishment.[54] In the struggle for the souls of men, the Auburn system had won out. The choice had been made to install a system of punishment that elicited obedience from its subjects rather than encouraged internal reform. But the Auburn system won its "victory" only by conceding that the fundamental form of punishment on which it was built was developed and first implemented in Pennsylvania. The Auburn system adopted the means of reform of the Pennsylvania system and, with a few changes in emphasis, made those means serve a new end.

The penitentiary system can be understood to have emerged during the

1830s as a system of means decoupled from any particular set of ends, or coupled only to whatever ends political authorities decided to put it. In the era of Jacksonian democracy, those ends could be said to have been the establishment of democratic despotism. Yet, as I will explore below, democratic despotism is an inadequate description of the ends of U.S. society. Those ends were then (and, it can be argued, are now) nothing more or less than a continual and unending pursuit, a drive that has no end. In such a society, means become ends.[55] The question is, what becomes of the souls of men in such a society?

### Democratic Despotism: Tocqueville and the New System of Authority

> The type of oppression which threatens democracies is different from anything there has been seen in the world before. Our contemporaries will find no prototype for it in their memories. I have myself vainly searched for a word which will exactly express the whole of the conception I have formed. Such old words as "despotism" and "tyranny" do not fit. The theory is new, and I cannot find a word for it. I must try to define it.[56]

Tocqueville's struggle to explain the manner in which oppression operates in a society of equals is among the masterpieces of political and social analysis. His theory of democratic despotism gathers together the disparate strands of his description of U.S. society and presents a seamless argument concerning its logic. That tyranny was, for Tocqueville, the greatest danger that democratic society presented to individual autonomy and freedom, the major benefits of living in democracy. Tocqueville's description is worth examining closely, because it was influenced by the fact that he had come to study the U.S. penitentiary system. To say that Tocqueville saw U.S. society through the prism of punishment would be to overstate the case. But a careful reading of his theory of democratic despotism, and the materials from which it was derived, reveals that he understood the absolute despotism of the penitentiary and the more ordinary despotism of the democratic majority to have a common ground. This common ground is not even hinted at by Tocqueville himself, and one could idly speculate concerning the extent to which he self-consciously derived his theory of democratic despotism from his study of prisons. What is important is that the parallels exist, to such an extent that it can be said that the penitentiary system was the most complete articulation of the Jacksonian system of political authority. To what extent punishment was responsible for the creation of that authority is addressed in the conclusion of this work. Here, it is sufficient to describe the parallels.

In their study of the penitentiary, Beaumont and Tocqueville claimed that the Pennsylvania system was the more philosophical of the two penitentiary systems. Yet in *Democracy in America* Tocqueville developed a different definition of the philosophy that operates in U.S. democracy. Tocqueville noted that "less attention . . . is paid to philosophy in the United States than in any other country of the civilized world."[57] But this does not mean that Americans lack a philosophy. Indeed, while most Americans pay little attention to philosophical questions, they all share a common philosophical approach to the world, which Tocqueville identified as being Cartesian.[58] Citizens of the United States follow Descartes's philosophy in that they all learn by relying on their individual effort and judgment. The importance of this reliance on Cartesian principles is manifold. It leads to inventiveness, to skepticism concerning the judgments of others, and to an overriding confidence in their own individual opinions. In the United States, noted Tocqueville, "there is a general distaste for accepting any man's word as proof of anything." Each person falls back on his or her own devices in order to know about the world. "Each man is narrowly shut up in himself, and from that basis makes the pretension to judge the world."[59]

The danger of this Cartesian "turn of mind" is the danger of Cartesian doubt. Mere anarchy may well prevail in the absence of common belief. Moreover, when people are so divided from each other,

> each man undertakes to be sufficient to himself and glories in the fact that his beliefs about everything are peculiar to himself. No longer do ideas, but interests only, form the links between men, and it would seem that human opinions were no more than a sort of mental dust open to the wind on every side and unable to come together and take shape.[60]

How could common beliefs emerge in a society in which such radical individualism prevailed? For Tocqueville, this dangerous situation was saved by the condition of equality that prevailed in the United States. He argued that the source of common belief was precisely the recognition of equality. Equality leads to the development of common beliefs on the basis of majority opinion. "In democracies public opinion has a strange power of which aristocratic nations can form no conception. It uses no persuasion to put forward its beliefs, but by some mighty pressure of the mind of all on the intelligence of each it imposes its ideas and makes them penetrate men's very souls."[61] In this way individualism and majoritarianism work together in democratic societies.

This depiction of the philosophy of U.S. citizens and the manner in which it is moderated recalls the earlier depiction of the relationship of the inmate to penal authority. A part of the problem of the Pennsylvania system was that it reinforced the isolation of the inmate or, in other words, strengthened the Cartesian leanings of the inmate. If the inmate remained totally isolated, his links with other men would be of precisely the nature that Tocqueville describes in criticizing the effects of that philosophy on the citizen. In the congregate system, these isolated men must associate with each other, they must conform, even as they preserve their individuality through silence. The Auburn system strikes the balance between individuality and conformity. Hence, the Auburn system, while remaining the less philosophical of the two, is nonetheless the more complete system. It responds to the requirements of balance in a way that the Pennsylvania system cannot.

Concern with the idea and practice of equality permeates *Democracy in America*'s sections on the mores of the U.S. citizenry. For Tocqueville, it was an all-encompassing and all-pervasive concept which, when put into practice, left no area of social life untouched. "Equality," he asserted, "puts many ideas into the human mind which would not have come there without it, and it changes almost all the ideas that were there before."[62] Perhaps the most important way in which equality affected U.S. society was through its encouragement of the idea of the indefinite perfectability of man. The idea of perfection, Tocqueville argued, was one of the chief ideas that the human mind could conceive, yet only under the social conditions encouraged by democratic equality could the pursuit of perfection be a serious social force. Aristocratic societies can suggest only the amelioration of existing conditions, because they cannot imagine a radical change in the conditions of society,

> but when castes disappear and classes are brought together, when men
> are jumbled together and habits, customs, and laws are changing,

when new facts impinge and new truths are discovered, when old conceptions vanish and new ones take their place, then the human mind imagines the possibility of an ideal but always fugitive perfection.[63]

This scramble has an enormous impact on the activities of the citizen. "His setbacks teach him that no one has discovered absolute good; his successes inspire him to seek it without slackening."[64]

This search for perfection in the face of failure is at the heart of the endeavor to reform the penitentiary system. In the face of the failure at Walnut Street, the Pennsylvania reformers carried on; confronted with a cell system that was destroying its inmates, the supervisors of Auburn established new principles of punishment that sidestepped the problems of solitary confinement. Failure stimulated. Crisis led to relief. Reform could be perpetual because it could never be complete.

The effects of democracy extend even to the manner in which U.S. citizens devote themselves to scientific studies. "Hardly anyone in the United States devotes himself to the essentially theoretical and abstract side of human knowledge." Tocqueville noted that the higher sciences required the ability to meditate above all else. The proclivities of U.S. citizens were in the opposite direction. "How can the mind," he asked, "dwell on any single subject when all around is on the move and one is himself swept and buffeted along by the whirling current which carries all before it?"[65] Indeed, the bias against theoretical investigations on the part of citizens in democracies represented a great danger for Tocqueville.

If the lights that guide us ever go out, they will fade little by little, as if by their own accord. Confining ourselves to practice, we may lose sight of basic principles, and when these are entirely forgotten, we may apply the methods derived from them badly; we might be left without the capacity to invent new methods, and only able to make a clumsy and unintelligent use of wise procedures no longer understood.[66]

This descent into ignorance might lead to the abandonment of improvement, the major driving force within U.S. democratic society.

The chief advantage of the Auburn system over the Pennsylvania system, many had argued, was its practicality. It used the method developed in the "more philosophical" Pennsylvania system, but in a more practical and immediate way. This shift to the practical parallels the process of scientific discovery that Tocqueville noted as a tendency in democratic societies. It is worth noting that, shortly after his return to France, Tocqueville reevaluated his position concerning the two penitentiary systems. An advocate of the Auburn system at first, he shifted to support the adoption of the Pennsylvania system. Some commentators have argued that he was motivated by a dislike of one of the proponents of the Auburn system in France, but the fears of the decline of innovation that he associated with the more practical, and less introspective, system of Auburn may very well have been the reason for his change of opinion.[67]

This sampling of characteristics of democratic citizens reveals a pattern that Tocqueville attempted to summarize in his final discussions of the influence of democratic ideas on society. In that final section of *Democracy in America*, he turned to examine the impact of democratic ideas on politics.

An initial glance at the chapter headings in this section might incline one to believe that Tocqueville was unable to make sense of the role of democracy in relationship to politics. One chapter is an analysis of how equality inclines citizens to want free institutions. The remaining chapters focus on how democratic ideas incline citizens to seek the constant centralization of political power. While on the face of it these inclinations may seem opposed, they are in fact complementary. Equality makes men independent of one another, and hence makes them suspicious of authority. But that is not the only tendency of equality: "Two tendencies in fact result from equality; the one first leads men directly to independence and could suddenly push them right over into anarchy; the other, by a more roundabout and secret but also more certain road, leads them to servitude."[68] Tocqueville argued that the anarchic tendency was the easier of the two to combat because its dangers were most obvious to the citizens of democratic society. The other tendency, however, was much more insidious.

It is not immediately clear why equality would lead citizens to seek the centralization of political power. Tocqueville's first argument concerning the adoption of central power is spurious—he argued that it is somehow natural for people to think of power in terms of its centrality. "The idea of a single central power directing all citizens slips naturally into their consciousness without their, so to say, giving the matter a thought."[69] But indirectly, another tendency among people of equal conditions leads to centralization in a logical, quite reasonable way: the tendency on the part of people in a democratic society to seek uniform legislation.

As each sees himself little different from his neighbors, he cannot understand why a rule applicable to one man should not be applied to all the rest. The slightest privileges are therefore repugnant to his reason. The faintest differences in the political institutions of a single people give him pain, and legislative uniformity strikes him as the first condition of good government.[70]

This desire for good government stems as well from the simple comparison that individuals are able to make concerning themselves and society: "As conditions become more equal among people, individuals seem of less and society of greater importance; or rather, every citizen, having grown like the rest, is lost in the crowd, and nothing stands out conspicuously but the great and imposing image of the people itself."[71] People come to seek an image of themselves in the political state. The state comes to inform them of what is right and wrong, of what they are capable of doing and failing to do. "They . . . freely agree that the power which represents society has much more education and wisdom than any of the men composing it and that it is its duty, as well as its right, to take each citizen by the hand and guide him."[72]

Government itself will tend to encourage the idea of equality because equality's implementation strengthens its power. "One can . . . assert that every central government worships uniformity; uniformity saves it the trouble of inquiring into infinite details, which would be necessary if the rules were made to suit men instead of subjecting all men indiscriminately to the same rule."[73] Thus a paradox emerges. "Democratic people often hate those in whose hands the central power is vested, but they always love the power itself."[74] The tendency toward increased power of the central government is exacerbated by the relative ignorance of the population. "If a nation is both democratic and ignorant, there is bound soon to be a huge difference between the intellectual capacity of the government and that of the governed."[75] All of these factors contribute to the absolute power of government over the citizenry.

If the structure of political authority takes on these characteristics it becomes despotic. But the question remains to what extent that despotism has anything to do with the clearly acknowledged despotism of the penitentiary system. Parallels exist, but do the same goals? Methods are similar, but are they the same? If one reviews the tendencies that lead to the establishment of despotism, the final linkage between the rulers and the ruled is missing. It is not until the actual mechanism at work is discussed that the connection between the one despotism and the other is clarified. That discussion occurs in two places in *Democracy in America*, at the conclusion of the second volume and in the more famous discussion in volume 1 of the tyranny of the majority. The connection, quite briefly, can be said to be made at the point where Tocqueville articulates his vision of the modern soul.

For Tocqueville, the soul was the symbol for the inner self, the space that determines the individuality of each citizen. It is that aspect of a person which most clearly is autonomous, least reachable by the power of others. When Tocqueville discussed the individuality of citizens in a democratic society, he referred to the "solitude in his own heart" that typifies the individual, who is isolated from others.[76] The soul is the spirit, the inner psyche of the person, and its content is the person's own. In a society with free institutions, that individual soul is protected; to be free, one's inner self must be free. In this sense, Tocqueville harkened back to the liberal vision of the individual expressed by Locke.[77] Indeed, he claimed that individuality is most pronounced in society immediately at the close of a democratic revolution, before certain powers of association are established.[78] But when the free soul of the individual is confronted by the institutions that grow out of the equal conditions of society, it can no longer hide, it becomes exposed, subject to the new tyranny, the tyranny of the majority. That tyranny operates in a way that the former tyranny could not.

> Princes made violence a physical thing, but our contemporary democratic republics have turned it into something as intellectual as the human will it is intended to constrain. Under the absolute government of a single man, despotism, to reach the soul, struck at the body, and the soul, escaping from such blows, rose gloriously above it; but in democratic republics that is not at all how tyranny behaves; it leaves the body alone and goes straight to the soul.

Tocqueville followed this striking passage with an example of how the tyranny operates. The example is important, because it shows how the structure of tyranny in public life parallels that which operates within the penitentiary.

The master no longer says: "Think like me or you die." He does say:

"You are free not to think as I do; you can keep your life and property and all; but from this day you are a stranger among us. You can keep your privileges in the township, but they will be useless to you, for if you solicit your fellow citizens' votes, they will not give them to you, and if you only ask for their esteem, they will make excuses for refusing that. You will remain among men, but you will lose your right to count as one. . . . Go in peace. I have given you your life, but it is a life worse than death."[79]

The tyranny of the majority thus operates as a form of psychic banishment. No concern needed to be given to the content of the attitudes and opinions of the dissenter. All that matters is that the dissenter is isolated from the community.

A series of inversions is involved in the translation of the discipline of the penal system to the community at large; but the logical structure and the content of the lessons learned are the same in both spheres of society. The tyranny of the majority operates out of two key assumptions: first, that it is possible to isolate the individual in society, and second, that it is desirable to have all individuals treated equally. The routinization of the operations that constitute the tyranny of the majority is nothing less than the establishment of democratic despotism. "Equality," wrote Tocqueville, "puts men side by side without a common link to hold them firm. Despotism raises barriers to keep them apart. It disposes them not to think of their fellows and turns indifference into a sort of public virtue."[80] The principle of isolation was, of course, central to the workings of penal discipline, and the Auburn system maintained that isolation even as men were put "side by side."

The communicative superiority of the penal authority has its parallel in the central power of administration of the state. This administration grows powerful because it exploits and encourages the dependence of the citizenry, through emphasizing the isolation of each. When the takeover of power occurs, it is subtle, but pervasive. Tocqueville described the operations and effects of this administrative power, which never directly asserts itself, in the starkest and most frightening of terms.

Having thus taken each citizen in turn in its powerful grasp and shaped him to its will, government then extends its embrace to include the whole of society. It covers the whole of social life with a network of petty, complicated rules that are both minute and uniform, through which even men of the greatest originality and the most vigorous temperament cannot force their heads above the crowd. It does not break men's will, but softens, bends and guides it; it seldom enjoins, but often inhibits, action; it does not destroy anything, but prevents much being born; it is not at all tyrannical, but it hinders, restrains, stifles, and stultifies so much that in the end each nation is no more than a flock of timid and hardworking animals with the government as its shepherd.[81]

Minute and uniform rules which inhibit action; a bending, not a breaking, of the will; in essence, the conditions of the Auburn penitentiary are writ large by the power of the administrative state in a society in which equality and individualism prevail. The Auburn system did not concern itself with the interior of the individual, but sought to effect only the individual's behavior. It inhibited the exercise of free will, but did not make the imposition of its discipline absolute, constraining rather than shutting off automatically the independent judgments of its inmates. It produced timid and hardworking animals, in the form of people who worked out of habit, not out of a self-conscious sense of the rightness of their actions.

The extension of the embrace of government is pursued through the same means that inform the penitentiary institution. Its end is the same, the establishment of a form of tyranny. Yet the two institutions are different because the penitentiary is assumed to have the power of tyranny legitimately, and the government is not. Still, one might ask, through what means is it possible to distinguish between the legitimacy of tyranny in one dimension and its illegitimacy in the other?

This question is of great concern for Tocqueville, and it is also the key for understanding the importance of the establishment of penitentiary discipline within a democratic society. The forces which temper the tendency toward the completion of a system of democratic despotism are what he labels "free institutions," such as local governments, juries, and state governments. Private professional associations and especially the system of lawyers also served as checks against the development of a strong central administration.[82] Tocqueville wished to make clear the distinction between centralization of government and centralization of administration; it was in administration that he saw the greatest danger to freedom in the United States. As long as townships and counties remained sovereign over the day-to-day habits and rules of the people, then the dominance by administration could not proceed to the point where tyranny would overcome freedom.[83] Since criminal punishment was administered largely at the local and state level, it would seem to present a case of the administrative decentralization that Tocqueville understood to be so necessary to preserve freedom.

But in fact this was not so. The spread of penitentiary discipline was uniform through the United States, at least through the northern United States.[84] The same model was adopted, which, it would seem, undercut Tocqueville's hope that the lack of a central administration would prevent tyranny from gaining an upper hand. Tocqueville looked upon centralization in *Democracy in America* as a macro phenomenon, perhaps because he was, after all, a citizen of France, in which the administration of government had reached new levels of centralization under the Napoleonic regime.[85] But the centralization that developed in the U.S. penitentiary was micro, in the sense that it was dispersed within the structures of individual states and also relied upon the administrative expertise of the personnel who ran the prisons. While one might look upon the variety of laws that existed in the criminal codes of the different states as an example of the plurality and lack of cohesion that Tocqueville sought, the inevitable singularity of the form of punishment adopted in them had a greater impact on the "souls of men," simply because it was designed to have that impact.

This uniform legal punishment underscored and supported a uniform model of behavior, so that there was less and less psychic space available for the growth of individuals, for the development and nurturance of variety. U.S. citizens would have one dimension in which they could develop. Tocqueville analyzed this dimension in his chapters concerning the development of industry in the United States,[86] as well as in his discussions concerning the major driving force that impels U.S. citizens to continually strive onward, namely, the desire for wealth. His discussion of industry is remarkably anticipatory of Marx's critique of the social consequences of capitalism (indeed, Marx was to cite Tocqueville as well as Beaumont in "On *The Jewish Question*").[87] There he also described the kind of labor that was to emerge as industrial order developed, in terms not of alienation but of mechanization.

In a succinct passage, Tocqueville explained how men in the United States rise above the crowd.

> In democratic countries where money does not carry its possessor to power, but often rather bars him from it, rich men tend not to know

what to do with their leisure. The restlessness and extent of their desires, the greatness of their resources, and that taste for the extraordinary which is almost always felt by men who rise, by whatever means, above the crowd, all urge them on to action. Trade is the only road open to them.[88]

Men rise through business because it is the only road open to them. Since this fact is implicitly recognized by all U.S. citizens, the entire mass of society is always anxious to engage in commerce. Farmers, unlike those of the Old World, will sell their land, or make farming a business enterprise itself. All are engaged in trade. The crises that the society faces are likely to be economic ones, because since all are "more or less engaged in industry, at the least shock given to business activity all private fortunes are in jeopardy at the same time and the state is shaken."[89]

But fortune cannot smile on everyone at the same time, and the wealthy themselves can become poor even as wealth concentrates in fewer and fewer hands. This concentration of wealth is simply a consequence of what Tocqueville called industrial science. This science has two principles. First is the principle of division of labor. "When a workman spends every day on the same detail, the finished article is produced more easily, quickly, and economically." Second is the principle of the economy of scale. "The larger the scale on which an industrial undertaking is conducted with great capital assets and extensive credit, the cheaper will be its products."[90] The social consequence of these two principles, when applied, is the emergence of a highly stratified society. The worker, while he becomes highly accomplished at very specific skills, "loses the general faculty of applying his mind to the way he is working. . . . The man is degraded as the workman improves." After years of such work, he contracts habits that make him unable to do anything beyond his specific tasks. "In a word, he no longer belongs to himself, but to his chosen calling."[91]

An industrial theory stronger than morality or law ties him to a trade, and often to a place, which he cannot leave. He has been assigned to a certain position in society which he cannot quit. In the midst of universal movement, he is struck immobile.[92]

Immobility, specific work, these are calling cards of penal discipline, which creates habits of industriousness in inmates.

What of the industrialist? He "daily embraces a vast field of his vision, and his mind expands as fast as the other's contracts." The industrialist needs a greater intellectual capacity as time goes by and the enterprise grows. He becomes "like the administrator of a huge empire, and the [workman] more like a brute."[93] The separation of intellect from physical labor serves the interests of the industrialist in the same way that the removal of the inmates' power to communicate serves the administrators of the prison. Possibilities of advancement are stopped when the workers are denied the opportunity to learn. What emerges is a form of aristocracy in which the permanent leaders are the industrialists and their progeny, and the permanent serfs are the laborers. The old form of aristocracy was deeply connected to the people it ruled through the corporate spirit which informed its actions, but in the new aristocratic system "there is no connection except that between the first and last links of a long chain."[94] The only common meeting ground of the industrialist and the worker is the factory, a situation of pure command and obedience.

Here again is the more general replication of the pattern established in penal discipline. Again, it exists, not at the level of a centralized state, but at the micro level of the industrial firm. Tocqueville could not imagine that the industrial firm could grow to the point at which it would be able to challenge and establish a common interest with the state. Hence he saw this aristocracy as being limited in scope and impact.[95] Yet the expansion was to come. The chain forged by discipline was to hold, even if bloodily.

The parallels between Tocqueville's analysis of democratic tyranny and Tocqueville and Beaumont's earlier study of the penitentiary can be summarized through a listing of the features of penal discipline. The penitentiary isolated the inmate, yet did so in such a way as to emphasize that isolation was a shared characteristic of all the inmates. Democratic tyranny operated through the principle of isolation, throwing the violator of majority will into a prison without walls, one maintained through the same silence that was imposed on the inmate, but inverted: while the violator might speak, he would not be heard. In addition to individual isolation, the penitentiary depended upon equality. All were to undergo the same experience in prison, learning the habits of industry and obedience necessary for their integration into society upon their release. Equality taught much the same lesson outside of prison walls, softening the effects of individualism, enabling the development of an industrial hierarchy, in a sense teaching the ignorance necessary for the monopoly of expertise that would enable the few to subjugate the many. The disconcern for the interior reform of the inmate, the simple teaching of habits in order to shape behavior, was echoed in the factory discipline of repetition and specialization that was to be the hallmark of U.S. industrial practice. Citizens were broken down into isolated individuals whose sole purpose was the accumulation and expansion of wealth. The drive for wealth had and has no end; neither did the system of discipline developed in the penitentiary.

Tocqueville taught all of this, but he misidentified the real source of the danger as lying within the administration of an increasingly centralized government. The "network of petty, complicated rules that are both minute and uniform" originated not in a central government, but in the penal institutions scattered across the landscape of the various states. The petty rules, the intricate procedures, the schedules, and finally the silence were born of an expressed desire on the part of responsible citizens to make responsible citizens out of others. Thus democratic despotism is born. The woof of time was broken, only to be reshaped into the regular and predictable time of the prison workday. It was not a neat and clean system, and never would be complete, but as a technique, as a means, it was effective enough. Tocqueville came to the United States to study the prison, and left to write *Democracy in America*. No irony need be made of that coincidence, nor should anyone be surprised. After all, the penitentiary was the ideal liberal democratic institution.

# Conclusion:
# From Danger to Fear

The establishment of disciplinary society in the United States was the restless end of a quest to ensure the safety of the subjects of the liberal democratic state. One need not claim that the state and disciplinary society are immediately coterminous. Nor can discipline's origin be traced to an original cause linking the powers of government, production, and meaning. One learns, when exploring the genealogy of danger, to focus on the banal habits of being which make intelligible, even if they don't explain, a set of practices. The various metaphysical claims of the practitioners of the moral sciences have obscured this banality. The hope so often expressed implicitly by such metaphysicians is that beyond practices are principles, and that an education in principles will protect humanity from the dangers that somehow well up, untamed and mature, from a savage, wild body.

Yet bad habits are hard to break.

I have so far tried to suggest why that might be the case. A series of displacements of danger in pursuit of the elusive goal of safety; the control of a subject which could not be articulated except as a consequence of that dangerous pursuit; such are the ironies which circumscribe the behavioral imperative lying within the bowels of disciplinary society.

A summary of this book would refer the reader to the desire of the early Quakers, the ambition of Benjamin Rush, and the practicality of the first warden of Sing-Sing prison. Desire—for a peace born of silence, a silence so great as to allow the whispered word of God to reach the ears of the sinner, and so transform the sinner's life. Ambition—to construct a machine that would regulate life and thus liberate the subject from the discomforts of imagination gone amuck, modulating, providing heat where there is

141

cold, calm where there is agitation, action and reaction, a balance wheel for the great orrery of being. Practicality—to take the imperfect material of being and make it work, not perfectly, but well enough, and thus to enable a seemingly delicate and limited device to insinuate itself into the fabric of social life, setting into motion the machinery of discipline in such a way as to make it seem to go of itself.

This seeming "overdetermination" of dangerous relationships is embedded deeply in the structure of contemporary policies of the United States. That the logic of the moral sciences has embraced this overdetermination as the bedrock of policies indicates the possibilities for movement, for ways of living that might reshape dangerous relationships. Hence, I now turn to the logic of the moral sciences for the answers they provide. I do so by remaining faithful to the task of the genealogist, distorting, indeed, torturing the material to make it reveal its secrets.

### Constitutive Policy and the Modern State

In 1964, Theodore J. Lowi wrote a review essay in which he developed a framework for organizing case studies of public policy. He suggested that three categories of policy can be distinguished in studies of the modern state—distributive, redistributive, and regulatory. In each policy arena, he argued, different political arrangements obtain. The organization and mobilization of groups, the recruitment and social bases of memberships within groups, peak associations and elites, and the relationships that predominate in interactions among various groups vary dramatically, he argued, depending upon the arena within which policy is formulated and implemented.

In delineating this typology, Lowi was not attempting to create an instrument by which technocratic policymakers might dominate the policy-making agenda. In fact, his ultimate goal was the practical realization of democratic ideals, a goal long sought by many citizens of the United States. But in his initial attempt to clarify the types of policy, Lowi was confronted with a much more immediate problem, one so intransigent that he only made note of it in passing. His problem was that the lines between the different types of policy were bound to blur over time. This peculiar temporal blurring was to haunt his subsequent work. But initially he straightforwardly noted the problem:

In the long run, all governmental policies may be considered redistri-

**Table 1. The Properties of Political Relations**

|  |  | LIKELIHOOD OF PEACEFUL ADJUSTMENT | |
|  |  | Low | High |
| --- | --- | --- | --- |
| LIKELIHOOD OF COERCION | Remote | Deadlock | Negotiation |
| | Immediate | "Coercion" | ? |

From Theodore J. Lowi, *The End of Liberalism*, 2d ed. (New York: Norton, 1979), p. 39.

butive, because in the long run some people pay taxes more than they receive in services. Or all may be thought regulatory because, in the long run, a governmental decision on the use of resources can only displace a private decision about a resource or at least reduce private alternatives about the resource. But politics works in the short run, and in the short run certain kinds of decisions can be made without regard to limited resources. Policies of this kind are "distributive."[1]

This temporal dimension of policy makes it difficult for either analyst or object of a policy initiative to fully trace out the meaning of the policy that they participate in developing and carrying out.

Lowi obliquely addressed this problem in his later formulations of the development of policy. Before pursuing further the development of his typology, however, it is worth noting that the temporal barriers to the ability of subjects *to know* is the essential stumbling block to achieving clear and cogent policymaking capabilities. One might say that the periodicity implied in Lowi's study of policy suggests that major shifts in the content of redistributive and regulatory policies are possible only over time spans that are generational in length or longer (the idea of *regime change* is crucial here).[2] It is important to note that the problem here goes to the core of the project of political science, because it suggests the impossibility of making the goals of *controlling* and *understanding* policy congruent.

In order to understand more fully this claim, and to better illustrate its implications for this study, it is necessary to be slightly roundabout. In elaborating upon Robert Dahl's categories of political relationships, Lowi, in *The End of Liberalism*, contemplated what policies might and might not be available to policymakers.[3] A summary of the way in which these initial relationships appear can be seen in Table 1. Interestingly enough, when

**Table 2. Political Relations and Types of Policy**

|  |  | LIKELIHOOD OF PEACEFUL ADJUSTMENT | |
|  |  | Low | High |
| --- | --- | --- | --- |
| LIKELIHOOD OF COERCION | Remote | (Deadlock) Distributive | (Negotiation) Regulatory |
|  | Immediate | ("Coercion") Redistributive | (?) Constitutive |

these initial relationships are posited, the "state" itself must be posited not as a meaningful actor, with interests of its own, but at best as a potential referee. The role it plays as a mediator of conflict, however, becomes exceedingly large as time goes by. This can be seen once the different policies initially delineated by Lowi are matched up to the specific political relationships that seem likely to predominate in each arena of power, as Lowi puts it.[4] A listing of these relationships appears in Table 2. The distributive, regulatory, and redistributive categories of policymaking might be said to constitute the way in which politics is conventionally limited in the modern era. But the sort of relationships that might predominate in constitutive policymaking is not immediately apparent. What relationships might obtain in situations in which it is very likely that people will concur on the substance of a policy and also realize that the sanctions against resisting the policy are bound to be high?

Lowi wrote of this arena of power,

It is a vast category. It must include virtually all of the public and private governmental processes in which people have internalized the sanctions that might be applied. The element of coercion may seem absent when in actuality the participants are conducting themselves in a certain way because they do not feel they have any choice. Since it is regular and systematic, it can be called administration, because an administrative component must be there if the conduct in question involves a large number of people making those peaceful adjustments. This immense fourth "great alternative" is missing from Dahl's scheme because it is beyond the confines of the theory of the perfect, self-regulating pluralist society. The fourth cell is actually the stable regime of legitimacy and effective administration without which neither the reality nor the theory of pluralism has any meaning.[5]

Lowi's arena of legitimacy and effective administration—of constitutive policy—is the arena that most clearly describes the continuing construction and reproduction of the modern state.

Policies that have constitutive components are those that shape the most widely accepted and most compulsory features of citizenship. These include (1) policies that encourage fidelity to the state, as opposed to fidelity to other, competing groups such as family, class, or group—i.e., ideological and legal forms that promote acceptance of the supremacy of national government, the sanctity of national frontiers, and the need for a national defense; (2) policies which contribute to the acceptance of the regular gathering of revenues by the state; (3) policies that contribute to the acceptance of and acquiescence in the regularization of political participation in the form of elections,[6] professionalization of bureaucratic administration, and the deployment of instruments of communication to provide rationales for the use of power on the part of the state; and (4), without presuming to exhaust the list, the sort of policies that contribute to the generalized acceptance of and particular participation in discipline, whether it be criminal legal codes and punishment, or the regularized use of disciplinary techniques in schools, factories, and offices.

Lowi's category of constitutive policy is an extension of and elaboration on the most widely recognized contemporary definition of the state, that made by Max Weber in *Economy and Society*. There Weber defined the state in constitutive terms: "A compulsory political organization," he wrote, "with continuous operations will be called a state insofar as its administrative staff successfully upholds the claim to the *monopoly* of the *legitimate* use of physical force in the enforcement of its order."[7] But it is important to note that Lowi includes *internal sanctions* as an element of the constitutive realm; Weber did not. He instead understood discipline as habitual, and categorized psychic coercion as a function of theocratic organizations, or churches.[8] Ironically, Weber, who had a sophisticated and subtle understanding of the secular consequences of the disenchantment of the world, failed to recognize the conflation of psychic and physical coercion that represents "the stable regime of legitimacy and effective administration," to use Lowi's language. The modern state is not merely the secular substitute of the church; it is a more generalizable instrumentality. While Weber recognized this instrumentality, he failed to follow it to its root, in the subjugated subjects who constitute the material reality of the modern state, who are the coerced, disciplined citizenry of regimes like that of the United States.

Throughout this book I have attempted to show some specific practices that can be said to have contributed to the constitution of this vast category of constitutive policy. In so doing, however, I have rendered those practices problematic. Yet one must ask why they should be considered as such. Lowi, for instance, celebrates constitutive policy, and in fact prescribes the expansion of the realm of constitutive policy, through what he refers to as "juridical democracy," as the major means for ameliorating the problematic dimensions of American political life.[9] At a more philosophical level, Richard Rorty might say, one must begin where one is.[10] So God is dead, and the modern state has as its constitutive function that of providing humanity with its value, of punishing and enabling human being. It distorts, it cramps, it hurts, but it enables nonetheless. Wherein lies the problem?

My own deep suspicion is that a disenchanted world cannot become reinhabited by a god who would save us now, *pace* Heidegger. And yet the logic of the moral sciences from Locke (at least) to Heidegger entails the continual pursuit of such a god. The instrumentality of the late modern state is not much influenced by suggestions in the tradition of Weber, which turn the affirmative defiance of Martin Luther's inner voice—"Here I stand, I cannot do otherwise"—into a desperate plea to assert *meaning* over power, in a state in which there "is power, but no motive."[11] The suggested development of an expanded intersubjective realm, one capable of sustaining *meaning* without degrading it into *value*, seems to me to depend upon an alternative reassertion of enchantment. To call for the completion of the project of modernity, to use Jürgen Habermas's apt and unfortunate phrase, is representative of the kind of valorization that risks all to achieve a dubious end, since the establishment of conditions of undistorted truth is ultimately dependent on a violence that might prevent, through its radical disallowance, life from continuing on the face of the earth.

The United States exists as the exemplary modern state precisely because it has so strongly relied upon capitalism, as a set of measures for controlling bodies en masse, on the one hand, and as a consumptive principle—self-ownership as self-consumption—on the other. Both are poles of danger—both inform the current dilemma of legitimacy.[12] Both are implicated in policies of the modern state. Policy is ultimately policing, and the late modern state, increasingly a constitutive state of forced consensus, of habitual obedience, matures into a police state.

The men and women who inhabit this state are constantly threatened by contradictory demands that, in the never-ending quest for normalization, break up coherent identities. This logic of infinite regress informs the disciplinary apparatus fundamentally. Simultaneously, consumer culture presents these burdened subjects with innumerable commodities, by which and through which they must live, seeking meaning through their collections. Margins disappear and reappear, at the level of fashion and at the level of self-knowledge. Like Benjamin's angel of history, the modern subject is blown toward the future, never once able to gather up the debris of a self-identity through which he or she might find rest or consolation.

A state constituted as a disciplinary society is one composed of subjects for whom the Hobbesian search for peace must always continue and always be frustrated. The disciplinary techniques that structure existence also create demands, in order to sustain the state's relationships, for assaults upon the body and, as a complement of those assaults, for the manufacture of obscure and empty desires. The state that must bear these relationships cannot be understood as separate from the society it shapes, just as it cannot be understood as merely repressive. Instead, it is the primary site for originating the techniques for shaping, making coherent, establishing the strictures through which the inchoate character of the world of things might be positively ordered and thus made available for destruction.

Those features of the modern era that escape the grip of this discursive field—the countermemories, the subjugated knowledges—do not weigh against these dangerous forces, but instead seemingly have no place to be, even as the discourse that seeks to legitimate modern existence begins to fail. Perhaps as well, these knowledges are subjugated precisely because of the ever-tightening grip of *danger*, which squeezes hard upon all knowledges to implicate them in a search for peace, a search for certitude, which being a search for safety is ultimately the most dangerous search of all. Such is the logic of the moral sciences.

But such need not be the constitutive force at work in the production of meaning in the ever-present future. Alternatives to *danger* always are found in the deconstruction of danger. For in an era of great danger, there is a surplus value available out of which new meaning might come to be. The surplus value of danger is fear.

## Fear and Freedom

*Fear* is a word rooted in the experience of being in transit. It shares a common root with the word *fare*, and in Teutonic languages it shares a root with danger, the word *fahren* expressing their common meaning as early as the ninth century. The word *far*, distant, is also associated with these words. *Fare* originally meant travel, and then came to mean the *price* of travel. The price of travel is removing oneself from protection (originally removing oneself from the jurisdiction of the *dan*), and can be thought of as fear, fear of calamity, of sudden disaster. The experience of fear is that of moving from protection to exposure, experiencing the vertigo of uncertainty, not knowing what threat to well-being might lay in wait. The farther one travels, the greater the fear.

While danger is a relationship, however strained and difficult it may have become, in which there is an ongoing possibility or existence of reciprocity (bear the lord, the lord protects), however uneven, fear has had more of the nature of an emotion, reactive, a response to the condition of peril. Fear is possibly (although there is no clear etymological connection) associated with *foreign*, a word which has as its first meaning "to be outside." In tandem with the meaning of danger, the meaning of fear has shifted. Danger expresses a relationship that is borne internally; fear is now the experience of being outside oneself, being profoundly self-alienated.

If one accepts the plausibility of the notion that *danger* may be a principal form of domination, a primary category for determining the viability of actions in the modern world, then one must also acknowledge that modern subjects weigh their movements in a world of others on the basis of fear. They evaluate the different actions they might take in terms of how such actions might lessen fear. But when danger so permeates the range of possible actions that there is no escaping it, then a point may have been reached in the human condition such that fear itself might undergo some change in meaning. The experience of fear might contribute to a rearrangement of the current regime of truth, which has so deeply problematized human existence.

The traditional means of *overcoming* fear, trying to confront danger so as to seek a new safe condition, are mistaken, because the elimination of the dangerous, as currently formulated, involves establishing new dangers that tighten the vise in which the human species is now trapped. The dangerous condition of being, however, is not coextensive with life. Instead, danger is very close to the condition that Foucault described as constitutive of bio-power.

> It is not that life has been totally integrated into techniques that govern and administer it; it constantly escapes them. Outside the Western world, famine exists, on a greater scale than ever; and the biological risks confronting the species are perhaps greater, and certainly more serious, than before the birth of microbiology. But what might be called a society's "threshold of modernity" has been reached when the life of the species is wagered on its own political strategies.[13]

The irony of danger is that it increases with every attempt to realize safety. The hopefulness implicit in fear stems from its immediate denial of the possibility of safety.

This depiction of fear and its relationship to danger parallels, in a limited but important way, Martin Heidegger's discussion of danger in "The Question concerning Technology."[14] One of the most important elements in Heidegger's discussion of danger is his depiction of a constantly closing gap between the world as it exists in what he calls its fourfold, and the ways in which technology turns the world into standing reserve, in a sense, reifying the world. The closer the world comes to being standing reserve, the greater the danger that humanity might lose the way toward a more primal truth than technology allows. This loss constitutes itself as a loss of coherent meaning, of any possible understanding of self and other. Such a loss resonates through all levels of existence. Yet this loss, in some readings, is not necessarily a bad thing, or at least is not troublesome enough to validate a rejection of modern humanism, especially when one considers what the alternative to modern humanism might be. In this reading, danger expresses the problematic situation of modern humanism in its attempt to valorize "man" as the object/subject to knowledge.

In an essay that focuses on the problems associated with the "rejectionist critique" of humanism, Nancy Fraser questions the value of problematizing modernity at the level of its foundations, and hence implicitly questions *how* problematic danger might be. Fraser, following Habermas, questions Foucault's rejection of humanism at three levels. At the philosophical level, while she concedes that rejectionism might not be antihumane, that it may indeed be seeking to find a way toward a higher sense of human being than humanism allows, she wonders, if "one abandons a foundationalist grounding of human values, then to what sort of nonfoundationalist justification can such values lay claim?"[15] At the strategic level, Fraser asks whether there might be a form of de-Cartesianized humanism, one not flawed so deeply as to be implicated in all exercises of power (presumably a Habermassian critical humanism), one that might operate as a critical force in the contemporary world. Such a humanism would be a better strategic alternative than a complete rejection of humanism, because such a critical humanism is able, as no posthumanist alternative has yet been able to do, to render distinctions among the various kinds and degrees of domination in the world.[16]

Finally, and most fundamentally in regard to a critique of danger, Fraser presents the ethical problem. The strongest rejection of humanism would render a project such as Habermas's suspect. Habermas's project of attempting more fully to realize an autonomous (though communicative) subject is the "completion" of the supposedly incomplete project of modernity; but in Foucault's analysis "even a perfectly anonymous subjectivity would be a form of normalizing, disciplinary domination."[17] In other words, the realization of the ideal speech act is synonymous with the realization of the panopticism Foucault criticized. But, Fraser goes on to ask, by what criteria can Foucault criticize panoptic society?

> Such a society only seems objectionable because Foucault has described it in such a way which invites the genetic fallacy. Because he has made the outcome of a historical process of hierarchical, asymmetrical coercion wherein people have been, in Nietzschean parlance, "bred" to autonomy. But this is a highly tendentious description. Why not describe it instead as a form of life developed on the basis of new, emergent communicative competences, competences that, while perhaps not built into the very logic of evolution, nonetheless permit for the first time in history the socialization of individuals oriented to dialogic political practice? Why not describe it as a form of life that is desirable since it no longer takes human needs and desires as brute, given *facta* to be either satisfied or repressed, but takes them rather, as accessible to intersubjective, linguistic reinterpretation and transformation, thereby widening the sphere of practical-political deliberation and narrowing that of instrumental-technical control and manipulation?[18]

Foucault is silent in response, Fraser argues, though she does suggest that the vocabulary of a response would have to be out of a language of some sort of authenticity, which is indeed an appeal to some version of autonomy. In other words, a posthumanist ethic requires a construction of "nothing less than a new paradigm of human freedom."[19]

Fraser identifies a need for a posthumanist ethic to contain a concept of freedom. But Foucault's intuition may well have been that the advance of such a concept would be a dangerous strategy. He may have been thinking (as I believe he often did) of Marx, who in his "Excerpt Notes of 1844" wrote, "We would not understand a human language, and it would remain without effect. On the one hand, it would be felt and spoken as a plea, as begging, as *humiliation* and hence uttered with shame and with a feeling of supplication; on the other hand, it would be heard and rejected as *effrontery* or *madness*."[20] Perhaps he was seeking a needed "slack" in order, as Connolly has suggested.[21] Regardless, no paradigm of freedom, no intelligible vision of autonomy has yet to have been identified with Foucault, or with any other rejectionist critic of the modern regime of truth.[22]

The paradigm Fraser seeks cannot be delivered. The imagination that provides paradigms is one that continues to identify freedom and necessity, insisting, with Engels, that freedom is necessity. But life is not; and, unfortunately, species-being is no longer. That great nay-sayer and affirmer, Nietzsche, permits no truthful philosophers to escape what they already know: the necessity of nihilism is not that of freedom, though freedom may indeed be becoming.

Foucault, however, less dramatically inclined than Nietzsche and perhaps more of this world, suggested points of study, and cautions to be exercised in the study of practice, that lend themselves to styling a rhetoric of freedom. First, he argued that one must avoid valorizing history by making it a repository of "meaning." Such an effort is futile if one desires to break with the ordering principles of disciplinary society:

> The history which bears and determines us has the form of a war rather than that of language: relations of power, not relations of meaning. History has no "meaning," though this is not to say that it is absurd or incoherent. On the contrary, it is intelligible and should be susceptible to analysis down to the smallest detail—but this in accordance with the intelligibility of struggles, of strategies and tactics. Neither the dialectic, as logic of contradictions, nor semiotics, as the structure of communication, can account for the intrinsic intelligibility of conflicts. "Dialectic" is a way of evading the always open and

hazardous reality of conflict by reducing it to a Hegelian skeleton, and "semiology" is a way of avoiding its violent, bloody and lethal character by reducing it to the calm Platonic form of language and dialogue.[23]

Foucault's reference to the "open and hazardous reality of conflict," his attempt to expose it as the intelligibility of modern existence, has as its end, I think, the assertion of a novel and humane, rather than humanistic, rhetoric of freedom, one grounded in a new right, a right to fear. Foucault argued, in attempting to counter those who seek the safety of rights grounded in the protection of the modern state, that "if one wants to look for a non-disciplinary form of power, or rather, to struggle against disciplines and disciplinary power, it is not toward the ancient right of sovereignty that one should turn, but toward the possibility of a new form of right, one which must indeed be anti-disciplinarian, but at the same time liberated from the principle of sovereignty."[24] By avoiding both "meaning" and sovereignty as the recourses to be followed in resistance to discipline, Foucault implicitly insisted that another way must be sought. That way is fear. If one wishes to problematize the panopticism of the modern state, whether it be in the form Bentham's utilitarian model, Rush's medical machine, or its most recent incarnation, Habermas's ideal speech situation, the freedom available is the freedom of fear.

Fear becomes, in a highly ordered system, the unreasonable reason that informs the desire to live, in the most fundamental way acting to unblock an imagination blocked by danger. To move outside of danger in this way is to experience fear. Alphonso Lingis describes this fear in semipoetic terms, referring both to the powerfully inauthentifying elements of fear and its liberating potential, a way out of the idiocy of the late modern experience. Fear, for Lingis, is a way to move beyond the condition of being "spacemen," beyond being American, in the most fundamental way possible:

> The one who longs to descend, himself, into the realm of the shark has known the fearful awe that watched the sharks moving in the layer of moonlit sea beneath him; he is seeking the terror that measures the shape and the size of its power, the stupor that knows what its watery speeds mean to the one its look has sought out, seeking to know what it means to find one's eyes steeped in the despotism of its look. Aristotle defines fear as "a kind of depression or bewilderment." Fear, Heidegger wrote, is inauthentifying, disperses out of reach whatever powers are

one's own, detaches one from a being that is one's own, disintegrates. The one that goes down to the deep goes for the fear.[25]

Fear contributes toward the understanding that the knowledge of experience exists as a transitory state, that modern subjects might learn to face the world with awe, to move away from and out of the experience of danger, to move out of the modern war of words.

Fear, as Heidegger depicted it, as a mode of state-of-mind, enables action in the world during the close of modernity, when there is an immanent collapse of order under the weight of order, when the value of objects is confounded through the commodification of the very imaginations that give rise to them, when the logic of modernity has reached the critical stage when what there is to fear most is *how humankind is to be protected*. The heart of protection is danger. Fear is a way of being between dangerous places, a way of gaining distance and perspective on the order of things and the processes through which they are made into mysterious entities.

In the past, the challenge issued by heroes has always been to overcome fear, so as to arrive at the next safe place. Overcoming fear under the current conditions of humankind would only place subjects in greater danger than before. Hence, modern subjects need to live through fear. Such an emphasis on the value of fear cannot mean valorizing it. Fear can act only as an arresting point, as a counter to valorization of any sort, for it is never an endeavor in its own right. The value of fear lies in this very fact, that it is a resistance to valorization, a value critical of value, resistant to teleology. Fear is only a way *toward* a value or a way *away* from a value. It is a way toward ways.

But neither is fear a starting point. Subjects realize fear only as a consequence of danger. It exists as a social construct, in that it is based upon the presumed benefiting and enabling (or debilitating and disabling) of selves. Fear, in a time when danger is the predominant form of power relationship, becomes a minimal social bond.

Fear, a disabling, incapacitating, paralyzing reaction to danger, constitutes a breaking point, a breaking off of the modern regime of truth. Death by perpetual motion, which is the most complete expression of life available in the modern episteme, requires a response that does not become implicated in the *telos* of death, that does not bind subjects to death. To be free is to fear. Fear is thus a way, a way to ameliorate the dangerous conditions of the late modern era.

## Conclusion

Here I conclude a book, which can remain an open site, until of course it is closed. I have traced strange documents, ones which outline, vaguely, some origins of this modern state, these United States. Some stories lend themselves quite readily to such rewriting. I think occasionally of the man who wished to emerge from prison alone, having made no dangerous acquaintances. Trading danger for danger, his choice to be alone may have been the best he could hope for at the time. But to accept the embrace of dangerous domination ultimately is an act of resignation, an act of succumbing to the seduction of an always false security.

Americans break the woof of time, Tocqueville claimed. That empty time is dangerous time. Such is one certain conclusion, that there is *danger* that the American subject will be lost, from himself or herself, from all others, from the face of the earth. If one is to reject the choices offered by dangerous relationships, one must betray the heritage of liberal democratic discourse. Yet even to speak of such a betrayal is to acknowledge what that heritage, as a practice, has left as its trace—the possibility of a next step, a move away from the tightening grip of danger, toward a situation in which danger is diminished, in which the war between life and death loosens its grip upon the imagination of the world of subjects which the American state has made.

# NOTES
# SELECTED BIBLIOGRAPHY
# INDEX

# Notes

## Introduction

1   Max Horkheimer and Theodor Adorno, *Dialectic of Enlightenment* (New York: Seabury Press, 1969), p. 226.

2   Jean-Paul Sartre, "Dirty Hands," *No Exit and Other Plays* (New York: Vintage Books, 1955), p. 142.

3   Etymologies used here are derived from the complete *Oxford English Dictionary*, and the *Oxford Dictionary of English Etymology*.

4   See Max Weber, "The City (Non-Legitimate Domination)," *Economy and Society*, Vol. 2, ed. Guenther Roth and Claus Wittich (Berkeley: University of California Press, 1978), p. 1214, especially. There Weber noted the growth of seigniorial authority in the early city as having a highly ambiguous relationship to politics and economics. Yet seigniorial authority was not traditional either, being dependent more upon both of the modern manifestations of power than on tradition.

5   John Wikse, *About Possession: The Self as Private Property* (University Park: Pennsylvania State University Press, 1977), p. 20.

6   See, for instance, Perry Anderson, *Passages from Antiquity to Feudalism* (London: New Left Books, 1974), and *Lineages of the Absolutist State* (London: New Left Books, 1974); and Barrington Moore, Jr., *Social Origins of Democracy and Dictatorship* (Boston: Beacon Press, 1966).

7   Wikse, *About Possession*, pp. 26–29, provides an etymology of behavior in order to illuminate this dimension of modern selfhood.

8   The underpinnings of almost all modern theories of commodity fetishism spring from Karl Marx. See *Capital*, Vol. 1, ed. Frederick Engels (New York: International Publishers, 1967), pp. 71–83. See also Walter Benjamin, "Unpacking My Library," *Illuminations*, edited and with an introduction by Hannah Arendt (New York: Schocken Books, 1969).

9   A thorough discussion of the transformation of the meaning of *habit* can be found in Chapter 5 of this book.

10  The best recent study of fetishism remains Herbert Marcuse, *One-Dimensional Man* (Boston: Beacon Press, 1964).

11  The language of "corruption" and disillusionment that informs so much of the rhetoric of American revolutionaries of the eighteenth century might reflect this nostalgia. Such is suggested by J. G. A. Pocock in chap. 15 of *The Machiavellian Moment: Florentine Political Thought and the Atlantic Republican Tradition* (Princeton: Princeton University Press, 1975). For a critique of Pocock, see Isaac Kramnick, "Republican Revisionism Revisited," *American Historical Review* 87, no.3 (June 1982): 629–64.

12  See Theodore J. Lowi, "American Business, Public Policy, Case Studies, and Political Theory," *World Politics* 16 (July 1964): 677–93. There Lowi adumbrates a theory of constitutive policy similar to what I am thinking of here. I elaborate upon his study in the conclusion of this book.

## Chapter 1: Liberal Democratic Discourse

1  Michel Foucault, *Discipline and Punish: The Birth of the Prison* (New York: Pantheon Books, 1977), p. 29.

2  I take this to be a primary insight of Giambattista Vico. See X 138, in *The New Science of Giambattista Vico*, trans. Thomas Goddard Bergin and Max Harold Fisch, rev. ed. (Ithaca: Cornell University Press, 1970). See also Edward Said, *Beginnings: Intention and Method* (Baltimore: Johns Hopkins University Press, 1975), "Conclusion: Vico in His Work and in This."

3  On fear of discourse, see Michel Foucault, "The Order of Discourse," *Language and Politics*, ed. Michael Shapiro (New York: New York University Press, 1984), p. 109. On the relationship of fear to philosophical discourse, see Alphonso Lingis, *Excesses: Eros and Culture* (Albany: SUNY Press, 1983).

4  Foucault, *Discipline and Punish*, p. 31; while this phrase is his, I have placed it in a slightly different context.

5  Michel Foucault, "Truth and Power," *Power/Knowledge*, ed. Colin Gordon (New York: Pantheon Books, 1980), p. 121.

6  See Thomas Hobbes, *Leviathan*, edited and with an introduction by C. B. Macpherson (London: Penguin Books, 1968), first published in 1651. "And Covenants, without the Sword, are but words," p. 223.

7  One way of thinking through the limits of such power is to understand the quest for security to be a way of furthering *danger*. In this sense, the only path toward freedom is the path of *fear*. I elaborate on this theme in the conclusion of this book.

8  On the intellectual atmosphere at the time of the Revolution see Christopher Hill, *The World Turned Upside Down: Radical Ideas during the English Revolution* (London: Penguin Books, 1975).

9  This argument is developed in much greater detail by Hans Blumenberg in "Theological Absolutism and Human Self-Assertion," part 2 of *The Legitimacy of the Modern Age*, trans. Robert M. Wallace (Cambridge: MIT Press, 1983), especially pp. 133–35.

10 There is nothing in Hobbes's texts to suggest that he was antiscientific, and, in fact, there is much to suggest that he fully advocated the science of such luminaries as Bacon. The idea that he would be concerned about protecting God from questioning can be found, however, by reading the last two books of *Leviathan*, in which he advances ideas concerning a Christian common-wealth. For an insightful reading of Hobbes in this regard, one which goes beyond the more limited concerns of this essay, see Eldon Eisenach, *Two Worlds of Liberalism* (Chicago: University of Chicago Press, 1981).

11 Eisenach, *Two Worlds of Liberalism*, pp. 67–71.

12 Hobbes, *Leviathan*, p. 105.

13 Ibid., p. 218. "He that owneth his words and actions, is the Author . . . . The right of doing any action, is called AUTHORITY."

14 Wikse, *About Possession*, p. 28. "Our word *behave* was formed in the late fifteenth century from the word *be* (an intensive, originally meaning 'about,' more figuratively in the sense of 'thorough'), and *have* (verb) in order to express a qualified sense of having, particularly in the reflexive: 'to have or bear oneself.' " The connection of being to *danger* should be duly noted here.

15 This argument is essentially C. B. Macpherson's, to be found in *The Political Theory of Possessive Individualism: Hobbes to Locke* (New York: Oxford University Press, 1962), especially chapter 2, section 5, "Penetration and Limits of Hobbes's Political Theory."

16 Hobbes, *Leviathan*, pp. 191–92.

17 Ibid., p. 223.

18 Ibid., p. 188. "The passions that incline men to Peace, are Fear of Death; Desire of such things are as necessary to commodious living . . . ."

19 Ibid., p. 340.

20 Ibid., pp. 341–42.

21 Ibid., p. 189. "The Right of Nature . . . is the Liberty each man hath, to use his own power, as he will himself, for the preservation of his own Nature."

22 Eisenach, *Two Worlds of Liberalism*, pp. 47–50, especially. There Eisenach introduces the necessity of a theological justification for laying down one's life if one adheres to the logic of liberal individualism. In the absence of such a justification, no liberal political order could exist, according to him.

23 The sovereign itself has become increasingly difficult to locate—it has become an abstraction, so to speak. This was one of Foucault's major points. But in placing the search for self in such a context, Foucault does not deny the alienating character of life in capitalist societies, as some have suggested.

24 This concept needs much elaboration, which it receives below. Useful as an introduction to thinking about Foucault's notion of the body politic is an essay by William E. Connolly, "The Dilemma of Legitimacy," in Connolly, ed., *Legitimacy and the State* (New York: NYU Press, 1984). In that essay, Connolly advocates the establishment of some "slack in the order," that is, the establishment of residual spaces in order to loosen tightly organized political systems.

25 Foucault, "Two Lectures," *Power/Knowledge*, p. 97.

26 Martin Heidegger, "The Question concerning Technology," *Basic Writings*, ed. David Farrell Krell (New York: Harper and Row, 1977), p. 291.

27 See Joseph A. Schumpeter, *Capitalism, Socialism, and Democracy*, 3d ed. (New York: Harper and Row, 1950).

28 Theodore Lowi, *The End of Liberalism*, 2d ed. (New York: Norton, 1979).

29 The most comprehensive compilation of documents concerning the history of liberal theory is E. K. Bramsted and K. J. Melhuish, ed., *Western Liberalism* (London: Longman, 1978). In regard to the question of Lockean liberalism and its role in dangerous relationships, see Chapter 3 of this book.

30 An attempt to take James Buchanan, for example, seriously as a political theorist reveals the shortcomings of such reductionism. See Norman P. Barry, "Unanimity, Agreement, and Liberalism: A Critique of James Buchanan's Social Philosophy," *Political Theory* 12, no. 4 (November 1984): 579–96. The critique of liberalism, especially in its pluralist incarnation, as being unable to advance to common sense of community values and standards, is central to Lowi's thesis.

31 See Isaac Kramnick, "Equal Opportunity and the Race of Life," *Dissent*, May 1982.

32 George Kateb, "Democratic Individuality and the Claims of Politics," *Political Theory* 12, no. 3 (August 1984): 338.

33 Michael Walzer, "Liberalism and the Art of Separation," *Political Theory* 12, no. 3 (August 1984): 320.

34 Ibid., p. 326.

35 Ibid., p. 329.

36 In that regard, see Francis M. Sim, Larry D. Spence, and Yoshimitsu Takei, "Telearchics: The Tightness of Loose Coupling," a paper presented at the American Sociological Association Annual Meeting, 1983.

37 Of course, there is little novelty in gesturing to this matrix at the most general level. Concordance of such diverse thinkers as Nietzsche, Heidegger, Marcuse, Adorno, Benjamin, and Habermas exists on this point. The trick, of course, lies in what is made of it, and at what level the basic relationships are understood as political.

38 Michel Foucault, *The History of Sexuality*, Vol. 1 (New York: Pantheon Books, 1979), p. 93.

39 Foucault, *Discipline and Punish*, p. 29. Kantorowitz's study was of the ritual aspects of the divine right monarchy. See *The King's Two Bodies* (Princeton: Princeton University Press, 1957).

40 Foucault, *Discipline and Punish*, p. 29.

41 Ibid., p. 31.

42 See *Lenin and Philosophy*, Louis Althusser, "Ideology and Ideological State Apparatuses," trans. Ben Brewster (New York: Monthly Review Press, 1971). See also *State, Power, Socialism*, Nicos Poulantzas, "The Ideological Apparatuses: Does the State Equal Repression plus Ideology?" trans. Patrick Camiller (London: New Left Books, 1978). While a major purpose of Poulantzas's study was to distinguish between class and state power, I think that he actually

confused the two areas. He presents a strong attack on Foucault, which might be of use to those who wish to gird themselves against abandoning the primacy of class conflict in the study of power relationships.

43  Foucault, *Discipline and Punish*, Plate 8. The auditorium of the prison at Fresnes.

44  Hobbes, *Leviathan*, p. 71.

45  Foucault, "Two Lectures," p. 81.

46  I take this to be a major premise of the important study by Gilles Deleuze and Felix Guattari, *Anti-Oedipus: Capitalism and Schizophrenia*, with a preface by Michel Foucault, trans. Robert Hurley, Mark Seem, and Helen R. Lane (Minneapolis: University of Minnesota Press, 1983). The critique often leveled against the refusal of genealogists to express positive support for programs is itself problematic. This work is positive, yet unprogrammatic.

47  Michel Foucault, "Intellectuals and Power: An Interview with Gilles Deleuze," *Language, Counter-Memory, Practice*, ed. Donald Bouchard (Ithaca: Cornell University Press, 1977).

48  For a provocative study of the phenomenon of nationalism, see Benedict Anderson, *Imagined Communities: Reflections on the Origin and Spread of Nationalism* (London: Verso Editions and New Left Books, 1983).

## Chapter 2: Genealogy versus History

1  Michel Foucault, "Nietzsche, Genealogy, History," *Language, Counter-Memory, Practice*, p. 164.

2  Friedrich Nietzsche, *On the Genealogy of Morals*, ed. Walter Kaufmann, trans. Walter Kaufmann and R. J. Hollingdale (New York: Vintage Books, 1969), pp. 77–78.

3  Ibid., p. 78.

4  See Nancy Fraser, "Foucault on Modern Power," *Praxis International* 1, no. 1 (October 1981): 272–96. On Nietzsche, see Mark Warren, "Nietzsche and Political Philosophy," *Political Theory* 13, no. 2 (May 1985): 183–212.

5  See the Introduction of this book. For another view, see George Kateb, "Thinking about Human Extinction: (1) Nietzsche and Heidegger," *Raritan* 6, no.2 (Fall 1986).

6  Foucault, "Truth and Power," p. 114.

7  Connolly, "The Dilemma of Legitimacy."

8  In *The Body in Pain: The Making and Unmaking of the World* (New York: Oxford University Press, 1985), Elaine Scarry attempts to undermine this merely metaphorical application of pain.

9  Jürgen Habermas, "Modernity—An Incomplete Project," *The Anti- Aesthetic: Essays on Postmodern Culture*, edited and with an introduction by Hal Foster (Port Townsend, Ash. Bay Press, 1983).

10  Foucault, *History of Sexuality* 1: 143.

11  David Rothman, *The Discovery of the Asylum: Social Order and Disorder in the New Republic* (Boston: Little, Brown, 1971), and *Conscience and Convenience:*

*The Asylum and Its Alternatives in Progressive America* (Boston: Little, Brown, 1980).

12  Rothman, *Discovery of the Asylum*, p. xvii.

13  Rothman, *Conscience and Convenience*, p. 11.

14  Ibid., chap. 1.

15  Foucault, *Discipline and Punish*, p. 208.

16  Ibid., p. 225.

17  The study of the relationships among social sciences and policymakers is perhaps the most important contribution that Rothman makes in *Conscience and Convenience*. There is a large literature concerning the relationship between social sciences and social policies, especially for the United States, but also for England and France. Among the best works in recent years, some of which share Foucault's concerns, are Jacques Donzelot, *The Policing of Families*, trans. Robert Hurley (New York: Pantheon Press, 1979): Samuel Bowles and Herbert Gintis, *Schooling in Capitalist America* (New York: Basic Books, 1976); Christopher Lasch, *Haven in a Heartless World* (New York: Basic Books, 1977); Judith Walkowitz, *Prostitution and Victorian Society* (Cambridge: Cambridge University Press, 1980); Thomas L. Haskell, *The Emergence of Professional Social Science: The American Social Science Association and the Nineteenth Century Crisis of Authority* (Urbana: University of Illinois Press, 1977); Anthony Platt, *The Child Savers: The Invention of Delinquency* (Chicago: University of Chicago Press, 1969); Michael Ignatieff, *A Just Measure of Pain: The Penitentiary in the Industrial Revolution* (New York: Columbia University Press, 1978); and R. Jeffrey Lustig, *Corporate Liberalism: The Origins of Modern American Political Theory, 1890–1920* (Berkeley: University of California Press, 1982).

18  See Michel Foucault, *The Order of Things: An Archaeology of the Human Sciences* (New York: Vintage Books, 1973).

19  Hubert L. Dreyfus and Paul Rabinow, *Michel Foucault: Beyond Structuralism and Hermeneutics*, 2d ed. (Chicago: University of Chicago Press, 1983), pp. 195–96.

20  See Richard F. Sparks, "A Critique of Marxist Criminology," in *Crime and Justice: An Annual Review of Research* 2 (1980), cited by John H. Langbein in "*Albion's* Fatal Flaws," *Past and Present*, no. 98 (February 1983), pp. 96–120. Both Anthony Barnett and Alan Stone brought this argument to my attention.

21  Langbein, "*Albion's* Fatal Flaws," pp. 119–20.

22  Foucault, *Discipline and Punish*, p. 224.

23  Perhaps my formulation is too simple and too sympathetic to Foucault. Foucault argued, "The real corporal disciplines constituted the foundation of the formal, juridical liberties. The contract may have been regarded as the ideal foundation of law and political power; panopticism constituted the technique, universally widespread, of coercion. It continued to work in depth on the juridical structures of society, in order to make the effective mechanisms of power function in opposition to the formal framework that it had acquired. The 'Enlightenment,' which discovered the liberties, also invented the disciplines." *Discipline and Punish*, p. 222.

24 Michel Foucault, *L'impossible prison* (Paris: Editions du Seuil, 1980), p. 37, as cited in Dreyfus and Rabinow, *Michel Foucault*, pp. 192–93.

25 Foucault, "Nietzsche, Genealogy, History."

26 Foucault, "Truth and Power," p. 121.

27 Ibid., p. 114.

28 Fredric Jameson, *The Political Unconscious: Narrative as a Socially Symbolic Act* (Ithaca: Cornell University Press, 1981), p. 54. I choose Jameson here, rather than a multitude of other Marxist critics of Foucault, in part because he is so familiar with the terms of discourse of the French, and in part because, despite that familiarity, he remains skeptical of them.

29 Ibid., p. 102. "History is therefore the experience of Necessity, and it is this alone which can forestall its thematization of reification as a mere object of representation or as one master code among many others . . . . History as ground and untranscendable horizon needs no particular theoretical justification: we may be sure that its alienating necessities will not forget us, however much we might prefer to ignore them."

30 The phrase is Michael Ryan's, delivered during an interrogation conducted at the conclusion of a seminar he delivered at the University of Massachusetts, Amherst, in July of 1984.

31 Michael Ryan, *Marxism and Deconstruction: A Critical Articulation* (Baltimore: Johns Hopkins University Press, 1982), pp. 78–79.

32 Ibid., p. 79.

33 Ibid., Preface.

34 See Murray Edelman, "Political Language and Political Reality," *PS* 18, no 1 (Winter 1985): 17. In context, Edelman might argue, that statement doesn't carry its extreme meaning, but is instead a rhetorical device designed simply to underscore the particularity of all social experiences and the ultimate exhaustion of reason as it attempts to incorporate them into itself. Nonetheless, in the analysis of power, that struggle is precisely what must be taken "seriously," whatever one might mean by serious.

35 Karl Marx, *Marx-Engels Collected Works* (New York: International Publishers, 1975), 5: 28.

36 Foucault, *Discipline and Punish*, p. 221.

37 Ibid., p. 30.

38 Ibid., p. 194.

39 Ibid., pp. 220–21.

40 Marx, *Capital*, 1: 335. "Co-operation ever constitutes the fundamental form of the capitalist mode of production; nevertheless, the elementary form of co-operation continues to subsist as a particular form of capitalist production side by side with the more developed forms of the mode of production."

41 That such a statement should even need a footnote is, I think, the consequence of the questioning of the class basis of conflict, which has led, not only to more sophisticated and clearer analyses of late capitalism, but also to the development of such ideas as Althusser's notion of capital without capitalists. See Karl Marx and Frederick Engels, *Manifesto of the Communist Party, The Marx-*

164 Notes to Pages 53–58

*Engels Reader,* ed. Robert C. Tucker, 2d ed. (New York: Norton, 1978). I am myself very ambivalent concerning the potentially central role of class in explaining late modern political conflict.

42 Marx and Engels, "Manifesto," p. 487.

43 A thorough discussion of this theme is Martin Jay, *Marxism and Totality: The Adventure of a Concept from Lukács to Habermas* (Berkeley: University of California Press, 1984). The following summary of positions held by Habermas and Foucault roughly parallels that made by Jay in his "Epilogue: The Challenge of Post-Structuralism," though my conclusions are different from his.

44 Jürgen Habermas, *Knowledge and Human Interests,* trans. Jeremy J. Shapiro (Boston: Beacon Press, 1971), pp. 290–300.

45 Ibid., p. 292.

46 Ibid., pp. 299–300.

47 Habermas, "Modernity—an Incomplete Project," p. 14. A critique of Habermas on this point is made by Nancy Fraser in "Michel Foucault: A 'Young Conservative'?" *Ethics* 96, no. 1 (October 1985): 165-84.

48 Habermas, "Modernity—An Incomplete Project."

49 "Structuralism and Post-Structuralism: An Interview with Michel Foucault," no. 55 (Spring 1983), p. 200. Foucault thus identifies himself with those whom Habermas tries to transcend.

50 Ibid., p. 201.

51 Ibid.

52 *The Foucault Reader,* ed. Paul Rabinow (New York: Pantheon Books, 1984), pp. 32–50.

53 Jürgen Habermas, "Taking Aim at the Heart of the Present," *University Publishing* 13 (Summer 1984): 5–6. This was a special memorial issue on Foucault, occasioned by his death in June of that year. "[Foucault] contrasts his critique of power with the analysis of truth in such a fashion that the former becomes deprived of the normative yardstick that it would have to borrow from the latter. Perhaps the force of this contradiction caught up to Foucault in this last of his texts, drawing him again into the circle of the philosophical discourse of modernity which he thought he could explode." The relationship between Foucault's essay and Habermas's critique is not completely clear. Here I have only tried to work out what I presume to be Habermas's continuing stance in opposition to Foucault.

54 *Foucault Reader,* p. 38.

55 Habermas, "Taking Aim at the Heart of the Present," p. 5.

56 Perhaps a clue as to the limits of Jameson's understanding lies in his continual recasting of dialectical materialism in terms that seem to be almost vulgar. For instance: "For Marxism, indeed, only the emergence of a post-individualistic social world, only the reinvention of the collective and associative, can concretely achieve the 'decentering' of the individual subject called for by such diagnoses; only a new and original form of collective social life can overcome the isolation and monadic autonomy of the older bourgeois subjects in such a

way that individual consciousness can be lived—and not merely theorized— as an 'effect of structure' (Lacan)." *Political Unconscious*, p. 125.

There would be little to disagree with in this passage were it not for the insistent use of such terms as "only" and "merely." Such rhetorical devices dramatically privilege a single discourse, and unnecessarily so, for here the question ultimately does not reduce to that of necessity. How can a Marxism be democratic when it insists upon a Tayloresque "one best way"? No doubt Jameson's call is made with great sincerity and veracity, but it nonetheless privileges a particular version of reality over all others. The gap between theory and practice, by the way, is also no excuse for academic Marxists to point accusing fingers at their protagonists. No one in the academy is "innocent" of theory that I know of, nor should they be.

57   I develop a comparison of the two below. My study of Walter Benjamin owes much to conversations with Susan Buck-Morss, although I would never hold her accountable since she finds my reading mistaken much of the time.

58   Charles Baudelaire, *The Painter of Modern Life and Other Essays*, trans. Jonathan Mayne (London: Phaidon, 1964), pp. 12, 11, as cited in *Foucault Reader*, p. 41.

59   *Foucault Reader*, p. 41.

60   Michel Foucault, *This Is Not a Pipe*, trans. James Harkness (Berkeley: University of California Press, 1982).

61   Walter Benjamin, "Theses on the Philosophy of History," *Illuminations*, pp. 253–64. See especially Thesis 9.

62   Benjamin, "Unpacking My Library," p. 67. On the *flaneur*, see "On Some Motifs in Baudelaire," *Iluminations*, pp. 155–201. The argument that Benjamin celebrates the *flaneur* must always be qualified by the observation that he expressed great ambivalence concerning all aspects of the modern age.

63   *Herculine Barbin: Being the Recently Discovered Memoirs of a Nineteenth-Century French Hermaphrodite*, introduced by Michel Foucault, translated by Richard McDougal (New York: Pantheon Books, 1980).

64   Foucault, *History of Sexuality*, Vol. 1, Pt. 5, "The Right of Death and Power over Life."

65   See Alexander Hooke, "The Order of Others," *Political Theory* 15, no. 1 (February 1987).

## Chapter 3: Friendly Persuasion

1   See *The Laws of Pennsylvania*, Vol. 1 (Philadelphia: Halls and Sellers, 1797); and *Charter and Laws of the Province of Pennsylvania* (Harrisburg: Commonwealth of Pennsylvania, 1871).

2   Louis Hartz, *The Liberal Tradition in America* (New York: Harcourt, Brace, Jovanovich, 1955), p. 6–8.

3   A discussion of Foucault's concept of the soul can be found in Chapter 1. Tocqueville's understanding of the soul is discussed in Chapter 5.

4  John Locke, *An Essay concerning Human Understanding*, ed. A. S. Pringle-Pattison (London: Oxford University Press, 1924), p. 267.

5  Ibid., p. 276.

6  Ibid., p. 277.

7  See John Locke, *The Reasonableness of Christianity*, ed. I. T. Ramsey (Stanford: Stanford University Press, 1958), pp. 42 and 67, for examples of how this persuasive process might work. In those passages, Locke argued for the use of parables that could be interpreted at several levels, depending upon the education and intelligence of the listener. Such a pedagogy would serve the end of persuading people of both the existence and reasonableness of God.

8  Locke, *Essay concerning Human Understanding*, p.1 280.

9  Locke, *Reasonableness of Christianity*, p. 42. "You may sooner hope to have day laborers and tradesmen, the spinsters and dairymaids, perfect mathematicians, as to have them perfect in ethics in this way: hearing plain commands, is the sure and only way to bring them to obedience." Locke thus limited his reasoning audience, but surely the Quakers demanded more than plain commands in order to obey.

10  John Locke, *Treatise of Civil Government and Letter concerning Toleration*, ed. C. L. Sherman (New York: Irvington Publishers, 1937), p. 191.

11  Ibid., p. 172.

12  Ibid., p. 193.

13  Ibid., p. 201.

14  John Locke, *Two Treatises of Government*, ed. Peter Laslett (New York: New American Library, 1963).

15  On the pacifism of the Quakers, see Hill *World Turned Upside Down*, pp.231–68, especially. There is a voluminous literature on the history of the Quakers, both in England and in North America. I have found one of the most interesting of recent works to be Digby Baltzell's *Puritan Boston, Quaker Philadelphia* (New York: Free Press, 1979). He accounts for the lack of attention paid to the Quakers' influence on the political development of the United States by arguing that their theology made them less visible as participants in the cultural development of the country. See pp. 57–176, especially.

16  William Penn, *A Letter from a Gentleman in the Countryside to His Friends in London, Upon the Subject of the Penal Law and Tests* (London, 1687 [?]), in the Rare Books Room, Olin Library, Cornell University, Ithaca.

17  On the evolution of Quaker theology during the late seventeenth century, the best source is George Fox, *A Journal* (Philadelphia: Friends Bookstore, 1849). Fox was the founder of the Quaker sect as well as William Penn's spiritual mentor, and his journal traces the stages of political compromise that the society went through in order to survive. On the relationships between Quaker theology and political organization, see Gary B. Nash, *Quakerism and Politics: Pennsylvania, 1681–1726* (Princeton: Princeton University Press, 1968).

18  Howard Brinton, *Friends for Three Hundred Years* (Wallingford, PA: Pendle Hill Publications, 1964), p. 184, as cited in Baltzell, *Puritan Boston, Quaker Philadelphia*, p. 131.

19  Hill, *World Turned Upside Down*, p. 256.
20  Baltzell, *Puritan Boston, Quaker Philadelphia*, p. 130. See also Thomas Haskell, "Capitalism and the Origins of the Humanitarian Sensibility," *American Historical Review* 90 (April and June 1985): 339–61, 547–66.
21  Nash, *Quakerism and Politics*, p. 58.
22  Ibid., pp. 78–82.
23  Ibid., pp. 97–114. This struggle contributed to the eventual dissolution of proprietary government.
24  See Foucault, *Discipline and Punish*. A more detailed treatment of punishment in this era can be found in a work Foucault himself cited, George Rusche and Otto Kirschheimer, *Punishment and Social Structure* (New York: Columbia University Press, 1939.)
25  For an overview of the English Criminal Code enacted at the beginning of the eighteenth century, see Douglas Hay et al., *Albion's Fatal Tree: Crime and Society in Eighteenth-Century England* (New York: Pantheon Books, 1975).
26  *Laws of Pennsylvania*, 1:136, provides an example of the clergy rule. On the origins and evolution of the practice of pleading clergy, see George Ives, *A History of Penal Methods* (London: Stanley Paul, 1918), p. 34.
27  Deterrence is broadly defined by criminologists to mean any act initiated by authorities to discourage commission of crimes. Specific deterrence is when the focus is on criminals; general deterrence is when the focus is on criminals and all potential criminals (i.e., everyone). One might say that the public execution of sentence served a general deterrence function, in that a lesson was presented to the subjects of authority concerning the consequences of fighting the sovereign. But this was usually subordinated to the larger lesson of resetting a disturbed moral balance. See Foucault, *Discipline and Punish*, pp. 58–59.
28  Ibid., pp. 54–55. This terror is produced, not merely or even primarily through the death of the condemned, but through the torture of the body leading up to death.
29  Ibid., pp. 59–64. Foucault's political economy of punishment is not as gross as I have implied here, although the general relationship does hold.
30  The isolation of the Quakers may not have been as great as I suggest, or as might be assumed from speculation on ocean travel during the era. A benign disinterest on the part of the Privy Council, especially as long as the colony was providing revenue without severe disruption, as well as the special relationship Penn enjoyed for a while with the crown, might have contributed to their having been left alone.
31  See Moore, *Social Origins of Democracy and Dictatorship*, p. 19.
32  For an example of the hagiographic tendency in historical studies of the Quakers, see Isaac Sharpless, *Quakerism and Politics* (Philadelphia: Ferris and Leach, 1905).
33  *Charter and Laws of the Province of Pennsylvania*, pp. 107–80.
34  Ibid., p. 84.
35  For a study of how the Quakers took advantage of "silent spaces" in law, see

N. C. Hunt, *Two Early Political Associations* (London: Oxford University Press, 1961), especially chap. 1.

36 Some scholars have suggested that the real author of the original frame of government for Pennsylvania was not Penn, but Furly, a Quaker merchant. Furly, given the argument I am trying to make here regarding the relationship between Quakerism and Lockean liberalism, is a particularly interesting figure because he was a friend of both Penn and Locke. See William Hull, *William Penn: A Topical Biography* (London: Oxford University Press, 1937), p. 229. See also Laslett, Introduction to Locke, *Two Treatises*, p. 65.

37 *Charter and Laws of the Province of Pennsylvania*, p. 83.

38 Ibid., p. 93.

39 Ibid.

40 Ibid., pp. 93–97.

41 Nash, *Quakerism and Politics*, pp. 11–13.

42 *Charter and Laws of the Province of Pennsylvania*, p. 105.

43 Ibid.

44 Locke, *Reasonableness of Christianity*, p. 58. There Locke discussed the seeming paradox of the rationality of the Athenians, who were not Christians, and reveals their heathenism to be a product of ignorance, not disregard.

45 *Charter and Laws of the Province of Pennsylvania*, p. 108.

46 Ibid., p. 154.

47 Hill, *World Turned Upside Down*, pp. 378–80. See also a nineteenth-century biography of Penn, Thomas Clarkson, *Memoirs of the Life of William Penn* (London: Longman, Hurst, Rees, Orme and Brown 1813), 2:428.

48 Clarkson, *Memoirs of the Private and Public Life of William Penn*, 2:438.

49 The Quakers were not to involve themselves in establishing the specific content of a new self at the level of modifying the behavior of subjects; it was to remain for their successors to do so. They instead focused on law as a codification of morality, relying upon the criminal, through reception of Inner Light, to realize morality in his or her life. The law served more as a monitor of behavior than as a set of instructions.

50 Clarkson, *Memoirs of the Private and Public Life of William Penn*, p. 428.

51 See Harry Elmer Barnes, *The Evolution of Penology in Pennsylvania* (Montclair, N.J.: Patterson-Smith, 1968), p. 33, for a summary of the differences between the two codes.

52 Ibid., p. 35.

53 *Charter and Laws of the Province of Pennsylvania*, pp. 109–13.

54 Attempts to rationalize criminal codes had begun in England as early as Cromwell. See Hay et al., *Albion's Fatal Tree*, and Christopher Hill, *God's Englishman* (New York: Pantheon Press, 1970), pp. 65–70.

55 *Charter and Laws of the Province of Pennsylvania*, p. 113.

56 For a study of the administration of law in meetings in Pennsylvania during this era, see Albert C. Applegarth, *The Quakers in Pennsylvania* (Baltimore: Johns Hopkins University Studies in Historical and Political Science, 1923), especially pp. 1–5.

57 *Charter and Laws of the Province of Pennsylvania*, p. 202.

58 Rusche and Kirschheimer, *Punishment and Social Structure*, pp. 63–64.

59 Ibid., pp. 41–43.

60 Ibid., p. 84.

61 On the influx of indentured servants to the American Colonies generally, and to Pennsylvania particularly, see Abbott Emerson Smith, *Colonists in Bondage* (Chapel Hill: University of North Carolina Press, 1947), p. 228.

62 Barnes, *Evolution of Penology in Pennsylvania*, p. 53.

63 John Howard's *The State of the Prisons* (New York: Everyman Editions, 1929), though published in 1777, over half a century later than the era under question here, nonetheless can be presumed to be reasonably accurate for this earlier era.

64 *Charter and Laws of the Province of Pennsylvania*, p. 202.

65 Howard, *State of the Prisons*, p. 12.

66 Ibid., p. 15–18. One irony of the system was that material witnesses, if indigent, would be put in jail and accrue such a debt to the jailer that they would remain there, often starving to death or dying of "gaol fever."

67 This was provided for in subsequently enacted legislation. *Charter and Laws of the Province of Pennsylvania*, pp. 139–40.

68 Barnes, *Evolution of Penology in Pennsylvania*, p. 57.

69 Ibid., p. 83.

70 Ibid., p. 63.

71 Ibid., p. 60.

72 Ibid., p. 58.

73 *Charter and Laws of the Province of Pennsylvania*, p. 200.

74 Nash, *Quakerism and Politics*, p. 313. On smuggling, see L. H. Gipson, *The British Empire before the American Revolution* (Caldwell, Idaho: the Caxton Printers, 1936), 3:180.

75 Affirmation laws permitted people to testify in legal proceedings without swearing oaths. They constituted the major statutory protection of the religious practices of the Quakers and other antinomian sects, who believed swearing oaths to be a sacrilegious subordination of faith to earthly government.

76 Nash, *Quakerism and Politics*, pp. 313–15. On the role of the Anglican church in Pennsylvania during this period see Winfred Root, *The Relations of Pennsylvania with the British Government, 1696–1765* (Philadelphia: University of Pennsylvania; New York; D. Appleton, 1912), chap. 8, "Anglicans and Quakers."

77 Root, *Relations of Pennsylvania with the British Government*, pp. 360–67.

78 Ibid., p. 368.

79 Barnes, *Evolution of Penology in Pennsylvania*, p. 38.

80 Nash, *Quakerism and Politics*, p. 241.

81 Ibid., p. 280 (Table A) and p. 326 (Table A) summarize this process.

82 Ibid., pp. 287–300.

83 *Laws of Pennsylvania*, 1:129n. These footnotes, from which Bradford is cited, provide one of the clearest summaries I have encountered of the evolution of criminal statutes during this era.

84 Quakers had attempted to settle in some of those other colonies. Their tragic

encounters with the Puritans of Massachusetts are discussed at length by Kai Erikson, *Wayward Puritans* (New York: John Wiley and Sons, 1966).

85 See Foucault, *Discipline and Punish*, p. 31, on the history of the present. Here I am arguing that the Quakers prepared the ground for the modern soul, for the establishment of mechanisms that would render the modern subjects of dangerous relationships possible.

86 See Wikse, *About Possession*, for an overview of the "pre-history of behavior."

87 This connection was first explained to me by Theodore J. Lowi.

88 See Lawrence Friedman, *A History of American Law* (New York: Simon & Schuster, 1973), for a discussion of law and commerce in the late eighteenth-century United States.

## Chapter 4: Republican Machines

1 See Marx and Engels, *Manifesto of the Communist Party*, pp. 477–78.

2 One way of gaining access to the suddenness and radical nature of the change that occurred, as well as to the continuities, is to read Washington Irving's famous short story "Rip Van Winkle," *Collected Works of Washington Irving* (New York: Graystone Press, 1921). The contrast between old and new political loyalties, but, more important, the shifts that occurred in the way in which citizens understood their role in the policy, are the themes of this relatively neglected work.

3 See Friedman, *History of American Law*, especially part 2, "From the Revolution to the Death of Chancellor Kent: 1776–1847."

4 See, for instance, Bernard Bailyn, *The Ideological Origins of the American Revolution* (Cambridge: Harvard University Press, 1967), and Perry Miller, *Errand into the Wilderness* (Cambridge: Harvard University Press, 1956). More recently, see Pocock, *Machiavellian Movement*, especially "The Americanization of Virtue." The argument here is not that there has not been extensive work done concerning the history of the American Revolution. On the contrary, the literature is extraordinarily rich and deep. The point here is instead that the various interpretations of that era hold that it was less a revolution and more a continuation of politics in Europe, a break with Great Britain only in a simple sense, and a consolidation of the separate states. It may have been all that, but, as will be shown below, important political leaders in the colonies weren't told that they were engaged only in a secessionist movement—they believed that they were involved in a moral revolution.

5 Penal historians have been far too modest in the claims they have made regarding the impact of punishment policies. For the most part, they have not analyzed with any sophistication the relationship between punishment and the broader issue of political authority, subsuming questions of ideology under the vaguer, and depoliticized, concept of general deterrence.

6 Friedman, *History of American Law*, p. 97. A fascinating analysis of the importance of this work, by a historical actor in the process, William Bradford, is contained in a footnote to *Laws of Pennsylvania*, 1:129nn.

7  See "Common Sense," *The Life and Major Writings of Thomas Paine,* Philip S. Foner (New York: Citadel Press, 1945), pp. 31–39.

8  Ibid., p. 36.

9  Ibid., p. 37.

10  The modern reader should be aware of the deeper meaning that the word "habit" carried during the late eighteenth and early nineteenth centuries. Habit meant, during this period, "mental constitution, disposition, custom," in short, the total attitude and disposition of a person as he or she related to a broader social context. The term began to refer to specific behavioral traits during the 1830s and 1840s. Indeed, this transformation can be related (and is in Chapter 5 of this work) to the development of a new concept of social order that emerged with the triumph of a specific form of penal discipline. See *The Oxford English Dictionary* for a more systematic discussion of the etymology of the word.

11  See "On the Defects of the Confederation," *The Selected Writings of Benjamin Rush,* ed. Dagobert D. Runes (New York: Philosophical Library, 1947), p. 26.

12  Rush, "Of the Proper Mode of Education in a Republic," *Selected Writings,* p. 92. Rush was very concerned in this essay to investigate the possibilities of developing "a new class of duties [for] every American. It becomes us to examine our former habits upon this subject, and in laying the foundations for nurseries of wise and good men, to adapt our modes of teaching to the peculiar form of our government," p. 87. Notice Rush's use of the term "habits."

13  Ibid., p. 92. Also see Ronald T. Takaki, *Iron Cages: Race and Culture in Nineteenth-Century America* (New York: Alfred A. Knopf, 1979).

14  See Rush's "Travels through Life," in *The Autobiography of Benjamin Rush,* George W. Corner (Princeton: Princeton University Press, 1948).

15  A list of Rush's various accomplishments is to be found in the preface to *Selected Writings,* pp. vi–ix.

16  This theme is addressed in some detail in Takaki, *Iron Cages,* " Diseases' of the Mind and Skin," especially p. 23.

17  Miller, *Errand into the Wilderness,* chap. 6, "Johnathan Edwards and the Great Awakening." The Great Awakening changed the status of American religion from a force in alliance with the crown (except, interestingly, for the Quakers), to a subversive force. The moral degeneration of the aristocracy of Britain that was a theme of writers as diverse as John and Sam Adams reflected the earlier themes of Edwards. (An extended discussion of the relationship between the Quakers and British political authorities is contained in Chapter 3 of this work.)

18  Education was a major concern of Rush, who wrote many essays on the subject aside from the one cited above. It is of interest to note that in recent years there have emerged studies that have focused on the role that education plays at a contributor to the social control of large populations. See, for example, the interesting work of Bowles and Gintis on the emergence of high schools during the late nineteenth century, *Schooling in Capitalist America.*

19 The idea that the penitentiary developed as a reaction to the dissolution of community during the period following the Revolutionary War is a major theme of Rothman, *Discovery of the Asylum*, especially his introduction, pp. xviii–xx.

20 Takaki, *Iron Cages*, pp. 30–35. The essay Rush wrote on this subject was presented to the American Philosophical Society in 1792, and was entitled "Observations intended to favour a supposition that the black Color [as it is called] of the Negroes is derived from the LEPROSY."

21 See Rush's *Medical Inquiries and Observations* (Philadelphia, 1812), especially the essay entitled "The Influence of Physical Causes upon the Moral Faculty," in Vol. 1.

22 For a discussion of this dilemma, and the difficulties it created for the diagnostician, see Rush, *Medical Inquiries and Observations upon the Diseases of the Mind* (1812; New York: Hafner Publishing Company, 1962), p. 360.

23 Rush structured his psychology so that the issue of conscious versus unconscious motivation was not relevant in assessing cause. While a patient might be under compulsion, the patient would, in the case of most forms of moral degeneration especially, always be aware of what he or she was doing. See Takaki, *Iron Cages*, passim.

24 Rush, *Medical Inquiries and Observations upon the Diseases of the Mind* (hereafter referred to as *Diseases of the Mind*), p. 11.

25 Rush, *Medical Inquiries and Observations* (hereafter referred to as *Medical Inquiries*), 2:146.

26 Rush, *Diseases of the Mind*, p. 360.

27 Ibid., p. 361.

28 Ibid., pp. 360–63.

29 Ibid., pp. 365–66. Rush's comment on the "imperfect manner with which the principles that suggested" the reform of the jail in Philadelphia were applied are made in reference to the principle of absolute isolation, which is addressed in the section that follows in this chapter.

30 Rusche and Kirchheimer, *Punishment and Social Structure*, passim. Theodor Adorno and Max Horkheimer make much the same observation in fragments concerning punishment in *Dialectic of Enlightenment*. See the Introduction of this book.

31 Garry Wills, *Inventing America: Jefferson's Declaration of Independence* (New York: Vintage Books, 1979), p. 131.

32 Rothman, *Discovery of the Asylum*, passim. Rothman never discusses Ruth. It is difficult to understand how his thesis could be sustained without reference to the foremost practitioner of the day.

33 Ibid., pp. 59–62.

34 Ibid., p. 62. "The faith of the 1790s now seemed misplaced; more rational codes had not decreased crime."

35 In this sense, a sort of Gramscian hegemony of the public discourse aided in the buttressing of the reformers' arguments. One might also examine Foucault's comments in *Discipline and Punish*, p. 232, concerning the "inevitableness" of the prison.

36  Rothman, *Discovery of the Asylum*, p. xviii.
37  Ibid., pp. xix–xx.
38  Barnes, *Evolution of Penology in Pennsylvania*, p. 106.
39  Ibid., p. 107.
40  William Bradford, an advocate of penal reform during this period, and one of the authors of the legislation of 1790, cited Beccaria as a major influence on the reformers in this regard. See his commentary on colonial penal law in *Laws of Pennsylvania*, 1:129nn.
41  See Cesare Becarria, *On Crimes and Punishments* (Indianapolis: University of Indiana Press, 1954), and Howard, *State of the Prisons*.
42  This model has been discussed in earlier chapters of this work.
43  As will be seen below, this problem was an immediate cause of the removal of convicted criminals to the isolation of prison.
44  Barnes, *Evolution of Penology in Pennsylvania*, pp. 85–86.
45  Negley Teeters, *The Cradle of the Penitentiary: Walnut Street Jail at Philadelphia, 1773–1835* (Philadelphia: Temple University Press, 1935), p. 11.
46  Barnes, *Evolution of Penology in Pennsylvania*, pp. 147–49.
47  Ibid., p. 148.
48  Ibid., pp. 80–83.
49  Ibid., p. 81. "Immediately following the peace of 1783 a number of prominent citizens of Philadelphia, led by Benjamin Franklin, Benjamin Rush, William Bradford, and Caleb Lownes, organized a movement for the reform of the barbarous criminal code of 1718, which was still in force." The only name with which the modern scholar might be unfamiliar among that group is that of Caleb Lownes. Lownes was to be the first warden of the reformed Walnut Street Jail.
50  Ibid., p. 82. It should be noted that references to most of the documents concerning this society and its memorials to the Pennsylvania legislature are derived from Barnes's work. Most of these proceedings have not been published and are available only to the visitor of the Pennsylvania Prison Society archives. See ibid., pp. 72ff.
51  Ignatieff, *Just Measure of Pain*, p. 86.
52  Memorials were akin to petitions, but they were more than that. It appears that in formulating laws the Pennsylvania legislature relied heavily on the resources of members of the community. In a sense, memorials served the purpose then that hearings and other information-gathering techniques of legislature play now.
53  Barnes, *Evolution of Penology in Pennsylvania*, p. 87.
54  Ibid., p. 89.
55  Ibid.
56  Ibid., p. 90.
57  Ibid.
58  Ibid., p. 89.
59  Ibid., pp. 90–91.
60  This claim would be dubious were it not for the fact that the first memorial had Rush as a signatory, that he was a founding member of the society, and

that, as has already been documented, he argued in *Diseases of the Mind* for the completion of the reforms suggested by the reformers. Rush did not, however, sign the memorial cited above. Perhaps because of his absence from the group of signatories he has been overlooked. Discussion of the specific reforms contained in the 1790 laws follows.

61 Barnes, *Evolution of Penology in Pennsylvania*, p. 91.

62 *Laws of Pennsylvania*, 3:802.

63 Ibid., pp. 802–4, sections 2–7.

64 Ibid., p. 805, section 8.

65 Ibid., section 10.

66 Barnes, *Evolution of Penology in Pennsylvania*, pp. 94–95.

67 *Laws of Pennsylvania*, 3:805–6, sections 11 and 12.

68 Barnes, *Evolution of Penology in Pennsylvania*, pp. 149ff. This citation is from Caleb Lownes, *An Account of the Alteration and Present State of the Penal Laws of Pennsylvania* (Philadelphia, 1796), pp. 32–33.

69 Barnes, *Evolution of Penology in Pennsylvania*, p. 97.

70 *Laws of Pennsylvania*, 3:808.

71 Many later practices derive from these early experiments, though the expansion of the penal system through parole had its genesis in other needs. The penal system of the Progressive Era requires a work of the scale of this present study in order to be fully understood.

72 *Laws of Pennsylvania*, 3:811, section 25. Other sections addressing the makeup of the board of inspectors are sections 22–24.

73 Ibid., p. 810, section 23.

74 See note 49.

75 Barnes, *Evolution of Penology in Pennsylvania*, pp. 97–98.

76 See Gustave de Beaumont and Alexis de Tocqueville, *On the Penitentiary System of the United States and Its Application in France*, trans. Francis Lieber (Philadelphia: Carey, Lea & Blanchard, 1833), pp. 3–4 (hereafter cited as *Penitentiary System*), and Barnes, *Evolution of Penology in Pennsylvania*, p. 97.

77 Barnes, *Evolution of Penology in Pennsylvania*, p. 95, citing a memorial from the Philadelphia Society.

78 The legislation was actually passed in 1817 for the construction of a prison near Pittsburgh, and in 1821 for construction of the Cherry Hill penitentiary, but funding was not provided for either until 1821. Beaumont and Tocqueville, *Penitentiary System*, p. 4, and Barnes, *Evolution of Penology in Pennsylvania*, pp. 138–41.

79 See Negley Teeters and John Shearer, *The Prison at Philadelphia: Cherry Hill* (New York: Columbia University Press, 1957), p. 2. The cost of the construction is discussed below.

80 Beaumont and Tocqueville, *Penitentiary System*, p. 276 (on the Walnut Street Jail) p. 277 (on Pittsburgh and Philadelphia).

81 Walnut Street was holding 576 prisoners in 1827; the combined population of Pittsburgh and Cherry Hill prisons was to be 452 prisoners. Ibid., pp. 276–77.

82 Ibid., p. 276 (on Walnut Street) and pp. 283–84 (on Philadelphia). The calculated cost of maintaining each prisoner in the Walnut Street Jail was estimated to be $1.99 per day, an extraordinary amount for the times; no figures were available on the cost per prisoner in the other prisons, though it would have been difficult for it to have exceeded that amount, and the Pennsylvania system advocates argued that the cost was essentially zero.

83 Rothman, *Discovery of the Asylum*, p. 104.

84 Beaumont and Tocqueville, Penitentiary System, p. 20.

85 Rothman, *Discovery of the Asylum*, p. 57.

86 There is a useful "law of first settlement" which, while ethnocentric, informs the work of historical and cultural geographers, to the effect that the impact of the first settlers in an "underpopulated" area is disproportionately greater than that of succeeding groups of settlers. As the earliest mass immigration following the Revolutionary War, these immigrants had considerable impact. On the "law of first settlement," see Wilbur Zelinsky, *The Historical Geography of the United States* (New York: Prentice-Hall, 1969), chap. 1.

87 Rothman, *Discovery of the Asylum*, p. 254.

88 Beaumont and Tocqueville, *Penitentiary System, passim.* The entire purpose of studying the prisons of the United States was to try to bring up the standards of the prisons of France to a more humane level.

89 This work is subject to the tyranny of secondary sources, which have gravely neglected the role of punishment of women during this period. It is not until the Progressive Era that a comprehensive literature on the punishment of women develops. For the most part, then, I have been limited in my capability to address this even more hidden dimension of the record.

90 Erving Goffman, *Asylums* (Garden City, N.Y.: Anchor Books, 1961), *passim.*

91 Beaumont and Tocqueville, *Penitentiary System*, pp. 39–40.

92 Barnes, *Evolution of Penology in Pennsylvania*, pp. 141–46.

93 Beaumont and Tocqueville, *Penitentiary System*, pp. 187ff.

94 Ibid., p. 188 and 189 (two different interviews with two separate prisoners).

95 While the language is stilted, obviously representing a creative rewriting of the original interviews, Beaumont and Tocqueville were partisans of the Auburn system of punishment at the time that the interviews were conducted. Hence, they had no reason to make the prisoners sound more articulate and clear about the favorable consequences of their punishment than they did.

96 Beaumont and Tocqueville, *Penitentiary System*, p. 189.

97 Ibid., p. 193.

98 Ibid., p. 188.

99 Ibid., p. 196.

100 Ibid., pp. 196–97.

101 Ibid., p. 196 (the complete story of this prisoner, pp. 194–96.)

102 Wills, *Inventing America*, p. 101.

## Chapter 5: The Woof of Time

1   See Benjamin Ginsberg, *The Consequences of Consent* (Boston: Addison-Wesley, 1982), p. 2, for example.

2   The number of references to Tocqueville and Beaumont's work in various studies of the history of prisons is truly overwhelming. Scarcely a study has been done without reference to their work, ranging from the most orthodox historical works, such as those of Teeters and Barnes, to the most radical, such as Foucault's *Discipline and Punish*.

3   The most comprehensive study of Tocqueville's trip to the United States, George Pierson's *Tocqueville and Beaumont in America* (New York: Columbia University Press, 1938), minimizes the relationship between the trip and study of prisons. Since Beaumont was most responsible for the report to the French government concerning the penitentiary, most scholars have assumed that Tocqueville's interests were not engaged by the penitentiary. The work that comes closest to making the connection between the two studies is David Rothman's *Discovery of the Asylum*, and even in this work the references are limited to Beaumont and Tocqueville's analysis of prisons, excluding larger relationship. Such neglect is disingenuous; even if Tocqueville was not largely responsible for the initial text, he was an extremely close associate of Beaumont, he contributed to the notes and appendices that went into the final report to the French government, and his subsequent involvement in French penal reform indicates that, even if he was initially uninterested in penal reform, his studies in the United States had a major impact on his attitudes.

4   Rothman, *Discovery of the Asylum*, p. 79–81.

5   Alexis de Tocqueville, *Democracy in America*, trans. George Lawrence, ed. J. P. Mayer, from the 13th, and final, edition of the work (1850; New York: Anchor Books, 1969), p. 250. (This edition is used rather than the earlier Reeves edition because of its acknowledgedly more faithful translation.) It is of passing interest to note that this reference to prison reform (the only direct reference in the work) appears in the chapter on the omnipotence of the majority, directly preceding Tocqueville's discussion of the tyranny of the majority.

6   It would be impossible to assess with any adequacy the differences between the North and the South in their penal practices without reference to the slave system. One important study has been done that makes such an assessment, Thorsten Sellin's *Slavery and the Penal System* (New York: Free Press, 1971). In this study, focus is necessarily on the northern and western states that were on the forefront of reform. The penal institutions that developed in the South were deeply influenced by slavery, and by what one might call the semifeudal social system that surrounded it. The essay that has had the most influence on me concerning the social structure of the southern United States and its differences from the north along politico-economic lines is Barrington Moore, Jr.'s "The American Civil War: The Last Capitalist Revolution," Chapter Three of *Social Origins of Democracy and Dictatorship*.

7  Tocqueville, *Democracy in America*, p. 508. This quotation appears in Marvin Meyers, *The Jacksonian Persuasion: Politics and Belief* (Stanford: Stanford University Press, 1960), pp. 37–38.

8  Beaumont and Tocqueville, *Penitentiary System*. The use of *The Penitentiary System* as a primary source has the distinct advantage of presenting the system as it was observed by Tocqueville. The fact that the accuracy of the report as a historical document is fortunately not in doubt makes such use easier.

9  Tocqueville, *Democracy in America*, pp. 614–16, "How the Aspect of Society in the United States is at Once Agitated and Monotonous." This theme is returned to later in this chapter.

10  A reproduction of the isometric drawing of the Eastern penitentiary appears in Rothman, *Discovery of the Asylum*, p. 98. For a detailed discussion of the construction of Eastern Penitentiary, see Teeters and Shearer, *Prison at Philadelphia, Cherry Hill*, chap. 2.

11  See W. David Lewis, *From Newgate to Dannemora: The Rise of the Penitentiary in New York, 1796–1848* (Ithaca: Cornell University Press, 1965), chap. 3.

12  Beaumont and Tocqueville, *Penitentiary System*, p. 5. The date of the beginning of this experiment is sometimes given as 1819. The reason for this confusion seems to be that 1819 was when the new wing was completed, even though isolation did not begin until later.

13  Ibid., pp. 151–52 (alphabetical note c).

14  Ibid., p. 6. A variety of descriptions of the emergence of this form of discipline have been made over the years. All of them seem to rely on the one given by Beaumont and Tocqueville.

15  Ibid., p. 10.

16  Comparative costs of the Pennsylvania and Auburn systems are contained in an appendix in ibid., pp. 275–86.

17  Ibid., p. 25. "The Auburn system gives the prisoners the habits of society. . . ."

18  Ibid., Appendix, conversation with E. Lynds, p. 202.

19  Ibid., p. 201.

20  Ibid., pp. 26, 201. A further discussion of this point appears below.

21  Ibid., p. 26.

22  Ibid. Francis Lieber had immigrated to the United States only six years prior to translating *The Penitentiary System*. His interest in publishing a study that favored the Auburn system over the Pennsylvania system stemmed from what he believed to be the evenhanded approach that Beaumont and Tocqueville used in their analysis. "Objective" observers, he felt, would reach different conclusions from the evidence presented in the report. Hence, the translation is liberally sprinkled with Lieber's comments, contained as translator footnotes. Yet the translation is not slanted itself.

23  The assumption of the close association of the prison with the conditions of society was so strong among reformers that they rarely even bothered to voice it. Rothman, *Discovery of the Asylum*, points this out as a general theme in his work. On paralleling the corrupting conditions of society through congregate

punishment, see Appendix—"Penitentiary System of Pennsylvania," by Francis Lieber, in Beaumont and Tocqueville, *Penitentiary System*.

24 Beaumont and Tocqueville, *Penitentiary System*, pp. 58–59.
25 Tocqueville, *Democracy in America*, p. 452.
26 Beaumont and Tocqueville, *Penitentiary System*, p. 10.
27 Ibid., p. 53.
28 Ibid., p. 59.
29 Ibid.
30 Ibid., p. 52.
31 Roberts Vaux, *Letter on the Penitentiary System of Pennsylvania* (Philadelphia, 1827), p. 3.
32 Beaumont and Tocqueville, *Penitentiary System*, p. 202. Beaumont and Tocqueville relied heavily on Lynds for their interpretation of the Auburn system.
33 Ibid., p. 202.
34 Tocqueville and Beaumont recognized this tendency of the Pennsylvania system when they noted, "The system of punishment appeared to us especially powerful over individuals endowed with some elevation of mind, and who had enjoyed a polite education." Ibid., p. 50.
35 Ibid., p. xlv.
36 Ibid., p. 92. This comment was made in reference to the viability of transferring the penitentiary principles of the United States to France.
37 For an interesting comparison of the social contexts of poverty in the United States as compared with France during this period, see Lawrence Clemmer's *The Discovery of Poverty* (New York: New York University Press, 1956), and Maurice de Chavalier, *Laboring Classes, Dangerous Classes* (Princeton: Princeton University Press, 1978). The scale of poverty in France as well as the social view of poverty was quite different, and understood in more overtly political terms than in the United States during this period.
38 Beaumont and Tocqueville, *Penitentiary System*, p. xlvi.
39 Tocqueville, *Democracy in America*, p. 615.
40 Each of these topics is addressed in turn, in *Democracy in America* in the sections entitled "Accidental of Providential Causes Helping to Maintain a Democratic Republic in the United States," pp. 279–81, "How Democratic Institutions and Mores Tend to Raise Rent and Shorten the Terms of Leases," pp. 581–82, and "Concerning Their Point of Departure and Its Importance for the Future of the Anglo-Americans," especially pp. 42–47.
41 Ibid., p. 281.
42 Ibid.
43 Meyers, *Jacksonian Persuasion*, pp. 42–64.
44 Tocqueville, *Democracy in America*, p. 614, quoted in Meyers, *Jacksonian Persuasion*, p. 43.
45 See Friedman, *History of American Law*.
46 Ibid., chap. 4.
47 A cursory examination of *U.S. Statutes at Large* for any year up until the 1870s

will reveal to the reader that the vast majority of national legislation had to do with the distribution of land, either directly or indirectly.

48  Tocqueville, *Democracy in America*, pp. 238–39. Theodore Lowi, in his introductory text to American politics, *Incomplete Conquest: Governing America* (New York: Holt, Reinhart, Winston, 1976), makes a similar point, listing property ownership as one of his "Seven Deadly Virtues."

49  Tocqueville, *Democracy in America*, p. 240. See also Ginsberg, *Consequences of Consent* chap. 2, for an analysis of the way in which the expansion of suffrage has been systematically used by political authorities to avoid more structural changes in policies.

50  There has been a recent trend in penal historiographic research to investigate the records of jails and prisons as documents that traced the movement of criminals and delinquents. See David Rothman, ed, *Crime and History* (Beverly Hills: Sage Publications, 1981).

51  James Madison was possibly the first political theorist in the United States to comment on the relationship between the limits of land and the limits of legitimacy of the government, though he addressed the question somewhat obliquely. See Federalist 10, in *The Federalist Papers*, ed. Clinton Rossiter (New York: Mentor Books, 1965).

52  Beaumont and Tocqueville, *Penitentiary System*, p. 59.

53  Ibid., p. 60.

54  Ibid., p. 20.

55  The recently published Lustig, *Corporate Liberalism*, discusses in depth the problem of the lack of meaningful ends that has haunted the political thought and practice of the United States. The creation of such a system is the consequence, for Lustig, of the emergence of corporate economic arrangements. Such arrangements, interestingly enough, can plausibly be said to have emerged out of what Tocqueville argued was the tendency in the United States for an industrial aristocracy to become dominant. The problem of such an aristocracy and its relationship to penal discipline is discussed below.

56  Tocqueville, *Democracy in America*, p. 691.

57  Ibid., p. 429.

58  Ibid. This Cartesian philosophy, however, is not explicitly adopted by U.S. citizens, but instead emerges quite simply and naturally as a result of the circumstances in which they find themselves.

59  Ibid., p. 430.

60  Ibid., p. 433. Given the contemporary sophistication of interest group theory in American politics, it is worthy of note that Tocqueville's use of the term, "interests" is completely compatible with the modern usage.

61  Ibid., p. 435.

62  Ibid., p. 452.

63  Ibid., p. 453.

64  Ibid.

65  Ibid., p. 460.

66  Ibid., p. 464.

67  See Foucault, *Discipline and Punish*, p. 318, for a discussion of Tocqueville's role in the controversy over the establishment of congregate versus solitary punishment. Tocqueville's views are said to have shifted, in the conventional history of penology, owing to his distrust of Charles Lucas, who advocated a congregate system. Such an explanation seems difficult to believe, given Tocqueville's background and reputation. Lucas is referred to in a translator's note in *The Penitentiary System* on p. 12.

68  Tocqueville, *Democracy in America*, p. 667.

69  Ibid., p. 668.

70  Ibid.

71  Ibid., p. 669.

72  Ibid.

73  Ibid., p. 673.

74  Ibid.

75  Ibid., p. 676.

76  Ibid., p. 508.

77  On Locke's concept of individualism, see Chapter 3 of this work.

78  Tocqueville, *Democracy in America*, pp. 608–9.

79  Ibid., pp. 255–56.

80  Ibid., p. 510.

81  Ibid., p. 692.

82  Ibid., pp. 262–76, "What Tempers the Tyranny of the Majority in the United States."

83  Ibid., pp. 262–63. The "absence of a central administration" was a primary safeguard against the tyranny of the majority for Tocqueville.

84  Admittedly the results were uneven at the level of implementation. But the point here is that at the level of government with which most of U.S. citizens were concerned, the penitentiary model was the one that was chosen in Ohio, Illinois, Iowa, Indiana, and throughout the remaining northeastern states as well. Rothman, *Discovery of the Asylum*, p. 100.

85  Tocqueville refers to this tendency toward centralization in the context of his discussion of democratic despotism, toward the end of Vol. 2 of *Democracy in America*, 679–89, "How the Sovereign Power Is Increasing among the European Nations of Our Time, Although the Sovereigns Are Less Stable."

86  Ibid., pp. 550–58.

87  "On *The Jewish Question*," *The Writings of the Young Marx on Philosophy and Society*, ed. Loyd D. Easton and Kurt H. Guddat (Garden City, N.Y.: Anchor Books, 1967). There it is their observations on religion that most interest Marx, but in the context of trying to discern the limits of liberation available to members of civil society.

88  Tocqueville, *Democracy in America*, p. 553.

89  Ibid., p. 554.

90  Ibid., p. 555.

91  Ibid.

92 Ibid., p. 556.
93 Ibid.
94 Ibid.
95 Ibid., p. 557. "[A business aristocracy's] object is not to rule the [working class] but to make use of it." For Marx, of course, such a distinction made no sense in the final analysis.

## Conclusion

1 Lowi, "American Business, Public Policy, Case Studies, and Political Theory," p. 690. I thank Ted Lowi here for his careful reading of this concluding essay. That I have not followed his good advice is due to my excessiveness, rather than his alleged conservatism.
2 Here I am specifically thinking of the work of such theorists as Walter Dean Burnham (*Critical Elections and the Mainsprings of American Politics* [New York: Norton Books, 1970].
3 On the original relationships posited by Dahl, see his *Modern Political Analysis* (Englewood Cliffs, N.J.: Prentice-Hall, 1963), p. 73.
4 Lowi does not associate these policies with the interplay of "coercion" and "peaceful adjustment." His study continually emphasizes a different play, between the "environment of conduct" and "individual conduct." From his perspective, I have inappropriately fused two separate dimensions of analysis into one.
   Of course, my study is concerned precisely with reclaiming the origins of a policy which has had as its goal the separation of these dimensions. By fusing together these categories, I am trying to show how they still inform a hidden politics, those concerned with protective, dangerous relationships. Only then can one posit distinctions between individuals and their environments of conduct.
5 Lowi, *End of Liberalism*, p. 39.
6 See Ginsberg, *Consequences of Consent*.
7 Weber, *Economy and Society*, 1:54.
8 Ibid., pp. 54–55.
9 Lowi, *End of Liberalism*, pp. 295–313.
10 Richard Rorty, "Postmodern Bourgeois Liberalism," *Journal of Philosophy* 10 (1983).
11 See Lustig, *Corporate Liberalism*, chap. 8. The citation is taken from Hartz, *Liberal Tradition in America*, p. 71.
12 This argument has much in common with that advanced by William E. Connolly. See his "Dilemma of Legitimacy."
13 Foucault, *History of Sexuality*, 1:43.
14 Heidegger, "Question concerning Technology," p. 309.
15 Fraser, "Michel Foucault: A 'Young Conservative'?" p. 172.
16 Ibid., p. 176.
17 Ibid., p. 179.
18 Ibid., pp. 179–80.

19 Ibid., p. 180.
20 Karl Marx, "From Excerpt-Notes of 1844," *Writings of the Young Marx on Philosophy and Society* p. 280.
21 Connolly, "Dilemma of Legitimacy."
22 John Rajchman, in *Michel Foucault: The Freedom of Philosophy* (New York: Columbia University Press, 1985), attempts to provide such an ethic. Much work can be done on this problem, particularly in the area of investigating "technologies of the selves" that may exist outside the asceticisms associated with the contemporary order.
23 Foucault, "Truth and Power," p. 114.
24 Foucault, "Two Lectures," p. 108.
25 Lingis, *Excesses*, pp. 14–15.

# Selected Bibliography

Althusser, Louis, "Ideology and Ideological State Apparatuses." In *Lenin and Philosophy and Other Essays*, trans. Ben Brewster, pp.127–88. New York: Monthly Review Press, 1971.

Anderson, Benedict. *Imagined Communities: Reflections on the Origins and Spread of Nationalism*. London: New Left Books, 1983.

Anderson, Perry. *Lineages of the Absolutist State*. London: New Left Books, 1974.

Anderson, Perry. *Passages from Antiquity to Feudalism*. London: New Left Books, 1974.

Applegarth, Albert C. *The Quakers of Pennsylvania*. Baltimore: Johns Hopkins University Studies in Historical and Political Science. 1923.

Bailyn, Bernard. *The Ideological Origins of the American Revolution*. Cambridge: Harvard University Press, 1967.

Baltzell, Digby. *Puritan Boston, Quaker Philadelphia*. New York: Free Press, 1979.

Barnes, Harry Elmer. *The Evolution of Penology in Pennsylvania*. Montclair, N.J.: Patterson-Smith, 1968.

Barry, Norman. "Unanimity, Agreement, and Liberalism: A Critique of James Buchanan's Social Philosophy." *Political Theory* 12, no. 4 (November, 1984): 579–96.

Baudelaire, Charles. *The Painter of Modern Life and Other Essays*. Trans. Jonathan Mayne. London: Phaidon, 1964.

Beaumont, Gustave de, and Tocqueville, Alexis de. *On the Penitentiary System of the United States and Its Application in France*. Trans. Francis Lieber. Philadelphia: Carey, Lea and Blanchard, 1833.

Beccaria, Cesare. *On Crimes and Punishments*. Indianapolis: University of Indiana Press, 1954.

Benjamin, Walter. *Illuminations*. Trans. Harry Zohn. Ed. Hannah Arendt. New York: Schocken Books, 1969.

Bowles, Samuel, and Gintis, Herbert. *Schooling in Capitalist America*. New York: Basic Books, 1976.

Blumenburg, Hans. *The Legitimacy of the Modern Age*. Trans. Robert M. Wallace. Cambridge; MIT Press, 1983.

Bramsted, E. K., and Melhuish, K. J., eds. *Western Liberalism*. London: Longman, 1978.

Brinton, Howard. *Friends for Three Hundred Years*. Wallingford, Penn. Pendle Hill Publications, 1964.

Burnham, Walter Dean. *Critical Elections and the Mainsprings of American Politics*. New York: Norton Books, 1970.

Clarkson, Thomas. *Memoirs of the Private and Public Life of William Penn*. London: Longman, Hurst, Rees, Orme, and Brown, 1813.

Connolly, William E. "The Dilemma of Legitimacy." In Connolly, ed., *Legitimacy and the State*, pp. 222–49. New York: New York University Press, 1984.

Dahl, Robert. *Modern Political Analysis*. Englewood Cliffs, N.J.: Prentice-Hall, 1963.

Deleuze, Gilles, and Guatarri, Felix. *Anti-Oedipus: Capitalism and Schizophrenia*. Trans. Robert Hurley, Mark Seem and Helen R. Lane. Minneapolis: University of Minnesota Press, 1983.

Donzelot, Jacques: *The Policing of Families*. Trans. Robert Hurley. New York: Pantheon Press, 1979.

Dreyfus, Hubert L., and Rabinow, Paul. *Michel Foucault: Beyond Structuralism and Hermeneutics*. 2d ed. Chicago: University of Chicago Press, 1983.

Edelman, Murray. "Political Language and Political Reality." *PS* 18, no. 1 (Winter 1985): 10–19.

Eisenach, Eldon. *Two Worlds of Liberalism*. Chicago: University of Chicago Press, 1981.

Erikson, Kai. *Wayward Puritans*. New York: John Wiley and Sons, 1966.

Foucault, Michel. *Discipline and Punish; The Birth of the Prison*. Trans. Alan Sheridan. New York: Pantheon, 1977.

Foucault, Michel. *The History of Sexuality, Vol. 1: An Introduction*. Trans. Robert Hurley. New York: Pantheon, 1979.

Foucault, Michel, ed. *L'impossible prison*. Paris: Editions du Seuil, 1980.

Foucault, Michel. *Language, Counter-Memory, Practice*. Ed. and trans. Donald Bouchard. Ithaca: Cornell University Press, 1977.

Foucault, Michel. "The Order of Discourse." In Michael Shapiro, ed., *Language and Politics*, pp. 108–38. New York: New York University Press, 1984.

Foucault, Michel. *The Order of Things: An Archaeology of the Human Sciences*. Trans. Alan Sheridan-Smith. New York: Vintage Books, 1973.

Foucault, Michel. *Power/Knowledge: Selected Interviews and Other Writings, 1972– 1977*. Ed. Colin Gordon. New York: Pantheon, 1980.

Foucault, Michel. "Structuralism and Post-Structuralism: An Interview with Michel Foucault." *Telos*, no. 55 (Spring 1983), pp. 195–211.

Foucault, Michel. *This Is Not a Pipe*. Trans. James Harkness. Berkeley: University of California Press, 1982.

Foucault, Michel. "What is Enlightenment?" Trans. Catherine Porter. In *The Foucault Reader*, ed. Paul Rabinow, pp. 32–50. New York: Pantheon, 1984.

Foucault, Michel, ed. *Herculine Barbin, Being the Recently Discovered Memoirs of a*

*Nineteenth Century French Hermaphrodite.* Trans. Richard McDougal. New York: Pantheon, 1980.

Fox, George. *A Journal.* Philadelphia: Friends Bookstore, 1849.

Fraser, Nancy. "Foucault on Modern Power: Empirical Insights and Normative Confusions." *Praxis International* 1, no. 1 (October 1981): pp. 272–96.

Fraser, Nancy. "Michel Foucault: A 'Young Conservative'?" *Ethics* 96, no. 1 (October 1985): pp. 165–84.

Friedman, Lawrence. *A History of American Law.* New York: Simon and Schuster, 1973.

Ginsberg, Benjamin. *The Consequences of Consent: Elections, Citizen Control, and Popular Acquiescence.* Boston: Addison-Wesley, 1982.

Gipson. L. H. *The British Empire before the American Revolution.* 10 vols. Caldwell, Idaho: The Caxton Printers, 1936–1962.

Goffman, Erving. *Asylums: Essays on the Social Situation of Mental Patients and Other Inmates.* Garden City, N.Y.: Anchor Books, 1961.

Gunnell, John. "The Idea of a Conceptual Framework: A Philosophical Critique." *Journal of Comparative Administration* (August 1969).

Habermas, Jürgen. "Modernity—An Incomplete Project." In Hal Foster, ed., *The Anti-Aesthetic: Essays on Postmodern Culture.* Port Townsend, Wash.: Bay Press, 1983.

Habermas, Jürgen. "Taking Aim at the Heart of the Present." *University Publishing* 13 (Summer 1984): pp. 5–6.

Hartz, Louis. *The Liberal Tradition in America.* New York: Harcourt, Brace, Jovanovich, 1955.

Haskell, Thomas L. "Capitalism and the Origins of the Humanitarian Sensibility." *American Historical Review* 90 (April and June 1985) pp. 339–61, 547–66.

Haskell, Thomas L. *The Emergence of Professional Social Science: The American Social Science Association and the Nineteenth-Century Crisis of Authority.* Urbana: University of Illinois Press, 1977.

Hay, Douglas; Thompson, Edward; and Hobsbawm, Eric. *Albion's Fatal Tree: Crime and Society in Eighteenth Century England.* New York: Pantheon, 1975.

Heidegger, Martin. *Being and Time.* Trans. John Macquarrie and Edward Robinson. New York: Harper and Row, 1962.

Heidegger, Martin. "Interview: Only a God Can Save Us Now." *Graduate Faculty Philosophy Journal (New School for Social Research)* 6 (Winter 1977): pp. 5–27.

Heidegger, Martin. "The Question concerning Technology," In *Basic Writings of Martin Heidegger,* ed. and trans. David Krell. New York: Harper and Row, 1977.

Hill, Christopher. *God's Englishman.* New York: Pantheon, 1970.

Hill, Christopher. *The World Turned Upside Down: Radical Ideas during the English Revolution.* London: Penguin Books, 1975.

Hobbes, Thomas. *Leviathan.* Ed. C. B. Macpherson. London: Penguin Books, 1968.

Hooke, Alexander. "The Order of Others." *Political Theory* 15, no. 1 (February 1987).

Horkheimer, Max, and Adorno, Theodor. *Dialectic of Enlightenment*. New York: Seabury Press, 1969.

Howard, John. *The State of the Prisons*. New York: Everyman, 1929.

Hull, William. *William Penn: A Topical Biography*. London: Oxford University Press, 1937.

Hunt, N. C. *Two Early Political Associations*. Oxford Clarendon Press, 1961.

Ignatieff, Michael. *A Just Measure of Pain: The Penitentiary in the Industrial Revolution*. New York: Columbia University Press, 1978.

Irving, Washington. "Rip Van Winkle." In *Collected Works*. New York: Graystone Press, 1921.

Ives, George. *A History of Penal Methods*. London: Stanley Paul, 1918.

Jameson, Fredric. *The Political Unconscious: Narrative as a Socially Symbolic Act*. Ithaca: Cornell University Press, 1981.

Jameson, Fredric. "Postmodernism, or the Cultural Logic of Late Capitalism." *New Left Review*, no. 146 (July–August 1984), pp. 53–91.

Jay, Martin. *Marxism and Totality: The Adventure of a Concept from Lukács to Habermas*. Berkeley: University of California Press, 1984.

Kantorowitz, A. M. *The King's Two Bodies*. Princeton: Princeton University Press, 1957.

Kateb, George. "Democratic Individuality and the Claims of Politics." *Political Theory* 12, no. 3 (August 1984): pp. 331–60.

Kateb, George. "Thinking about Human Extinction:(1) Nietzsche and Heidegger." *Raritan* 6, no. 2 (Fall 1986): pp. 1–28.

Kramnick, Isaac. "Equal Opportunity and the Race of Life." *Dissent* (May 1982).

Kramnick, Isaac. "Republican Revisionism Revisited." *American Historical Review* 87, no. 3 (June, 1982): pp. 629–64.

Langbein, John. *"Albion's* Fatal Flaws." *Past and Present*, no. 98 (February 1983), pp. 96–120.

Lasch, Christopher. *Haven in a Heartless World*. New York: Basic Books, 1977.

Lewis, W. David. *From Newgate to Dannemora: The Rise of the Penitentiary in New York, 1796–1848*. Ithaca: Cornell University Press, 1965.

Lingis, Alphonso. *Excesses: Eros and Culture*. Albany: State University of New York Press, 1983.

Locke, John. *An Essay concerning Human Understanding*. Ed. A. S. Pringle-Pattison. Oxford Clarendon Press, 1924.

Locke, John. *The Reasonableness of Christianity*. Ed. I. T. Ramsey. Stanford: Stanford University Press, 1958.

Locke, John. *Treatise of Civil Government and Letter concerning Toleration*. Ed. C. L. Sherman. New York: Irvington, 1937.

Locke, John. *Two Treatises of Government*. Ed. Peter Laslett. New York: New American Library, 1963.

Lowi, Theodore. "American Business, Public Policy, Case Studies, and Political Theory." *World Politics* 16 (July 1964): pp. 677–93.

Lowi, Theodore. *The End of Liberalism*. 2nd ed. New York: Norton, 1979.

Lowi, Theodore. *Incomplete Conquest: Governing America*. New York: Holt, Reinhart, Winston, 1976.

Lownes, Caleb. *An Account of the Alteration and Present State of the Penal Laws of Pennsylvania*. Philadelphia, 1976.

Lustig, R. Jeffrey. *Corporate Liberalism: The Origins of Modern American Political Theory, 1890–1920*. Berkeley: University of California Press, 1982.

Macpherson, C. B. *The Political Theory of Possessive Individualism, Hobbes to Locke*. New York: Oxford University Press, 1962.

Madison, James; Hamilton, Alexander; and Jay, John. *The Federalist Papers*. Ed. Clinton Rossiter. New York: Mentor Books, 1965.

Marcuse, Herbert. *One Dimensional Man*. Boston: Beacon Press, 1964.

Marcuse, Herbert, and Olafson, Peter. "Heidegger's Politics." *Graduate Faculty Philosophy Journal (New School for Social Research)* 6 (Winter 1977):28–40.

Marx, Karl. *Capital*. Ed. Frederick Engels. Vol. 1 New York: International Publishers, 1967.

Marx, Karl. *The German Ideology*. In *Marx-Engels, Collected Works*, Vol. 5. New York: International Publishers, 1975.

Marx, Karl. *The Marx-Engels Reader*. Ed. Robert Tucker. 2d ed. New York: Norton, 1978.

Marx, Karl. *The Writings of the Young Marx on Philosophy and Society*. Ed. and trans. Loyd D. Easton and Kurt H. Guddat. Garden City, N.Y.: Anchor Books, 1967.

Meyers, Marvin. *The Jacksonian Persuasion: Politics and Belief*. Stanford: Stanford University Press, 1960.

Miller, Perry. *Errand into the Wilderness*. Cambridge: Harvard University Press, 1956.

Moore, Barrington, Jr. *Social Origins of Democracy and Dictatorship: Lord and Peasant in the Making of the Modern World*. Boston: Beacon Press, 1966.

Nash, Gary B. *Quakerism and Politics: Pennsylvania, 1681–1726*. Princeton: Princeton University Press, 1968.

Nietzsche, Friedrich. *On the Genealogy of Morals*. Ed. Walter Kaufmann. Trans. Walter Kaufmann and R. J. Hollingdale. New York: Vintage Books, 1969.

Paine, Thomas. "Common Sense." In *The Life and Major Writings of Thomas Paine*, ed. Philip S. Foner. New York: Citadel Press, 1945.

Penn, William. *A Letter from a Gentleman in the Countryside to his Friends in London, Upon the Subject of the Penal Law and Tests*. London, 1687[?].

Pennsylvania, Commonwealth of. *Charter and Laws of the Province of Pennsylvania*. Harrisburg: Commonwealth of Pennsylvania, 1871.

Pennsylvania: Commonwealth of. *The Laws of Pennsylvania*. Philadelphia: Halls and Sellers, 1797.

Pierson, George. *Tocqueville and Beaumont in America*. New York: Columbia University Press, 1938.

Platt, Anthony. *The Child Savers: The Invention of Delinquency*. Chicago: University of Chicago Press, 1969.

Pocock, J. G. A. *The Machiavellian Moment: Florentine Political Thought and the Atlantic Republican Tradition*. Princeton: Princeton University Press, 1975.

Poulantzas, Nicos. *State, Power, Socialism*. Trans. Patrick Camiller. London: New Left Books, 1978.

Rajchman, John. *Michel Foucault: The Freedom of Philosophy*. New York: Columbia University Press, 1985.

Root, Winfred. *The Relations of Pennsylvania with the British Government, 1696–1765*. Philadelphia: University of Pennsylvania; New York: D. Appleton, 1912.

Rothman, David. *Conscience and Convenience: The Asylum and Its Alternatives in Progressive America*. Boston: Little, Brown, 1980.

Rothman, David. *The Discovery of the Asylum: Social Order and Disorder in the New Republic*. Boston: Little, Brown, 1971.

Rothman, David, ed. *Crime and History*. Beverly Hills: Sage Publications, 1981.

Rusche, George, and Kirschheimer, Otto. *Punishment and Social Structure*. New York: Columbia University Press, 1939.

Rush, Benjamin. *The Autobiography of Benjamin Rush*. Ed. George W. Corner. Princeton: Princeton University Press, 1948.

Rush, Benjamin. *Medical Inquiries and Observations*. Philadelphia, 1812.

Rush, Benjamin. *Medical Inquiries and Observations upon the Diseases of the Mind*. 1812; New York: Hafner Publishing Company, 1962.

Rush, Benjamin. *The Selected Writings of Benjamin Rush*. Ed. Dagobert D. Runes. New York: Philosophical Library, 1947.

Ryan, Michael. *Marxism and Deconstruction: A Critical Articulation*. Baltimore: Johns Hopkins University Press, 1982.

Said, Edward. *Beginnings: Intention and Method*. Baltimore: Johns Hopkins University Press, 1975.

Sartre, Jean-Paul. *No Exit, and Three Other Plays*. New York: Vintage Books, 1955.

Scarry, Elaine. *The Body in Pain: The Making and Unmaking of the World*. New York: Oxford University Press, 1985.

Schumpeter, Joseph. *Capitalism, Socialism, and Democracy*. 3d ed. New York: Harper and Row, 1950.

Sellin, Thorsten. *Slavery and the Penal System*. New York: Free Press, 1971.

Sharpless, Isaac. *Quakerism and Politics*. Philadelphia: Ferris and Leach, 1905.

Sim, Francis; Spence, Larry; and Takei, Yoshimitsu. "Telearchics: The Tightness of Loose Coupling." Paper presented at the American Sociological Association Annual Meeting, 1983.

Smith, Abbott Emerson. *Colonists in Bondage*. Chapel Hill: University of North Carolina Press, 1947.

Sparks, Richard F. "A Critique of Marxist Criminology." In *Crime and Justice: An Annual Review of Research*, 1980.

Takaki, Ronald T. *Iron Cages: Race and Culture in Nineteenth Century America*. New York: Alfred Knopf, 1979.

Teeters, Negley. *The Cradle of the Penitentiary: Walnut Street Jail at Philadelphia, 1773–1835*. Philadelphia: Temple University Press, 1935.

Teeters, Negley, and Shearer, John. *The Prison at Philadelphia: Cherry Hill.* New York: Columbia University Press, 1957.

Tocqueville, Alexis de *Democracy in America.* Ed. J. P. Mayer. Trans. George Lawrence. New York: Anchor Books, 1969.

Vaux, Roberts. *Letter on the Penitentiary System of Pennsylvania.* Philadelphia, 1827.

Vico, Giambattista. *The New Science of Giambattista Vico.* Ed. and trans. Thomas Goddard Bergin and Max Harold Fisch. Ithaca: Cornell University Press, 1970.

Walkowitz, Judith. *Prostitution and Victorian Society.* Cambridge: Cambridge University Press, 1980.

Walzer, Michael. "Liberalism and the Art of Separation." *Political Theory* 12, no. 3 (August 1984):315–30.

Warren, Mark. "Nietzsche and Political Philosophy." *Political Theory* 13, no. 2 (May 1985):183–212.

Weber, Max. *Economy and Society.* Ed. Guenther Roth and Claus Wittich. Berkeley: University of California Press, 1978.

Wikse, John. *About Possession: The Self as Private Property.* University Park: Pennsylvania State University Press, 1977.

Wills, Garry. *Inventing America: Jefferson's Declaration of Independence.* New York: Vintage Books, 1979.

Wolin, Richard. "The Bankruptcy of Left-Wing *Kulturcritik.*" *Telos,* no. 63 (Spring 1985): pp. 168–77.

Zelilnsky, Wilbur. *The Historical Geography of the United States.* New York: Prentice-Hall, 1969.

# Index

DESIGNED BY MARY MENDEL
COMPOSED BY BIRMY GRAPHICS OF AMERICA, INC.
MIAMI, FLORIDA
MANUFACTURED BY BRAUN-BRUMFIELD, INC.
ANN ARBOR, MICHIGAN
TEXT IS SET IN PLANTIN, DISPLAY LINES IN LUBALIN GRAPH

**Library of Congress Cataloging-in-Publication Data**
Dumm, Thomas L.
Democracy and punishment.
Bibliography: pp. 183–189.
Includes index.
1. Prisons—United States—History.   2. Liberalism—
United States—History.   3. Punishment—United States—
History.   4. Power (Social sciences)   I. Title.
HV9469.D86   1987      364.6′0973      87-40147
ISBN 0-299-11400-7
ISBN 0-299-11404-X (pbk.)